Spiritual Awakening...

*Walking A Path
Of Light & Love...*

Robin Morris

A Spiritual Awakening…

Published in 2022

This work is an updated version of the original title:
I See Therefore I Am I Think...

Robin Morris

PUBLISHING
JEFFREYS BAY

P O Box 1588 Jeffreys Bay 6330 South Africa
www.assegaipublishing.com

*Assegai Publishing is based in Jeffreys Bay, South Africa. It is a non-profit
organisation dedicated to spreading goodwill and spiritual direction via the
printed word. All proceeds go to **J/Bay Pet Rescue** who feed, heal and provide
medication for destitute and abused animals*

Cover Design: Craig Mackay

ISBN: 9798842423767

Aloha...

Writing is a wonderful experience. For this book, I used real life experiences and adventures based on my travels and the incredible people I've had the pleasure to meet. Surrounded by a very *'tasty'* world, I know how difficult it is to follow a positive *'Life'* path and stay focused, whilst still enjoying life, but enjoying life really is the key. We live in an interesting period with time having little value. Everyday slips by so effortlessly.

I like to motivate people to release themselves from their *'life boxes'*, set themselves free and re-look at life again with new eyes. Maybe it's due to the current state the world is in but it's awesome that people are aware of the need for change in their secular lives. Hopefully, with this book you'll desire to seek deeper within, enhance your awareness and walk your life path with new purpose and meaning.

When it comes to life and the meaning of life, it is infinite. You can never learn it all. I know I'll still be forever learning but that's the joy. It's so stimulating. The more I meditate and deeper I go to explore my Subconscious, being ever mindful of the abundant Universal energy and earth's vibrational resonance, the more I get to appreciate the path I am walking to discover who I am.

From home, I overlook the timeless surf breaks of Jeffreys Bay and draw inspiration from the bowling right-hand waves breaking endlessly in flawless lines; magical sets of cylindrical corduroys, powering across exposed reefs. For me - this is *'Perfectly Balanced'* energy. When the wind blows onshore, I'm sensated with the ocean's salty spray. What more to ask for in this age. Life is indeed virtuous...!

Robin Morris

www.robinmorris.co.za

Foreword – *Professor Ian Schulz*

It's a matter of personal choice when deciding what spiritual path one should walk in life. Sometimes the horizon gets tainted, one can be led astray. In this fascinating book the author has provided a broad perspective on life, enhanced with many words of wisdom in his dynamic approach to create a more positive and moral attitude towards life.

Taking cognisance of the push/pull effect of our magnificent Solar System's gravity induced magnetic field of energy, including the Circadian effect of Earth's Geomagnetic field, we have a planetary environment of perfect equilibrium. Robin Morris has produced a God driven book on life to illustrate how one can use this power of dualism or balance of opposites, to engage in everyday life, awaken spiritually and walk a more enlightened path.

The left versus right brain plus the intriguing brainwave patterns open up a whole new dimension of thinking for the more liberal players in life. There are also many angles and some interesting takes on how one can use the various consciousness levels to one's advantage, consequently improving one's lifestyle.

This is a self-motivational book on life. What makes it different are the wonderful life stories and anecdotes, spiced with humour, to illustrate and reinforce the author's opinion on various subjects.

Robin Morris has created a deep and profound read, which is captivating and mesmeric.

I Rescued A Human Today...

His eyes met mine as he walked down the corridor, peering apprehensively into our kennels. I felt his need instantly and knew I had to help him. I wagged my tail but not too exuberantly, I didn't want him to be afraid.

As he stopped at my kennel, I blocked his view from a little accident I'd incurred at the back of my small cage. I didn't want him to know I hadn't been walked today. Sometimes the shelter keepers get too busy and I didn't want him to think poorly of them.

As he read my kennel card, I hoped he wouldn't feel too sad about my past because that's all behind me now. I only have the future to look forward to and I want to make a difference in someone's life. I know I can do it.

He got down on his knees and made little kissy sounds. In return, I shoved my shoulder up against the cold steel bars to comfort him. Gentle, probing fingertips caressed my neck in return. He was desperate for unconditional companionship. A tear fell down his cheek so I raised my paw to assure him. I wanted him to know he could trust in me. Slowly my kennel door opened. His smile was so bright; I instantly leapt into his arms. I would promise to keep him safe and always be by his side. I would promise to do anything, just to feel his warmth and see that radiant smile and sparkle in his eyes.

He was so fortunate he came down my corridor today. There are so many more out there who haven't walked these corridors. There are so many more humans still to be saved...

I'm glad I was able to save one today...!

Fido...

I Believe...

How do you know God exists...? Because I believe in creation and the mighty Universe. I believe in our Solar System and our incredible planet with all its perfection. I believe in Mother Nature, our exquisite oceans, our magnificent wildlife, the amazing human population and the very air we breathe. I believe God created all this because I believe it could never have happened by coincidence...

A Meditation...

What am I...Who am I...Where am I...? I am nothing and yet I am everything I need to be. I am within, I am without, existing only in the moment, in the absolute stillness around me. I hear the distant beating of my heart, the light breaths of my lungs but they are mere fleeting sounds of no consequence for I am drawn into the beautiful white light before me, into the centre of the Lotus flower as it enfolds tranquil petals of abundant shimmering colours all around me, embracing me in pure unconditional love. I shiver involuntarily with delight, with sheer exhilarating ecstasy. It is joy beyond joy. I have arrived with grace. Thank you, Universal Consciousness...for sharing your infinite love and everlasting light...!

Robin Morris

For Irma and her incredible team, who devote their time and energy to saving destitute animals in the surrounding townships of Jeffreys Bay...

Contents

Part One

Life's Origins

'If it's true we are here to help others, then what exactly are the 'others' here for...?'

Back in the day, Earl and Bart met for their usual once a month business update. "So, Bart, what's currently going down that's new and exciting in the international business arena...? Things are kinda quiet here in New York. Hope you got something good to tell me. I'd like to invest and make a bunch of cash like that last one we did with your coffee bean." Says Earl, stirring his fresh cup of coffee. "Well," replies Bart, "this one's big Earl, in fact it's gonna be huge, worldwide. We gotta climb in now and tie up the rights for the USA market before anybody beats us to it because this one's already gaining ground in parts of Asia...!"

"What is it...?" Earl snaps, excitedly.

"It's called tobacco, Earl."

"Tobacco, Bart…! What in hell is that…?"

"It's a leaf, grown in Africa Earl."

"A goddamn leaf…! Must be some kinda special leaf Bart, cause we got loads of 'em around here. What does it do…?"

"Well basically, you roll it up, stick it in your mouth, set the end of it on fire and then inhale the smoke Earl."

"Holy crap…! And people do this voluntarily…? Surely there are health risks Bart…?

"Yup, there certainly are Earl. The leaf produces some kinda highly toxic and extremely addictive drug called nicotine, which slowly clogs up your lungs, affects your breathing and you eventually die a slow and terribly painful death from emphysema. A doc has to drill a hole through your neck just so you can breathe."

"That's insane. You reckon this one's gonna go big…? People will voluntarily commit to this of their own free will Bart…?"

"Yup Earl, they sure will. It's addictive. Once tried, they're totally hooked."

"What else can people do with this leaf Bart…?

"Well Earl, this one's really good. They can chew it and suck out all the nicotine."

"No way Bart. Surely not. Does it taste good…?"

"Nah Earl. It tastes like shite, turns your teeth and gums brown and your teeth all eventually fall out because your gums rot."

"Geez, I don't know about this one Bart. Can't see it catching on in America. What else you got…?"

"Well Earl, there's this African animal, they call it a cow. It's a very meek and mild animal, has the most adorable eyes. Every time it has a baby, you take the baby away from the mother and drink all the mother's milk. When it can no longer have babies, you murder it and eat it. This one's gonna be even bigger Earl."

"Sounds revolting Bart. Must be side effects…?"

"Well Earl, because cow's milk wasn't designed for human consumption, when you drink the milk it clogs up your breathing system, your sinuses decay, it causes asthma, plus lotsa stomach and digestive problems from the milk curdling and rotting in your stomach."

"Wow…! And what about from eating the flesh Bart…?"

"Aah, this one's not good either. Everyone eventually dies a wicked death from heart attacks."

"You gotta be kidding me. How we gonna convince folk to do this Bart…?"

"It's all in the blood Earl. Once they've tasted the cow's blood, they're hooked; line and sinker, we got 'em. The big problem is, we'll need a massive and I mean massive amount of prime land for the cows to roam and feed, which means we'll have to wipe out all the Native American Indians and steal all their land."

"No way Bart that's not good, those guys are tough, we could get hurt."

"And there's another issue Earl; the cows fart and burp a

lot, producing mountains of methane gas and cow poo. The gas creates really bad carbon dioxide in mind blowing quantities, which destroys our atmosphere and eventually our planet. But no worries, we'll be long gone by then…!"

"And the poo Bart, what about all the smelly cow poo you mentioned…?"

"Aaahhh, as soon as it starts raining, all that poo mostly ends up polluting our rivers Earl. This is before it gets to the ocean and similarly pollutes the ocean."

"That's sad Bart, so far I'm not convinced. Hope you got something else…?"

"Just one more Earl. This one's really good. Kept the best for last. It's a liquid you can drink."

"A liquid Bart…? You mean like a lemonade…?"

"Well, no Earl, not like lemonade. They call this one whisky, comes from a tiny country called Scotland, which is a little piece of turf on the northern tip of the UK. The men wear tartan skirts, I kid you not…!"

"That's real kinky Bart. So how do they make this whisky…?

"It comes from a grain Earl, which is a mix of barley, corn, rye and wheat."

"Wow Bart, now you're talking, sounds healthy."

"It would be Earl, except they ferment the grain, which means they let it rot."

"What do you mean they let it rot Bart. Just why in cotton pickin' hell would they do that…?"

"To get the alcohol out Earl."

"Alcohol…! What in carnation is that Bart…?"

"Well Earl, they mix all the healthy ingredients with water and let the mix age until it's rotten. This process produces alcohol. Then they store this alcohol in oak casks for years, until it becomes whisky."

"That's downright disgusting Bart. What does whisky do…?"

"Ah Earl, this is the good part. When you consume enough of this whisky, you lose all your senses, talk gibberish, your knees cave in, you can't walk properly and you make a complete dick of yourself in front of your family and friends. If you consume regularly, you become what they call a *'drunk'*. You lose your job, break up your family and friends, lose everything you own and eventually die a very painful death from cirrhosis of the liver. We gotta get onto this one soonest Earl, it's gonna be a killer…!" *(Reference - Bob Newhart's original tobacco story)*

Okay, we have to accept, humans are indeed a weird but wonderful species. We'll happily destroy each other and the planet for self-gain, just to be one better than our neighbour. We have to have the latest fashion, the latest gadgets, the latest everything, so we can be seen as *'Mr. Cool'*.

Why do we do this…? Mainly, because we have out of control egos. We're also pretty weak minded, easily misled by others and will jump into a fire if necessary, just to prove a point. However, our history, our past, our early survival instinct, encrypted into our DNA, has obviously determined to a large extent, who we are as a species today.

Evolution...

Darwin magnificently postulated, all life originated from non-life and evolved in a purely natural manner with minor body changes over time, in fact, a long period of time. A process Darwin aptly named: *'Natural Selection'*.

Darwin posed these slight body changes were then continually passed on to the next generation. Over time, these changes accumulated to such a degree, the result was an entirely different species. Not just a variation of the original, but an entirely new species...!

For example: If a member of a species developed wings and learnt to fly, the species would originally have begun developing tiny back bumps, which over time emerged as small wings, eventually growing into larger wings, enabling the species to actually lift off the ground and fly. Its offspring naturally inherited this advantage and passed it onto their offspring in a continuous cycle. Eventually the inferior or disadvantaged members of the same species gradually died out, leaving only the superior or advantaged members of the species to continue.

Neuron scientists tell us the only reason we still don't have a tail is because our brain no longer recognizes that part of the body. This is known as neuroplasticity or cortical remapping. It is the brain's ability to change as a result of an experience in life, meaning the brain is actually malleable. Natural brain stimuli and thought energy can be re-routed. People suffering from strokes for example, have been able to fully recover due to the brain's ability to re-map cortical routes. This evolution of the human brain over time, is a prime example.

Would a mother gorilla pick up an infant boy and mother it in the wild like the mythical story of Tarzan...? She might, since most social animals are not stupid; they can tell if an animal is threatening or if it's a harmless infant. A female gorilla who'd recently given birth herself, would likely pick up the baby and mother it. The evolutionary maternal instinct is strong in all social beasts. She could very well bring the kid back to her den and rear him. He would not however, learn speech like Tarzan did but he would most likely learn all gorilla traits, mannerisms, etc. He would evolve naturally with the gorillas.

Palaeontologists tend to agree on the overall theory of evolution but there are still many varying viewpoints re the extent of the various species historical progressions.

Homologous versus Analogous...

Evolutionary biologists prefer to make a distinction between homologous and analogous anatomical structures. Two structures are said to be homologous if they have a common embryonic and phylogenetic origin. For example, a human being's forearm, a bird's wing and a dolphin's pectoral fin are all composed of the same bones, probably inherited from a common distant ancestor and are therefore, considered homologous structures. In contrast, analogous structures are structures fulfilling the same functions in different species but are derived from two completely different evolutionary lines. An insect's wings and a bird's wings offer a good example. Both are used to fly, but taxonomically, they have nothing in common with each other. Analogous structures are the product of convergent evolution; they represent differing solutions that various organisms developed independently to cope with the same constraints in their respective environments.

The more science analyses nature's historical progress, the more they discover the intrinsic evolutionary progress of all life on earth. Specifically, when they're able to achieve fundamental inroads into the varying cell formations of all life forms. If only Darwin had known…!

The theory of evolution is based on all species being related and gradually changing over time. Accordingly, life began in the ocean as bacteria and evolved from there. Various DNA traces mixed together and produced life forms, which eventually evolved into non-vertebra fish and reptile species. Algae washed up on land and so plants and trees evolved. Insects evolved from crustaceans. Reptiles sought refuge on land and so began the entire 'Life' evolution.

There are those who say: If people evolved from apes, why are apes still present? Why are apes still thriving as a separate species? It's a valid question. No doubt, Darwin had an answer with his evolution theories and postulations.

It's indeed a deep subject. Some of us however, feel a little uncomfortable with the basic evolution theory that we all originated from pieces of seaweed or similar as this concept somewhat tones down a superior divine presence or creator.

Some scientists believe life on earth originally arrived from space in the form of ice particles, which converted into rain once the ice penetrated earth's atmosphere. Interestingly, this alien water transformation process still happens today.

Whether life originated from water with divine intervention or not, archaeologists have found sufficient fossils of the human race to prove we've been around for eons and evolved with time from a very basic upright walking type of Homo Sapiens' like structure into the sophisticated human status we enjoy today.

The origin of modern humans, according to Mitochondrial DNA and fossil evidence discovered, indicates we (Homo Sapiens) originated in Africa about 200,000 years ago, replacing populations of Homo Erectus in Asia and Homo Neanderthalensis in Europe. According to Wikipedia, Archaic Homo Sapiens (wise man) evolved between 250,000 to 400,000 years ago, which again illustrates the varied discrepancies that abound.

However, the recent discovery of a hominid skeleton

by a nine-year-old boy in early 2010 puts a whole new slant on human's existence. The skeleton was discovered in *'The Cradle of Mankind'*, which is a world heritage site situated about 55 kilometres North West from Johannesburg in South Africa. Palaeontologists claimed the skeleton to be around 1.95 million years old…!

Darwin's evolutional concept, re all physical life forms on earth, continually evolving over time, is real, to a point where gradual evolution in species has been proved. There is too much archaeological proof to deny this. However, the question remaining, which baffles scientists is the human eye debate. The medical Gurus are convinced the incredible complexity of the human eye could never have merely evolved. This question still remains unanswered but, in all fairness, the entire animal kingdom equally boasts implausible senses and other extreme bodily capabilities that defy our imagination.

Fact is - all forms of life on earth, including humans, will evolve with time, in order to adapt, according to their surroundings, lifestyles, needs, wants, desires, etc., including their consciousness.

The average human body contains enough sulphur to kill all the fleas on an average dog, enough carbon to make 900 pencils, enough potassium to fire a toy cannon, enough fat to make seven bars of soap and enough water to fill a 50-litre barrel…!

The Breaking Up of Pangaea...
According to psychists, around sixty-five million years

ago, a huge comet hit our planet. The theory originates, all land on earth was one big continent until this huge comet struck earth and split the land mass up into separate continents and subcontinents, finally settling more or less as they are today. What's fascinating about this, is all the continents fit perfectly into each other like a jigsaw when you put them together as one land mass.

When the new earth settled after the collision, new species of life inhabited Mother Earth. This was of course a process spread over many millions of years. With every recurring Ice Age, most life species became extinct but this is the mind blast: After every Ice Age, the new life species introduced to earth, were smaller, ate less, had more intelligence and were more evolved. In addition, each species had a significant role to play in Mother Nature's Balance, once again reinforcing the belief of an incredibly powerful higher *'God'* source of consciousness, constantly creating and perfecting all around us.

In 1960, satellites were able to photograph earth, enabling scientists to construct a map of the entire world below the ocean. They discovered the surface land was still moving, which means our earth hasn't settled as yet. It's still evolving; energy never relaxes…!

The biggest discovery breakthrough occurred when Palaeontologists were able to date rock and fossils, by recording the Uranium, Radiation and Carbon deposits, using sophisticated Radiometric methods. Fossils were then dated far more accurately by the *'strata'* they were found in.

This fascinating subject is constantly being debated by scientists throughout the world and no doubt will continue to be debated infinitely. Human origin doesn't really affect life in today's modern world with so much happening all around us but it is interesting to know how life began, considering there are so many dogmatic religions completely ruling people's lives, each with their own *'Life'* theory and belief. Throughout history, religious wars have been fought. Blood has been spilt by the bucket load, all in the name of one's faith and it's still happening today. So sad…

Our destiny will always lie in front of us, not behind us but in life, we do get to learn from our past because this is one way of determining **'Who We Were'**.

Whether you claim the past as, *'Evolution'*, *'The Big Bang'* or *'Divine Intervention'*, with man's incredible genes of survival and a competitive desire to succeed at any cost, we wouldn't have got to where we are today, if we didn't have a mind-boggling past.

In the following chapter, we have a look at, **'The Big Stuff'** and the balance effect it has on life, on Mother Earth…!

'Today is only yesterday's tomorrow' – Uriah Heep

The Big Stuff

'Treat the Earth well. It was not given to you by your parents; it was loaned to you by your children. We do not inherit the Earth from our ancestors, we borrow it from our children' - Ancient Indian Proverb

To get a mental picture of *'The Big Stuff'*, look up and observe that massive expanse of space above. To the casual observer this vast Universe, this immense void of seemingly infinite intergalactic activity looks remote and kind of creepy and it is. Space is a cold and eerie place.

Let's begin with our home – Planet Earth. We live only on the surface of this planet, not inside it. Our entire civilised world is contained within a thin layer that exists around the surface of the earth. This thin layer is protected by an atmosphere, which is wrapped around the sphere of the earth, just above the surface, about as thick as the skin of an apple, as a visual comparison.

This complex atmosphere consists of layers of gases, surrounding earth. These gases are retained within the atmosphere by earth's gravity. By volume, dry air contains 78.09% nitrogen, 20.95% oxygen, 0.93% argon, 0.04% carbon dioxide, plus small amounts of other gases. It's quite incredible to comprehend, our atmosphere consists of only 20.95% oxygen, considering oxygen is the life-giving source, most living entities breathe. Too much oxygen on earth and we burn up, too little and all life dies.

When we breathe, we breathe in oxygen and some carbon dioxide. When we exhale, we breathe out mostly carbon dioxide plus some oxygen. The end products of oxidation are carbon dioxide and water. Carbon dioxide is dissolved in the blood, carried to the lungs by circulation and breathed out. Almost all life forms require oxygen. In reverse, plants and trees breathe in carbon dioxide and breathe out oxygen. All mammals breathe in oxygen, which is used to break down carbohydrates into energy in a process called respiration. Note the balance affect here…

Some oxygen comes from photosynthetic organisms like plants and trees. However, the majority of the oxygen we breathe comes from organisms in the ocean like phytoplankton and various seaweed plant species, which help to process and store carbon by transferring carbon dioxide from the atmosphere to the ocean. Both use carbon dioxide, water and energy from the sun to create food for themselves, releasing oxygen in the process.

In other words, they photosynthesize. And they do it in the ocean. Together, these humble plants play an important role. They are the primary producers of organic carbon, which all animals in the ocean food web need to survive. They also produce more than half of the oxygen we breathe on earth. This is one of the reasons why there is more water than land on earth. Without water or air, there would be no life and therefore, no balance. Earth, like the other seven planets in our Solar System, would be uninhabitable…!

Beneath our feet, the sand we walk on every day, is no more than a few tens of kilometres thick. Below that is what Christians would imagine their hell looks like. We literally float on a hot, molten interior.

Earth's newest ocean is the Atlantic. It is remarkably only three percent the age of Planet Earth and is widening as the America's move away from Africa and Europe. Africa is busy splitting apart. In future millions of years, East Africa will hive off to become a separate continent. Over time, while the Atlantic Ocean increases in size, the Pacific Ocean will reduce.

Scientists tell us earth's rocky outer crust solidified billions of years ago, soon after the earth formed. However, this crust is not a solid shell; it is broken up into huge, thick plates (Tectonic Plates) that drift atop the soft, underlying mantle. These plates are made of rock and drift all over the globe. They move both horizontally and vertically. Over long periods of time, the plates also change in size as their margins are added to, crushed together, or pushed back into the earth's mantle.

Most of earth's seismic activity (volcano's, earthquakes, tsunamis, etc.) occurs at these plate boundaries as they interact, sometimes with catastrophic consequences. The explanation for the earth's plate movement is mainly due to the gravitational pull from all the planets, especially the Sun. For this reason, earth's dynamism needs to be flexible, enabling it to react on magnetic demand.

It's the same with the tides. Tides are the rise and fall of sea levels caused by the combined effects of the rotation of the earth and the gravitational forces exerted by the moon and the sun. The tides occur within a period of approximately six and a half hours and are influenced by the shape of the near-shore bottom. At spring high and spring low (every 14 days on the full moon and new moon when the sun, moon and earth are in line) the shape of the earth actually alters, going more oval than round as the oceans shift predominantly to each outer end of the earth, due to the huge planetary gravitational forces wielded.

We know sea levels rise and fall over time and we all probably disagree about the causes but the proof is all around us. The amount of water on our planet doesn't change, it just depends on where it is stored. Either in the atmosphere as water vapour/clouds or on land as water/ice.

In an ice age, sea levels fall, as more water is stored as ice. During a warming phase, ice at the extreme poles, melts, causing sea levels to rise. More water is then stored in the atmosphere due to evaporation. Sea levels have risen about one hundred and thirty metres since the last ice age and will continue to rise over time with the onset of Climate Change.

'Dinosaurs didn't believe in Climate Change either...!'

Gravity...

What we are beginning to see here is there's a powerful force of energy existing throughout our Solar System, controlling and creating a balance for Mother Earth. When we start looking for the source of all this energy that affects our earth so radically, another whole dimension unfolds.

As already mentioned, if we look above earth, we initially encounter the atmosphere, which consists of layers of gases retained by earth's gravity. Gravity, is defined as a force that attracts a body towards the centre of the earth, or towards any other physical body having mass. On earth it is created by the downward pressure exerted, due to the earth spinning on its axis. It has been said, should you fall out of a tree, it doesn't matter if you're good or bad, you'll hit the ground. This is gravity.

For a basic example of how gravity works, consider throwing a tennis ball through the air. The ball spins as it soars. As it spins, the spin creates a force of downward pressure around the ball. The faster the ball spins the more pressure exerted. Likewise, the slower the ball spins, the less pressure applied. This downward pressure is the relative gravity. It's only contained within a minute area around the ball. Further outward (away from the ball), the pressure quickly diminishes.

And here's the mind blast. To keep us all on the ground, our planet has to spin consistently at exactly the right speed and angle. Too fast and we'd be literally planted into the ground. Conversely, too slow and we'd lift off the ground. It's that precise, that exact, that balanced. You can pick up a handful of soil and think you're holding a piece of earth but the reality is, earth holds you. As long as earth continues to spin on its perfectly balanced axis, there will be gravity on earth. And these are just some of the incredible *'Balance Dynamics'* at work on Mother Earth...!

Minor asteroids, space rock debris and so on, randomly flying around our Solar System and occasionally targeting earth, have to penetrate the earth's rotational force (Atmosphere) in order to reach earth. Most of it fails and burns up because it doesn't enter at the right degree of the rotational direction. These are known as shooting stars, which we regularly see at night. Our earth is protected...!

Our sensitive atmosphere has an additional function. It protects all life on earth by absorbing ultraviolet solar radiation, which warms the surface of earth through heat retention (the greenhouse effect) and reduces temperature extremes between day and night.

The extent of the earth's atmosphere varies but it

becomes progressively thinner with increasing altitude. An altitude of 120 kilometres (75 miles) is where atmospheric effects start becoming noticeable during atmospheric re-entry of spacecrafts. Although, the Karman line, at 100 kilometres (62 miles), is often regarded as the boundary between the atmosphere and outer space.

What this all means is our planet is actually surrounded by an invisible *'magnetosphere'*, which is the reason earth behaves like a powerful magnet. The entire Universe is in fact inundated with magnetic fields and powerful gravitational forces exerted from rotating Galaxies, Solar Systems and Planets, all contained within one humungous vacuum we call our Universe. Notably, only five percent of the Universe is made up of matter such as planets, stars and galaxies. There's a lot of empty space out there…!

So, our entire Universe is a magnetic wonder of push/pull dynamics. On earth, we have yet to fully utilise this free electro-magnetic energy existing all around us. Astronaut Michael Collins, on viewing earth from space for the first time, remarked how small, delicate and fragile earth looked in contrast to the immensity of space. We are just a mere spec in the big arena, yet another tiny magnetic rock swirling through space and we're all riding on it…!

Solar System...
Closer to home, our Solar System is considered to be very

stable compared to our scary Universe. The earth's axis is tilted at a perfect angle of 23.45 degrees. This is to enable different parts of the globe to receive varying amounts of sunlight during the year, which in turn creates the seasons.

The term *'Earth Rotation'* refers to the spinning of our planet on its axis. One rotation takes twenty-four hours and is called a mean solar day. Earth's rotation is responsible for the daily cycles of day and night. At any one moment in time, one half of the earth is in sunlight, while the other half is in darkness. The orbit of the earth around the Sun takes 365.26 days to complete one cycle, which is our calendar year. Furthermore, earth's orbit around the Sun is not circular, but oval or elliptical. The Sun rotates at an angle of 7.25 degrees and is precisely the right distance from earth to allow water and sufficient heat to exist on earth. Think about that for a moment. The speed of the earth's rotation around its axis is around 1,664 km/hr. While this is happening, the earth is also systematically hurtling around the Sun at a rather spectacular 107,800km/hr. Our Solar System rotates even faster. It spins around the centre of the Milky Way at an astonishing 791,700km/hr. Incredibly, even at this phenomenal speed it takes 225 million years to complete an orbit, which gives one an idea of the gargantuan size of space and how small earth actually is.

By now you have to be asking yourself how incredible is planet earth…? How precise is it…? The earth rotates on an axis of 23.45 degrees…? Why not 24 degrees or even 22 degrees…? Because it's all about balance…perfect balance.

When we start looking at the bigger picture, it's even more mind blowing. Our Solar System is made up of eight planets, nine if you include the Sun. This void actually consists of a volume of space where the Sun's gravitational pull dominates everything. Its outer limits stretch as far as ten trillion kilometres. A distance that is difficult for us to define logically.

It is however, split into two sections. The first section is known as the *'Inner Solar System'* and contains the four smaller planets. The second section is known as the *'Outer Solar System'* and contains the four larger planets. In between the two sections is the *'Asteroid Belt'*. It consists of minor planets and large chunks of rock and space debris. The Asteroid Belt completely separates the Inner Solar System from the Outer Solar System.

Mercury, the smallest planet, is closest to the Sun. It has an eighty-eight-day orbit, which almost resembles a perfect circle and has a 7.00-degree ecliptic tilt in comparison to earth's 23.45 degrees. The planet is only fifty-eight million kilometres away from the Sun so it is incredibly hot and humid. Venus, the second planet is almost the size of earth and is one hundred and eight million kilometres from the Sun. It is surrounded in a thick and dense atmosphere of deadly carbon dioxide with deep white layers of cloud covering its surface.

Earth is the third rock from the sun with Mars our

closest neighbour, in fourth position. Mars is smaller than earth. It is the last of the four inner rocky or *'terrestrial'* planets contained within the Inner Solar System. Mars is known as the *'Desert Planet'* or sometimes as the *'Red Planet'* because this aptly describes this barren and inhospitable planet. Past Mars we get the *'Asteroid Belt'* with all its minor planets and space debris rotating in a constant orbit around the Inner Solar System.

After the Asteroid Belt we get the Outer Solar System. The four Outer Planets are giants in comparison to the four inner planets. Their orbit around the sun is huge. We have Jupiter, Saturn (with its distinctive rings), Uranus and Neptune. They are all largely composed of liquid hydrogen with no solid surfaces. Encircled by rings and moons, each one is so large they almost represent a mini Solar System on their own. Jupiter is the largest planet, more than ten times the diameter of planet earth. Saturn is the most beautiful planet of them all, surrounded by a ring system that consists of shiny ice particles. The rings are ultra-thin, only about a hundred meters thick.

Uranus is covered in dense cloud and always appears featureless. It takes eighty-four years to complete one Sun orbit. Neptune, the outermost planet, known as the *'Blue Planet'*, is covered in a deep cloud with a distinctive *'blue'* colour. It takes sunlight over four hours to reach this planet. Neptune is slightly larger than Uranus.

Similar to the four planets of the Inner Solar System surrounded by the Asteroid Belt, so the Outer System planets are surrounded by what is known as *'The Kuiper Belt'*. This is an expanse consisting of countless dwarf planets that are constantly in orbit. Among the larger dwarf Planets, is the well-known mini planet, Pluto.

This is just our Solar System. Our Solar System belongs to a Galaxy, which includes billions of other Solar Systems that all contribute to our *'Milky Way'*. When you look up at the sky at night, every twinkling star you see represents yet another Solar System. The planets don't twinkle, only the stars do. You can also look up during the day but due to the Sun's reflection you can't see the stars. Our galaxy belongs to a Universe of which there are billions of spinning Galaxies contained within this Universe. So, just how small and insignificant are we in the big picture...? Humbling, isn't it...? And there are those among us who still think this all happened by chance...!

Within our Solar System, our Sun is gigantic in relation to the planets orbiting around it but compared to other Solar Systems within our Galaxy, our Sun is considered fairly moderate. There are some really big Sun's with even larger Solar Systems existing in our galaxy. Obviously, there are many planets with life as we know it, existing throughout similar Solar Systems in this gigantic Universe.

We'd be extremely naïve to think our tiny earth was the only *'life'* planet within this humungous Universe. Astronomers are finding planets similar to earth every other day and that is just within our galaxy.

On November 4, 2013, astronomers reported, based on Kepler space mission data, there could be as many as 40 billion planets similar to earth, orbiting in the habitable zones of Sun-like stars and red dwarf stars within our Milky Way galaxy. And there are billions of other galaxies out there.

In *A Brief History of Time* by the late cosmologist and author, Stephen Hawking, who was one of the leading scientists in physics, based at NASA, illustrates how our wonderful Universe works. Hawking scientifically peels back the Universe, layer by fascinating layer, providing an illuminating insight into the dynamics of the intergalactic gravitational pushes and pulls, which help maintain balance within our mighty Universe. According to Hawking, with our limited current space travel ability, it would take astronauts something like three hundred and fifty thousand years to reach other Solar Systems. This certainly puts that dream out of our sights for now.

Big Bang Theory...
Hawking and fellow scientists, suggest the Universe literally exploded into being. NASA scientists discovered the *'Doplar Shift'*, which led to this theory, based on the colour of energy. Take for example an approaching car. It is bluish as it approaches you but turns reddish as it passes and leaves you. This same principle equally applies in space. NASA scientists discovered, all the galaxies are reddish in colour, meaning they are moving away, which

means our Universe is still expanding. Reverse this situation and everything (the entire Universe) compacts into a dot...or nothing.

Therefore, the entire Universe began as a microdot (or nothing) and simply exploded into existence. The catalyst was one massive explosion. This happened from a substance smaller than an atom, which exploded in size to say an orange in less than a trillionth of a second. The entire Universe was then created atom by energised atom, via gravitational push/pull energy forces caused from the initial explosion. Conversely, if we reversed the process, could we go back in time...?

According to Hawking, the majority of our Universe originally consisted of hydrogen gas. Gravity exerted from the initial explosion compressed independent volumes of hydrogen gas to fuse into helium, which is heavier (denser) than hydrogen and so the cosmic evolution process began. Hydrogen then fused into Lithium and eventually into carbon and finally, into iron and so the stars were born.

The evolution process in forming a star is infinite. Other heavier metals like gold and platinum are also produced from further fusing. The iron core of a star eventually implodes on itself due to the heat created and then explodes in an amazing array of colour, which is called a 'Supernova' or the death of a star. It's not quite as simple as all this though because everything (all the elements) have to be perfect before it happens but we're talking about this all happening over billions of years in time, in fact 13.7 billion years, for this is when they predicted, the Universe commenced.

However, stop the bus – it's a great theory and probably works cosmically but if the Universe had a beginning, then surely someone or something originally started it. Even the *'Big Bang'* would have initially required someone or something to initiate it. It's kind of difficult to imagine *'time'* just starting.

Considering the incredible density and complexity of the Universe, the perfection of the planets and Solar Systems, it's surely way too complex, too precise, to just haphazardly fall into place with no steering wheel.

In addition, accepting this theory would obviate the presence of a superior Celestial Consciousness, constantly creating and controlling our hurtling *'earth'* rock through space. If we accept this theory of a Godless Universe, then do we also accept the absolute brilliance of DNA for example...? Its intricate complexity is unexplainable. It could never have naturally occurred or originated on earth without a superior intellect in control. The design and coding behind DNA reveal an intelligence beyond our imagination. A mere pinhead volume of DNA contains information equivalent to a stack of paperback books that would encircle the world five thousand times.

DNA has its own language, a language far more complex than any language man has ever produced or probably ever will be capable of producing. For these reasons, many Quantum Physicist's believe the coding within a DNA molecule points to an intelligence far exceeding anything that could have possibly occurred by natural causes on a dirt filled, crusty earth, let alone in stringent and clinical laboratory conditions. They believe the creation of all life and the magnitude of the entire Universe, have the justifications and obvious fingerprints of a vastly superior celestial creator at work.

Back to space. If we could travel at the speed of light (we can't) we'd reach the outer extremities of our Galaxy in around eighty years. By achieving this we'd then be able to travel into the future as one day in space would equal one year on earth under those conditions.

On the 16 August 1977 a radio telescope station based in Ohio in the USA, recorded a radio wave from a star system located over two hundred light years away. It became famously known as the 'WOW' radio wave and consisted of six letters and numerals. If the guys at the radio station had to reply, it would take a further two hundred light years for the reply to reach its destination, meaning the aliens who sent the original message would only receive a reply four hundred and something years later. Consequently, the original senders would no longer be alive...!

Re our Solar System – one needs to understand how complex and yet how perfect and balanced our Solar System is. Let's take a moment here and re-cap: Our Solar System has eight planets of various sizes plus several moons all specifically positioned and all orbiting on their individual perfect axis. In addition, they're all orbiting around the Sun, which is also spinning. Plus, our Solar System, which represents one of many Solar Systems, revolves within a huge Galaxy. And finally, our Galaxy is one of untold billions of Galaxies, all rotating within a gigantic Universe. This constant rotational movement of everything, creates continual gravitational forces and magnetic energy pulses throughout our entire Universe.

The significant difference here though, is our mighty Universe is not exactly a human friendly place, considering we have supernovas (exploding stars), black holes, dodgy comets, asteroids and so on, constantly orbiting throughout our Universe. Whereas, when we zero in on our Solar System, a very distinctive picture emerges. Our Solar System consists of absolute perfection, absolute balance. Each planet within our Solar System is a definite size, in order to guarantee just the right amount of gravitational pull to maintain the overall system and keep all the planets orbiting perfectly in sync and in position. Our Solar System is that balanced.

The various planet' moons have many functions but with their respective sizes and positions they also serve an additional function. Similar in effect to the weights attached to motor car wheels to balance the wheel, the various planet's moons are incredibly, absolutely perfect in size with exacting orbital rhythms, to sustain a perfect balance, by providing the precise amount of gravity to maintain their respective planet's orbits.

And all of this for planet Earth to perfectly exist...!

Earth is the only planet within our Solar System that is perfectly positioned within the Solar System, suitable for life with the ideal oxygen/nitrogen mix, fresh water, arable land, an ocean filled with life, a protective atmosphere and perfect gravity to keep us earth-bound and so on. The other planets within our Solar System are totally in-hospitable for human life. This means we have only one planet within this vast arena we call our Solar System, meeting all the criteria and therefore perfectly suitable to sustain life, as we know it. The other seven planets are flawlessly positioned within our Solar System to deliver the ideal mix of gravitation and whatever else it takes, to precisely position earth within our Solar system and maintain its axis, thereby creating a Perfect Balance. Take a minute and absorb these phenomena…

Armed with this knowledge and the absolute perfection of our Solar System and planet earth, makes it very difficult for anyone to deny the presence of an incredibly powerful higher source of Universal Consciousness, constantly controlling, designing and creating, with specific focus on the many *'earth'* planets orbiting within perfectly balanced Solar Systems, throughout the Universe.

We call this higher source of energy **'God'** because this is the accepted word. In later chapters, we get a lot deeper into this sensitive subject.

How does this affect *'Life'* on earth...? As much as we have a powerful force of gravitational energy controlling the balance throughout our Solar System, likewise, it impacts directly on Mother Earth with a magnetic energy force known as the Geomagnetic Field, causing all magnetic needles to point due North. This vitally important field is used by nature, humans, animals, insects and marine life, to *'tune in'* and circumnavigate their way.

In the following chapter we have a look at *'Balance'* and the incredible effect it has on all of us in life...

'Gravity explains the motion of the planets but cannot explain who set the planets in motion' - Isaac Newton

Balance

*'The main reason Santa is so jolly is because he
knows where all the bad girls live...!'*

Santa is this enchanting, colourful character who flies
around the world in one night and delivers toys to every
child on Christmas Eve, or so the fable goes. It's this story
of being able to fly around the world in one night that is of
interest to us, sort of makes the world seem like this
minute place. Fact is, it is small and this realisation was
driven home in depth just the other day of how
diminutive it is.

We live in Jeffreys Bay, South Africa. While out in the
ocean enjoying our favourite passion, which is surfing, a
fellow surfer who hailed all the way from New Zealand,
on the other side of the world, paddled over for a chat
while waiting for a wave. He spent the next ten minutes
describing in detail how he'd travelled around Africa,
chasing the African coastline in search of the perfect wave.

He couldn't prevent himself from repeatedly explaining how he felt about Africa: the pulse, the magnificent wildlife, Black Africa, poverty, appalling corruption, the vast plains, the heat, the arid conditions, the few who *'have'* and the many who *'have not'*, rampant crime, abundant natural resources, a harsh reality where life has little value and yet to him, the African eastern and western coastlines were so incredibly exquisite to behold, he couldn't believe Africa was all one magnificent continent with so many extraordinary diversities.

We thought about what he'd said and replied that it must have been a difficult transition to make coming from New Zealand where everything was disciplined, clean and orderly, neat and tidy, the scenery breathtakingly beautiful with clean, mountain air and a safe protected environment.

His reply was instant. He said it had nothing to do with having to make any type of transition. As far as he was concerned, we are all one world. We all belong. No matter where we come from or how we live, we all walk on Mother Earth. He said, "It's just sand you know, just sand, it doesn't matter where you are, it's just the same old earth's crusty sand and we all walk on it…!"

He's so right. Whether we're walking on a continent in the Southern Hemisphere or on a continent over in the Northern Hemisphere, we're still walking on sand, essentially still walking on Mother Earth. And it's the same with life. We're all humans existing in one world.

Yes, we are all vastly different with diverse cultures and outlooks on life but fundamentally we all eat, sleep and survive on this amazing God given planet called Earth.

The sages say human life is like a river, begins as a small stream and steadily matures, joins other streams (partners/ friends/marriage), unites, meanders, takes many turns, has many adventures, faces challenges, enjoys wonderful discoveries and glorious moments, eventually runs into the ocean with all the other streams and finally settles. Once it begins, it completes its journey. This is Life. It is what it is...

It doesn't matter if you're English, Russian, Japanese, Chinese, European, Indian, Hispanic, African, American or other, for this is just our exterior appearance; on the inside we all consist of the same divine energy. It's no different with the sand we walk on. No matter where we are in the world, it's all just sand and we're all heading for that big ocean. Yet we still choose to fight over it...!

When we look at a perfect triangle it always represents *'Perfect Balance'* because no matter which way it stands, it'll always be on a base with the central pivot point of the triangle at the top. If we cognitively incorporate this image to symbolise *'Life'*, it represents a typical yin and yang conflict of how we strive for **'Balance'** in our lives, from the day we are born until we pass on and leave this earth plane because achieving a consistent balance in life is a major part of our daily life challenges. If we understand this and accept these vital energy forces of opposites exist in life, we can use them to our advantage.

However, achieving a relative balance in life can be complicated, considering our complex emotions; life's many twists and turns; our indomitable ego; plus, the various challenges and opportunities we face ad infinitum. In fact, the deeper we progress on our life path, the more difficult and confusing it can be.

For example: We have day and night; male and female; black and white; good and evil; hot and cold; positive and negative; and so on. These opposite energy forces are all direct and indirect balances we deal with in everyday life.

Yin & Yang – Perfect Balance

For mankind, opposites often exist for the purpose of communication. Without heat how would we define cold...? Remove one element and the other automatically becomes an empty, lifeless word with no meaning. They are simply a human fabrication to describe how we feel but they are still opposing balances that affect our everyday lives.

Many guru's use the *'Three Roads'* metaphor to define balance in life. The high road is when life is supreme, business is rocking, your love life is solid, companions and fame are at an all-time high, etc. The low road is exactly the opposite, nothing works for you, everything is against you. The middle road is when you have balance. However, one needs to initially experience both the high and the low roads in life in order to appreciate how special the middle road is.

Sadly, it's normally only at the end of our journey or circle of life, when we discover, all that we seek is actually within us already. In reality, we need only awaken from our dream of separation and imperfection to realise our spiritual God (the Collective Consciousness) is within us all. When we have Oneness, spiritual balance flows in abundance.

The following is a lovely story, which metaphorically explains this *'yin and yang'* concept: At a certain college, there was a professor with a reputation for being tough on those who believed in God. At the first class every term he'd ask if anyone was a believer and then proceed to degrade them and mock their faith. One semester, he put a question to the class:

"Who can answer, did God make everything...?"

A student raised his hand and replied, "Yes sir, God did!" The professor responded, "If God made everything, then God made evil." The student didn't have a response and the professor was happy to have once again proved all faith is a myth. Then another student raised his hand and asked, "May I ask you something, sir...?"

"Yes, you may." The professor responded. The student stood up and said, "Sir, is there such a thing as cold...?"

"Of course, there is. What kind of question is that...? Haven't you ever felt cold...?" The professor snapped back. The young man replied, "Actually sir, cold doesn't exist. What we consider to be cold is really an absence of heat. Absolute zero is when there is absolutely no heat. Cold does not really exist. We only created the term to describe how we feel when there is no heat." The student continued, "Sir, is there such a thing as dark...?" Once again, the professor responded, "Of course there is...!" To which the student replied, "Actually sir, darkness doesn't exist either. Darkness is the absence of all light. Darkness is only a term man developed to describe what happens when there is no light present." The professor was silent. Finally, the young man said, "Sir, with regards to your earlier question about evil, do you really believe there is such a thing as evil...?" The professor smirked, responding confidently, "Oh yes I do. We have rapes, murders and violence everywhere in this world. We are terrorised regularly with evil." To which the student replied, "Actually sir, evil doesn't exist. Evil is simply the absence of God. Evil is a term man developed to describe the absence of a Godly presence. God did not create evil. It isn't like truth, or love, which exist as virtues such as heat or light. Evil is simply a state where God is not present, like cold without heat or darkness without light." The professor shook his head and abruptly changed the subject.

Nice story to depict the concept of opposing energy forces in balance. Without trying to confuse the issue, as already mentioned, you need to understand; as long as we have the 'one', we'll always have the 'other'. This is how opposites work. When they are in sync, there is balance. When they are out of sync, there is chaos.

From a more positive perspective, in the same way we get rid of darkness by producing light or overcome cold by introducing heat, so we can also get rid of evil and negative thoughts by exercising good thoughts. Try it…!

Are there both good and bad people on mother earth…? Well yes and no. From a physical, society point of view, we can easily determine right from wrong, good from bad. We can point fingers and say those people are bad because they commit wicked acts and we can likewise point fingers and say those people are good because they do acts of love and kindness. However, from a spiritual point of view, there are no good or bad people, there are merely those have 'seen' and those who have yet to 'see'.

This is balance. Mindfully realising this quality, is

when you've opened the door – you're now walking a path of light and spiritual love…!

On this earth plane and on the *'Other Side'*, we experience many levels of spiritual development, which we refer to as *'climbing the ladder'* from one spiritual level to the next. In life, as we progress, we see, we learn, we add knowledge and wisdom. We gradually transcend up the ladder, hopefully as better people, balanced people.

Kind of like the experienced guitarist who plays effortlessly and yet the one still learning to play has difficulty in connecting all the dots but eventually gets his fingers working cohesively. He gradually improves with time, moves up the musical ladder. And the bonus is, once he starts to improve, he wants only more, aspiring for the highest level, knowing full well there is no highest level because learning and developing, like seeking balance, is infinite.

It doesn't always mean the gifted guitarist is a better person than the learner because we all have our skeletons in the cupboard. It's like people who were once chain smokers but managed to give it up. Ironically, these same people become the biggest anti-smoker campaigners, when all that's actually happened is, they've *'seen'* the light, they've understood, they've discovered balance in their lives. Without realising it, they've moved up the ladder, leaving the die-hard smokers behind but if they continue campaigning against the smokers, then they're still attached, so they lose their balance. They need to break free completely and move on in order to safely transcend the ladder and find their balance again.

The recent Covid19 virus that smashed the world and brought it to a complete standstill is a prime example of how balance affects us all. For every country, those in authority had to find a balance, a delicate balance between the defined lockdown time period and when to let go and kick-start the economy. Too early and the virus wins, too late and the economy fails.

When the balance is right, all is good and harmonious, we go forward. Whereas, when one side of the scale is loaded, the reverse happens, we regress. And it happens in life and in everything we do. Whether it's the world, the environment or it's personal, without balance the situation stagnates, progress is one sided, which means 'one' has taken from the 'other' and tilted the scales, leading to conflict, destruction, intolerance, disharmony, dissonance, etc. Difficult for one to escape the effects of balance...!

It's like the concept of 'time', which we use to balance our day. In reality, time doesn't exist. Every day is just another day, merely one more earth revolution on its perfect axis. We only measure time to organise our lives, like getting to work on time, attend meetings on time, etc. Whereas our Universe works unconditionally, it's not dependent on issues like time or any other human production or invention but even our mighty Universe reacts to balance.

Another example would be hunters or poachers (same thing really...!). There are those who feel it's their given right to murder an innocent animal and feast on its flesh. And then there are those who have *'seen'*, realised all life is precious, all life has a right to live, all life belongs only to God and therefore has an equal right to exist in God's world.

However, the equalization (the Spiritual Balance of Karma), guarantees, whatever you put out, you will receive with interest. Take an innocent life and you will pay dearly until you finally learn to *'see'*. Always bear in mind – our Solar System works in Perfect Balance. Likewise, Mother Earth functions cohesively when in Perfect Balance, as does your personal life function perfectly when you're in Perfect Balance.

Finding a balance is an eternal search. It happens with everything you do; from spiritual, to work, to your love life, your sport and even your social life. Don't overdo the work; keep time for the family. Don't over commit to sport; keep some time for socialising and so it continues. It's a constant juggle with time being the parameter because you only have so much time so you try and use it the best you can. You need to enjoy life but don't go overboard (you may not come back...!). We live in a society that promotes an impulsive and sometimes chaotic lifestyle. We strive to:

- Work to get to the top of our field
- Cook gourmet meals from scratch

- Stay supremely fit
- Volunteer for everything
- Be active on all social media, write a blog, etc.

And so on...

It can at times be a struggle to find a moment of downtime, a moment for *'self'*. As life becomes increasingly more hectic, even the activities that bring us joy can feel like just one more thing to do, one more mountain to climb.

Often, we look for some external solution to make us better, stronger, more spiritual or happier but once again, even the search itself can leave us feeling busier, more stressed and ultimately, even less fulfilled. So, how do we bring balance into our hectic lives...?

Balance is ideally about getting centred, grounded, bringing everything back to normality. We do this by seeking within, living in the present moment, ensuring a consistent and even energy flow. Energy constantly flows throughout our body via our sensitive nervous system, including our subtle Chakras (energy centres).

The essential ingredient however, is to honour our body's internal messages. We do this via meditation or by spending time in nature. Sometimes being alone or doing things creative. Principally, partaking in activities that bring us joy. Ideally, we can return to our centre if we make a concerted effort to reconnect to our inner wisdom by letting go of life's clutter for a while. It's about slowing life down.

It can affect us physically as well. Unfortunately, via bad eating habits, bad posture, lack of daily exercise, alcohol and nicotine abuse and so on we tend to build up unwanted toxins. We call these toxin build-ups *'energy blocks'* because they're not only a health hazard; they also prevent the even flow of energy throughout the body, which ultimately upsets our balance. Muscle spasms, which inflict pain, are also energy blocks. If we ignore them and don't confront them, they'll imprint on our Subconscious. We then end up living with these problems instead of dealing with them.

Yoga is the study of balance and if balance is our comfort zone, a balanced spiritual yoga practice can bring us full circle, offering both peace of mind and physical fulfilment. Doing yoga is one way of getting rid of those unwanted energy blocks as yoga exercises are specifically designed to stimulate the overall body and revitalise the nervous system plus doing yoga is remedial for restoring overall balance. You'll soon find your centre and get grounded.

Breathing techniques as well as a good body massage are also methods that will assist in clearing the energy paths throughout the body and help restore balance. Sometimes we just need to look at things from a different perspective in order to mentally understand how to create a balance in life. It's about thinking laterally as opposed to thinking vertically or thinking *'outside the box'*, which is another way to describe alternative thinking.

This is how opposites work. They create a balance, which is the core of the cosmic vibration for seeking *'Balance'* in life. It's a definition, which features indefinitely because almost everything throughout life ultimately revolves around a system of balance, or direct cause and effect. It's also the equivalent of Newton's third law: *'For every action there is an equal and opposite reaction'.* In the east, people refer to it as Karma.

We will always have those who have *'seen'* and those who have yet to *'see'* and it applies to every aspect in life. If we take time to pause for a moment, mindfully think about it and mentally come to terms with these phenomena, accepting there are magnetic energy forces of opposites constantly at play throughout the cosmos with resultant consequences for upsetting the balance, then we can use these vibrant energy forces to our advantage, merely by being conscious they exist and acting accordingly.

One of our life objectives therefore, is to create a reasonably consistent balance in life, both physically and spiritually. It's not about living in constant fear because you're worried, you'll upset your balance, it's rather about being aware, everything has a consequence. Often, it's not only you who suffers from the result of your imbalances, it's your loved ones as well. So, tread a little more warily before leapfrogging into anything without carefully thinking it through. Rather look for the balance in life. It's like the old Doctor's quote, *'Everything in moderation…!'*

When it comes to meditation, balance is high on the list of must haves because we need both mental and physical balance in order to find inner peace for a completely relaxed meditation session.

Magnetism...

Magnetism in all its dynamics, embodies balance because it not only represents positive and negative forces of energy, it's actually one of the components driving our Universe.

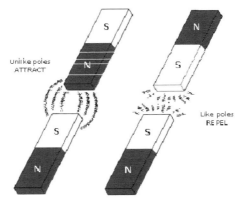

To understand this further, we need to look at how basic magnets work. A magnet has two ends that are referred to as poles. One pole is called North, the other is referred to as South. Scientifically, these poles represent either a positive or a negative mode. To attract magnets towards each other, you have to place the opposite ends (North & South) of two magnets near each other. Placing like ends (North & North or South & South) of two magnets together, causes the opposite to occur; the magnets repel.

The dynamic we have here, is the *'energy'* existing between the two poles of each magnet. This simple yet powerful form of energy is infinite. As long as the magnets remain magnetised, the energy exists and it's perfectly balanced.

As an energy source, magnetism equally plays a significant role, even in simple everyday industrial use. A magnetised piece of iron (electro-magnetic) has the energy to lift many times its own weight. If you switch off the power and demagnetise the same piece of iron, it becomes just another piece of iron, unable to move anything.

In Japan, they have high performance trains running on magnetism. Opposites will always attract. Take the majestic lightning bolts you witness preceding a storm. Lightning begins within a storm cloud, comprising minute water droplets and ice crystals. As they propel around within the cloud at high speed, they collide with one another, creating an electrical charge. The positive charges rise to the top of the cloud while the negative charges descend to the bottom of the cloud. On the ground below, positive charges build up on trees, poles, rooftops and other exposed areas. These opposite charges then attract. Negative charges from the bottom of the cloud, bolt towards earth while positive charges from the ground stream upwards. When these highly charged opposite electrical pulses collide, lightning occurs, creating massive bolts of energy.

There's the story of the Swiss physician, Franz Anton

Mesmer who in 1976 amazed the medical world, healing patients by stroking their bodies with magnets. Plus, we have the *'Bermuda Triangle'*, a region in the Western part of the North Atlantic Ocean (Bermuda, Florida and Puerto Rico) where aircraft and surface vessels occasionally disappear. Scientists believe this is due to an inordinate amount of magnetic activity in the area, affecting sensitive navigation instruments.

This is *'Magnetic Energy'*. You cannot see it with the naked eye but if you drop a few iron filings between the two magnets, you'll immediately see the push/pull combination.

These mysterious effects also explain the enigmatic behaviour of molecules and how their atoms, consisting of electrons, protons and neutrons, create constant push/pull patterns of perfectly balanced magnetic energy.

And this is the lightbulb moment - everything throughout our Universe, all life, including all of us, consists of atoms. Therefore, everything is magnetically bound and connected. Please, take a moment and mindfully absorb this phenomenon.

The following is a lovely story about life and balance and how we tend to lose sight of our objectives when we're faced with daily challenges that upset our balance. We so easily ignore the opportunities we have right on our doorstep: A small fishing boat docks in at a tiny Mexican fishing village. An observant tourist approaches the boat and compliments the fisherman on board for the quality of his fish and asks him how long it took to catch the fish.

"Not very long." The fisherman replies.

"Why didn't you stay out longer and catch more...?" The tourist enquires further.

"Because this small catch is sufficient to meet my needs and those of my family." The fisherman explains with a smile.

"Then what do you do with the remainder of your time...? The tourist probes.

"I sleep late, fish a little, play with my children and take a siesta with my wife. In the evenings, we go into the village to visit our friends, have a few drinks, play a little guitar and sing some songs. We have a full life."

The tourist quickly interrupts, "I have an MBA from Harvard University. I can help you. You should ideally be fishing longer every day. You can then sell the extra fish you catch. With the extra revenue, you can buy a bigger boat."

"And after that...?" The fisherman asks, shaking his head.

"With the extra money the larger boat will bring, you can purchase a second boat and then a third one and so on until you have an entire fleet of trawlers. Instead of selling your fish to a middleman, you can then negotiate directly with the processing plants and maybe even open your own plant. You can then leave this little village and move to Mexico City, Los Angeles, or even New York City. From there you can direct your huge new enterprise."

"And how long will that take...?" The Mexican asks.

"Perhaps twenty to twenty-five years." The tourist replies.

"And after that...?" The fisherman asks, shaking his head.

"Well my friend, that's when it gets really interesting," the tourist answers and starts to chortle, "when your business gets really big, you go public, you can start buying and selling stocks. You will make millions...!"

"Millions...? Really...? And after that...?" The fisherman asks incredulously.

"After that you'll be able to retire, live in a tiny village near the coast, sleep late, play with your children, catch a few fish, take a siesta with your wife and spend your evenings drinking and enjoying time with your friends."

"But that's what I am already doing now." The fisherman replies, laughing...!

Lovely story. Don't walk in the dark. It's so much easier if you know where you're going in life, especially if you're able to maintain an equal balance. The simple but effective anatomical balance of a positive and a negative reaction, is the basic primary protocol for all energy forms to exist, which brings us to the subject of *'Electro-Magnetic Energy'* and how it affects us on Mother Earth.

*'Balance is not something you find
it's something you create'*

Electro-Magnetic Energy

'In the end you won't remember time spent in your office or mowing your lawn every Saturday. Climb that mountain, write that book today...!' -J. Kerouac

In a previous chapter, we established how our Universe produces electro-magnetic energy, created from the gravitational forces of the billions of rotating planets, Solar Systems and Galaxies, throughout our Universe. To take this concept earth bound, magnetism as an energy source equally plays a significant role.

More than 3.5 billion years ago, embryonic life first arrived on earth. As primitive life evolved, it encompassed the earth's magnetic frequency and tuned in, essentially using the frequency to navigate. When human life finally arrived, another relationship began, a relationship that science is only recently beginning to understand and accept.

The Schumann Resonance...

You naturally feel happier and more peaceful when you're out in nature, away from noise, traffic jams, and neon lights. This is because when you're outside, breathing fresh air, with that pungent earthy smell beneath your feet or experiencing soft rain splashing on your face, your body tunes into the earth's frequency and restores, revitalises and heals itself. This is due to the earth behaving like a gigantic electric circuit. Its electro-magnetic field surrounds and infuses all life with a natural frequency pulsation of 7.83Hz.

This pulse (The Schumann Resonance), is named after physicist Dr Winfried Otto Schumann. The frequency circulates in the cavity bounded by earth's surface and the ionosphere, surrounding the earth. The ionosphere is the ionized part of earth's upper atmosphere, from about 60 km to 1,000km altitude, a region including the thermosphere and parts of the mesosphere and exosphere. The ionosphere is ionized by solar radiation from the sun. It plays an important role in atmospheric electricity and forms the inner edge of the magnetosphere.

It has practical importance because, among other functions, it influences radio propagation to distant regions on earth. The area below the ionosphere is called neutral atmosphere, or neutrosphere. Earth's electro-magnetic field is created by the clashing of the ionosphere, which is positively charged by the sun, and the earth's surface, which carries a negative charge.

Interestingly, the 7.83Hz Schumann resonance falls precisely in the middle where human Alpha brainwaves and Theta brainwave ranges meet. This range of brainwaves facilitate a deep coupling of human physiology with the earth's resonance. These brainwave frequencies induce relaxation and meditation; a state that enables us to tap into the wealth of creativity lying just below our conscious awareness, but more about that subject in a later chapter.

Dr Wolfgang Ludwig discovered, while earth's vibration could be clearly measured in nature and in the ocean, it was difficult to measure anything in the city, due to the massive manmade and destructive signal input from radios, TVs, cars, smart phones, etc. He was concerned how this radiation affected humans because his mother suffered frequently from Foehn symptoms, caused by certain weather phenomena such as low pressure and high winds. Her symptoms were so strong she had absolutely no energy and could hardly move. In 1974, Ludwig created a small magnetic pulsar, imitating earth's magnetic fields. It was a small hand-held box, which emitted the Schumann frequency of 7.83Hz. As soon as his mother applied the device to her solar plexus or on the back of her neck, the symptoms disappeared.

The good doctor then proved that human health was related to geophysical parameters and variations in naturally occurring patterns, which produced mild to disastrous health and behavioural changes. He and others, later documented this relationship in various experiments.

Notably, Professor R. Wever, from the Max Planck Institute for Behavioural Physiology in Erling-Andechs, built an underground bunker that completely screened out magnetic fields. Between 1964 and 1989, this bunker was used to conduct 418 studies using 447 human volunteers. Student volunteers lived for four weeks in this hermetically sealed environment. Professor Wever observed; the students' circadian rhythms diverged and they suffered emotional distress and migraine headaches. Since they were young and healthy, no serious health conditions appeared but older people or people with a weak immune system had a different response. After only a brief exposure to 7.83Hz, the volunteers' health stabilised. Astronauts and cosmonauts out in space, when no longer exposed to the Schumann waves, report similar symptoms.

Electro-magnetic fields are dynamic entities, causing charges and currents to move and respond accordingly because electro-magnetic fields embody and store patterns of information. They become a connecting bridge between matter and resonant patterns. The Schumann Resonance and the natural electro-magnetic patterns of earth, act like a tuning fork, not just for the biological oscillators of the brain but for all processes of life. The bridge that connects resonances and brain frequencies, resides in our DNA helix, developed since early life began in the earth's environment.

In 1981, Dr Richard Alan Miller, published a detailed scientific paper, showing how human beings are coupled with the isoelectric field of the planet and how everything alive responds to the subtlest changes in the magnetic and electro-magnetic fields surrounding it. However, with all the vibration frequencies caused by the super accelerated manmade technological developments of our time, we are creating an environment that is out of tune with nature itself.

Ample anthropological evidence shows how humans have intuitively synchronised with the planetary resonance throughout human history. There is cross-cultural evidence demonstrating a variety of ritualistic practices, which enhance this harmonisation with the planetary field. Perhaps the most obvious *'drivers'* of these trance states are shamanic drumming, trance dance and the chanting of mantras, which have been in use for over 50,000 years.

Scientist, Robert Beck, researched the brainwave activity of healers from various cultures and religious backgrounds (he enumerates psychics, shamans, dowsers, Christian healers, seers, ESP readers, kahuna, Santeria, wicca practitioners plus others). Independent of their belief systems, each exhibited nearly identical EEG signatures during their *'healing'* moments: a 7.83-8Hz brainwave activity, which lasted from one to several seconds, which was phase and frequency-synchronised with the earth's geoelectric micro-pulsations, i.e. the

Schumann Resonance.

All life comes from life, we can only exist where life was once before. It's a widely accepted fact in science, life cannot exist without life to initially bring it about. Therefore, scientists have yet to create *'something'* into life from *'nothing'*. Luc Montagnier, the Nobel Prize award-winning scientist, found how DNA strands in separate test tubes, communicated at low frequencies and even exchanged nucleotide information (something that had never been accomplished before in a lab). These frequencies were found to create the very building blocks of life. This was the first time the building blocks of life came together into something from nothing. What did Montagnier do that was different...? He applied the resonant earth frequency of 7.83 Hz.

Everything on this planet, including animals, plants, and water is made of atoms, which produce, emit, and receive energy and they all operate at a specific frequency. Our tissues, cells, organs, emotions and thought patterns, have their own unique electro-magnetic fields, as do allergens, viruses, bacteria and fungi. Like a subtle spider's web, everything is connected in one way or another. It may not be all harmonious or equal but the electro-magnetic earth connection with everything, definitely exists.

We tend to reduce our bodies' anatomy down to a simplified version that consists of only flesh and blood. Grasping the intangible is something we cannot immediately experience via our senses. It can be challenging. This limited understanding of the intangible has led us to ignore therapies and practices, which have the capability to heal our bodies from disease by reading and correcting, resonating with our magnetic field and subsequent frequencies.

Quantum physicists are constantly discovering the intangible laws of electro-magnetism, which will inevitably change the way we currently practice conventional western medicine. Many areas of the world have been using this invisible energy for diagnosis and healing for thousands of years in acupuncture and other ancient healing therapies. Imbalances residing in our bodies and minds are detected and reduced via the correction of their particular electro-magnetic fields, through the means of biofeedback.

The beginning of biofeedback belongs to Claude Bernard, who proposed way back in 1865, how the body strives to maintain a steady state in the internal environment and how humans can take control over their physiologic functions to achieve a level of constant wellness.

After World War II, a mathematician named Norbert Wiener developed 'Cybernetics', which is the scientific study of control and communication. Healthy tissue responds in a predictable manner, while unhealthy tissue conducts erratic pulses. Traumatised, inflamed or degenerative tissue all produce abnormal readings compared to a patient's baseline norm. In the cybernetic loop, a biofeedback machine measures the body's frequencies and produces feedback for wound healing, pain reduction, relaxation and stress reduction via electro-magnetic stimulation.

During biofeedback therapy, electrodes are attached to the patient's skin, which in turn send an in-depth analysis to the equipment. Once the imbalances and stresses have been identified, the machine's program selects from a vast database of vibrational biofeedback therapies, to help return balance and relief for the patient.

In the late 1920's, Dr Royal Raymond Rife invented the Rife Machine – one of the first frequency generators. According to Dr Rife, every disease has a frequency. He found certain energy frequencies prevented the development of disease and others could even destroy it. Dr Rife's machine was tested with cancer patients at Pasadena County Hospital. The doctors put patients under treatment for 90 days and found 86.5% of the patients were completely cured of cancer. The remaining patients were further tested and underwent additional treatment; they too were cured. In other words, an astounding 100% of patients included in the program were cured of cancer.

The Rife machine was a total hit during the time due to these impressive cancer cure rates. Major pharmaceutical companies tried to buy the technology to conduct more research on his equipment but Dr Rife refused to sell.

It's well known, toxic substances (alcohol, tobacco, drugs, consuming animal flesh and dairy, plus radiation from cell phones, gamma rays from computers, TV's, etc.) distort the negative equilibrium existing in a living cell.

Due to these toxins, the cell becomes depolarized, losing its ability to magnetise and divide normally. The cells either die or they corrupt and divide abnormally, invading nearby tissues. These malignant cells then spread to other parts of the body through the blood and lymph systems.

American inventor Nikola Tesla (1856 – 1943) who pioneered electrical technology said, "If we could eliminate certain outside energy frequencies interfering with our bodies, we would have greater resistance toward disease."

Bees (including many insects/birds/animals) are incredibly sensitive to man-made electro-magnetic energy fields. The USDA estimates, a whopping 80% of crop pollination is accomplished by bees. The busy bees are exceptionally important to Mother Nature in so many ways. Sadly, worldwide, bee colonies are currently collapsing.

Physicist, Dr J Kuhn conducted experiments and discovered, mobile phone radiation as one of the major problems, considering there are now over four billion mobile phones in use worldwide. Man's interference with microwave ovens, X-Ray machines, mobile phones, especially cell phone towers, computers, television's, etc., have seriously clashed with the earth's natural electro-magnetic field, with devastating results.

In 2011, the World Health Organisation reclassified mobile phones as carcinogenic to all life on earth - and yet we still use them...? *RadiationHealthRisks.com* observes that 1G, 2G, 3G and 4G use between 1 to 5 gigahertz frequency. 5G uses between 24 to 90 gigahertz frequency and then asserts that *'Within the RF Radiation portion of the electromagnetic spectrum, the higher the frequency, the more dangerous it is to all living organisms.'* These man-made Gamma rays effect our health (as well as animal and plant life) by eroding our immune and sensitive nervous system, to the point where a common cold soon becomes bronchitis and even worse, pneumonia. Be aware...!

In 1940, during WW2 the British used Radar, which is *'Radio Detection and Ranging'*, to pinpoint German planes en route to bomb the UK. The signal works when a magnetic field is established between two objects. One object sends out a signal to the other object. When the signal reaches the other object, an image of the object is returned. It works purely on an electro-magnetic signal, sent on a specific frequency, a magnetic vibration. It's magnetic because the signal is instantly returned, once it hits the other object.

Pacific salmon are born with an inbuilt *'magnetic map'* that helps them migrate over thousands of kilometres. USA researches believe the fish are capable of sensing the changes and intensity of the earth's magnetic field to establish their position in the ocean. They use the earth's magnetic field to navigate their way. The epic journey of the Pacific salmon is one of nature's greatest migrations. The fish hatch inland in rivers and streams, before swimming many kilometres to reach the open ocean. After several years of foraging at sea, they make their way back to the same freshwater sites where they spawn and die. Such is the magnetic influence of the earth's energy field...!

This same phenomenon, affects migrating birds and insects throughout the world. They cover vast distances, from continent to continent for seasonal changes, relying solely on the earth's magnetic field to tune in and reach their destinations safely.

In the human body, magnetism is the power source of the entire nervous system. Information delivered from the brain travels throughout the body in the form of electrical signals, called nerve impulses. When no impulse is transmitted, the ions outside a membrane of a nerve cell are positive whilst those impulses on the inside of the membrane are negatively charged. This positive/negative attraction then polarizes (magnetises), allowing the information (impulse) to magnetically pulse through the membrane and continue. Nerve impulses sent from the brain move at an astonishing speed of 274 km/h. Can't imagine how they measured it...!

We already have Climate Change with Tsunami's, earthquakes, hurricanes, raging fires, extended droughts, a polluted ocean and so it continues as man liberally extends his footprint for maximum self-gain.

For continual survival, man needs to protect earth's existing magnetic energy field and not erode it with his manmade electromagnetic fields, which he is currently exercising his right to actively do so.

That '*Space*' Thingy...

In life, we often sense an invisible but very real, almost existential entity, which we refer to as that '*Space*' thingy. It appears throughout life. Although vastly different to an *Auric* space, which is defined, other '*Space*' entities exist and they are omnipresent. Earth's magnetic force creates push/pull dynamics that at times generates rather strange effects on earth. As already defined, everything is made of atoms, which consist of molecules, consisting of protons, neutrons and electrons that are all magnetically charged. It's this positive and negative field that often creates these unseen subtle forces on earth.

Take for example the '*Silence*' that sometimes occurs in a conversation. It's an awkward and even uncomfortable moment. Everyone in the conversation feels it intuitively. It cannot be seen or touched but it's definitely there. People will subconsciously scratch their head, fidget or whatever until the moment passes and the conversation continues.

The unpleasant nature of such silences is associated with feelings of anxiety as the participants feel pressure to speak but are unsure of what to say next. This *'Silence'* or *'Space'* entity in this situation is a nervous reflex generated from the ego (negative ions) because the ego is very aware of its self-esteem (positive ions). Although we can't see it, we all know this intangible polarity of energy exists.

Ben Thouard, winner of the coveted 2019 Red Bull Illume Award for photography, is an avid waterman, capturing photographic images above and below the waterline. He claims his photography lives and breathes in the space above the water and the abundant energy lying under the waterline. Says, "It's all about the light, which gets reflected for this is where the texture, the substance, the matter, is created between this timeless and surreal meeting point, just above and just below the surface". The dynamics here, both above and below, are either negatively or positively charged, creating an energy release at the meeting point, for it was at this eclipse of the meeting point when the magic for Thouard happened. This was the *'light bulb'* moment that made him see the light so to speak. He says this was the pinnacle focus he'd been searching for to create a platform for a unique and creative perspective. For him, it was an enlightening experience. He pursued this unique take on his photographic journey with passion, which eventually earned him his photographic awards. This subtle blending of the above and below the waterline dimension, climaxing in an existential meeting point, was the polarised or magnetic *'Space'* existing between these two entities.

The *'Space'* thingy comes in many guises…! Musicians are often judged by the genre they play. However, there is a silent understanding, a certain respect between musicians, re those who are classically trained, read music, play in orchestras or big multi instrument jazz bands as opposed to musicians who play by ear, write some lovable tunes, play the club circuits and manage to sell their songs, get radio play and earn a bunch of fans. They're all professional musicians (earn a living from their music) but there is a distinct dividing line, almost a respect between them. It's unspoken but revered and once again, about that surreal *'Meeting Point'*. Joe Soap in the public domain cannot see this line, this *'Space'* that exists between the classical musician and the rock musician. People might say, 'Once you're a musician you can play anything.' That's like being a Jack of all Trades but master of none. Most musicians will stick to their genre's, seldom venturing out of their comfort zone, almost as if there is a barrier of sorts prohibiting them from crossing an unseen line. This is that *'Space'* thingy. There is of course the fact that they don't share the same musical knowledge but that invisible wall, that intangible negatively and positively charged *'Space'*, still exists.

Keith Richards of the Rolling Stones fame, in his Bootleg series on *'You Tube'*, talks about a powerful electro-magnetic wall of energy that exists between the stage and the audience, whenever the Stones perform. He says the combined energy projected from the audience plus the band's energy, projected outwards towards the audience meets in this unseen *'Space'* or *'Meeting Point'* in an explosive magical euphoria. He claims, 'It's the most incredible high one could ever experience, there's a euphoric feeling of unconditional love, enveloping everything and everyone, almost like you've been transported into another dimension or zone, drowning in dopamine as the brain's pleasure centre is overwhelmed with joy…!'

Richards claims he understands the polarity and science, creating the incredible electro-magnetic energy forces but he says the love and joy created from the *'Space'* could only descend from a superior Celestial Being because it's a love that is beyond any kind of love man experiences in everyday normal life. This is what happens when a massive positive and negative polarity of energy is created, completely unseen, invisible but felt by everyone present. These are highly charged vibrations…!

And then there is the actual *'Space Between the Notes'* paradigm, originally claimed by both Claude Debussy and Arthur Rubenstein back in the day, now used liberally from Miles Davis to Maya Angelou. It's an esoteric issue but actually reality because it's all about feel and timing. Some have it from birth, born with it, others have to work at it, some sadly never get it. Musicians feel the notes on a fretboard or a keyboard or a sax or whatever, but use the space between the notes to create the timing. Let's take a saxophone, for example, if you blow a series of notes, they're just notes but when you play them in a melodic scale pattern and insert the right spaces between the notes, you produce beautiful music.

Evolved musicians, like Miles Davis, are emotionally aware of this elusive negatively and positively charged '*Space*' that exists between musical notes. Emotionally, because they '*feel*' it within. This isn't something one can touch. It's more of a sonic feeling because music is this wonderful enigma that beams us up into that eclectic vortex of the brain where dopamine is released in pleasurable quantities.

One cannot describe the personal experience of hearing a piece of music and what it means to each of us because it's different for everyone. As individuals, we always have this esoteric need to hear the musical piece for ourselves, to understand the nuances, the melody and the lyrics. It's our individual interpretation of the music that matters. Music is a personal thing with a particular vibration, each of us feel and experience personally, differently but sincerely.

For most of us, this is a time to momentarily stop whatever we're doing and mentally tune in, completely absorbed in the melody, the lyrics, the rhythm, the feel of the song and often, we're able to recall sublime personal memory reflections. With our feet tapping away and head bobbing rhythmically, we slide into that pleasurable, lazy mental zone. Busy Beta brainwaves are replaced with slower Alpha brainwaves. Our active left brain effortlessly slips over into our dreamy, creative right brain mode and we simply let go, all life problems are gently released until the music slides to a close. Its paradise - earphones are such a blessing…!

When guitarists play a solo by ear, they mentally only hear that specific space between the notes. Their fingers touch the fretboard but that's only to feel and play the right note. What they're mentally hearing is the space between the notes because that micro space is all about perfect timing and perfect timing is what creates a meaningful solo. Listen to the greats playing the blues, you'll get it. They feel every note. Their continual flawless delivery is an expression of their passion for the blues, a passion for that distinctive sound that resonates deep within all of us and it's all about that 'Space'.

Eric Clapton was affectionately referred to as 'Slow Hand', not because he couldn't shred with the best, it was because he had an instinctive ability to stretch a specific note past the time period. When Clapton bent a string an octave up, he held it there for at least a semiquaver past the bar, tickling it with a slight vibrato before slowly releasing the note and effortlessly sliding back down the scale with those nimble fingers to fall into time with the next bar and he did it without thinking about it because it was all about that intangible 'Space between the notes' that held his attention. In these situations, he'd obviously completely slid over into his creative, automated right brain mode because he didn't need to think, he just did it. To him, it felt right and that's what it's really all about in music; when you start feeling it, when you start feeling those magnetically charged *'Spaces'*.

Yogi's talk about the space between the breaths. Inhale, hold it *'Space'*, exhale. A central part of yoga is about breathing. Each tension and release are breath controlled. With yoga, as you go into a stance, you breathe in and breathe out as you let go. A tangentially similar scenario to what meditation gurus refer to as focusing on the *'Space Between the Breaths'*, to reach a meditative state of being. In meditation, you focus on your breath to still your busy mind. In a deeper meditation you focus on the *'Space between the Breaths'*. This is what brings you into the present moment, allowing you to look within.

These subtle energy forces are negatively and positively charged vibrations we resonate with subconsciously. Whether they are the *'Silent'* moments or the *'lightbulb'* effect or the intangible *'Space between the Notes'* or even the *'Space between the Breaths'*, we all know these energy centres exist but didn't realise their frequency was in the 7.83Hz. range.

The discovery that humans are tuned to the natural harmonic frequency of the earth is relatively recent in science circles, built upon the same principles of Nikola Tesla's electro-magnetic understanding of the Universe, which surely starts (magnetically) connecting all the dots…! Our health, clarity of mind and also our mood and inner balance, depend very strongly, on the frequencies we are exposed to or absorb into our body, by way of food or liquid.

Living in a world of frequencies and vibration, or electro-magnetic energy, makes us part of the whole system. Every cell of our body vibrates at an optimal frequency. When we are in tune, each cell of our body vibrates at the frequency it was designed to, there is no effort, no conflict.

A state of balance is also achieved when the cells, the body and the mind resonate at their natural frequency. When you're positively feeling good, then your frequency is obviously right. When you're in your natural state with no stress or emotional disorder, your frequency levels are neutral, compared to someone who is in disarray. Laughter raises your frequencies. Happy people have higher frequencies and for this reason, are less prone to disease.

When we look at our health conditions from an energy point of view, we're able to feel the imbalance and disharmony. By simply re-balancing our frequencies, we have the power to improve our situation. We can control our emotions with simple breathing exercises, as taught in yoga, to calm the mind and restore the balance.

Understanding what is happening around you will avoid you feeling uncomfortable or awkward in situations plus there are many ways where the 'Space' entity can be a huge advantage, like in sport, music, work or when you're in your lazy creative zone. Live the moment, feel the space, it's real…!

We conclude this chapter with a story to illustrate transparency or more appropriately, things in life are not always as they seem. The way we initially look at issues with a left-brain point of view is sometimes way off course. This story is about a blind woman who was flying from Singapore to Bali. Unexpectedly, the plane was diverted to Jakarta. Having landed in Jakarta the Captain informed the passengers there would be a delay before taking off again.

"If anyone wants to get off and stretch their legs you should do it now". The Captain confirmed over the intercom. Everybody got off the plane except the blind lady. The Captain approached her and gently stroked the guide dog that lay curled up at her feet. "Madam, we are going to be in Jakarta for almost an hour. Would you like to get off and stretch your legs?" He enquired. The blind lady replied, "No thanks Captain, but maybe Roxy would like to stretch her legs, can you take her please."

Now you have to visualise the next scene. All the passengers waiting in the gate area came to a complete standstill when they witnessed the Captain wearing his sunglasses, slowly exit down the plane ramp with a guide dog at his side. The passengers were almost frantic in their haste to not only change planes but to even change airlines, no matter the cost…!

Things are not always as they appear. Try thinking alternatively. Preferably, allow Mother Earth's electromagnetic energy to flow through you with a natural frequency pulsation of 7.83Hz. It's all good. Most of all, enjoy life and dance with the fairies...!

50,000 cells in your body died and were replaced by new one's while you were reading this sentence...!

Energy

'The sensation of energy expands with increasing relaxation'
~ Ilchi Lee ~

Who Are We...? Just one of the intangible questions everyone wants to know. In this chapter, we try and answer this deep, deep question by focusing on energy. We've now seen how energy exists in many forms. Of particular interest here though, is the existence of energy as a life source on earth. However, to try and understand energy as a life source, we first need to look at what energy's subject matter consists of.

To be fair, in Darwin's day they didn't know too much about energy and energy composition whereas today, we know a bit about our Universe, our Galaxy, our Solar System, Mother Earth and most of the composite energies surrounding us.

As already discussed, but repeated here in a little more depth - basic science tells us energy is a composition of atoms and infinitesimally minute particles. Taking cognisance of this, let us begin with life forms that live on our planet, like the human body. Here we have delicate and intricate organ systems, which consist of cells and stem cells. Cells are created from a composition of molecules, consisting of atoms. Atoms arrive from a composition of magnetic activity consisting of protons, neutrons and electrons. The protons and neutrons are in the core of the atom, called the nucleus. The nucleus is surrounded by an infinite rotating wave of energy because the electrons buzz frenetically within the nucleus (at various energy levels) in what is called an electron cloud, producing a positive and negative field for the molecule. Molecules then combine magnetically together to form cells. The number and shape of the electrons and their continual orbits provide cells with a specific set of vibrational frequencies. And so, it begins...

Cell Formations...

Almost all your cells get replaced every seven years. This might explain the seven-year itch because by then you're a completely different person compared to the one you were when you originally got married...yeah, right...!

Cells have only one objective and that is to multiply. This is how we get our human block building cell-structure format. Cellular body mass is a composition of

Amino Acids, Fatty Acids, Proteins, Carbon and other elements plus, Genes like RNA and DNA, i.e. the basic ingredients of our life form.

The cell theory, developed in 1839 by microbiologists Schleiden and Schwann, succinctly describes the properties of cells. It is an explanation of the relationship between cells and living things. The theory states:

- all living things are made of cells and their products
- new cells are created by old cells dividing into two
- cells are the basic building blocks of all life

Scientists have since discovered there are in fact tens of thousands of complex systems that exist on just one miniscule human cell and all life (including early life on earth), consists of cell formations. There are zillions of them and they get replaced as quickly as they die off.

According to well-known author, Paul Hawken, humans consist of around a quadrillion-cells, 90% of which are not even human cells. In addition, each human cell has four hundred billion molecules conducting millions of processes between trillions of atoms within the body. The total cellular activity at any one moment in a human body is a mind boggling one septillion actions (that's a '1' with 24 zeros after it...!).

Molecular biologist Michael Denton wrote, 'Although the tiniest bacterial cells are incredibly small, each cell is in effect a veritable micro-miniaturised factory containing an unfathomable amount of exquisitely designed pieces of intricate molecular machinery, far more complicated than any machinery ever built by man and absolutely without parallel in the non-living world'. Proving once again, there is a Universal higher Celestial Consciousness, designing and creating.

In one way this is exciting, because we're obviously making huge inroads into cell technology; like genetic pollination and engineering in life forms such as plants, flowers and animals. Animals can even be cloned. Advanced science technology is rapidly enveloping humanity every day in every way. Early life's evolution path is now studied within and without. Everything is exposed in fascinating 3D detail.

We even have CRISPR. This is a technique allowing scientists to make precision edits to any DNA, whether bacterial, animal or human. Scientists discovered the technique when studying a certain bacteria's immune system. They gave it the acronym CRISPR, which stands for *'Clustered Regularly Interspaced Short Palindromic Repeats'*. Who even knows where this direction will take us in the future because CRISPR kind of allows biologists to play at being a Deity…? Just by slightly altering a species' DNA structure, biologists can create whatever they want. It's as simple as copy, edit and paste. Existing experiments done on mice and dogs have produced muscle bound specimens. It's incredibly cruel and a very scary prospect for the future of our world.

Imagine this power getting into the wrong hands. Comic book futuristic super-beings are here...!

Note: this is not about having the ability to write new DNA (we are nowhere near that), this is about copying strands of existing DNA and pasting them into another DNA but it is still mind boggling that man can do this.

Consider for a minute the life of a common insect. In their little world they also have minute insects or parasites that live on them and those parasites also have parasites, ad infinitum, but now we're reducing the life size to the point where it's only bacteria. It's all life though. Blood is as much the lubricant of a tiny insect's body as it is in a human body and equally plays its part in reproduction. It's all about cells and cell formation...!

Divine Energy...

As a species, we are indeed complex. To re-cap - our bodies (our life form) consist of energised atoms morphing into molecules that reproduce into block building structured human cells. It's a lot more complicated but this is the basic format. How then does this energy form (our human body), inherit a spirit energy force (a soul) from conception and take life...?

As already discussed, the human body consists of complex cell structures, which can be created or destroyed. However, the actual spirit energy (the soul, which is you) within the body, consists of *'divine energy'* created via *'divine thought'*, by God, the Universal Consciousness. We are created in God's image (a spirit energy force). This is the *'Real You'*, your soul, your spirit. You are divine energy.

There isn't a surgeon available who can dissect your head, surgically remove your brain and extract your soul because you cannot see it, taste it, feel it, or smell it. It's almost as if your soul doesn't exist. If you could see God, you'd be able to see your soul because your soul is a finite part of the Universal Consciousness, which is God.

If you can accept this and understand and believe, your soul consists of divine energy, then obviously your soul cannot be recreated or destroyed; only the *'Life Form'* (your body) will eventually expire. You, your soul, lives on indefinitely. You are a spiritual being, an energy field, an eternal source of infinite energy, created in God's image, which is divine energy.

'And so, God created man in his own image' - Genesis 1:27.

God is **NOT** human therefore our human form cannot resemble God, only our spirit form can. This divine energy is trapped inside a human form/body. We have bodies so we can play the *'Game of Life'* on earth, where we get to experience joy, hardship, pain, ecstasy, love and so on. It's called *'Life'*…!

'And Jesus said, the greatest power in heaven and earth is thought. God made the Universe by thought and paints the lily and the rose with thought' - Chapter 84.22/23 The Aquarian Gospel

We are referred to as Spiritual Beings, *'Beings'* because we are *'born'* into our bodies. In other words, we have taken *'form'* plus the deep internal awareness we have of our thoughts, is surely proof, our *'Spirit'* (the Real You) is indeed within us, which means our *'Ego'* (thoughts) therefore, cannot be Spirit. Both of these mirror entities subsist in co-existence. This is what gives our *'Spirit'* its substance, it's balance. This is the living proof...

'And Jesus said, The Kingdom of the Holy One is in the soul; men cannot see it with their carnal eyes; with all their reasoning powers they comprehend it not. Its recognition is the work of inner consciousness' - Chapter 75 15:16 The Aquarian Gospel

Consciousness...

The resonance theory of consciousness builds upon the work of Pascal Fries, a German neurophysiologist with the Ernst Strüngmann Institute, which helps explain not only human and mammalian consciousness, but consciousness more broadly, i.e. the nature of consciousness as a general phenomenon of all matter. This is based on the observed behaviour of the entities surrounding us, from electrons to atoms to molecules to bacteria to paramecia to mice, bats, rats, etc. According to Fries, all things may be viewed as at least having some consciousness.

This is known as *'Pan Psychism'*. It's an increasingly accepted position with respect to the nature of consciousness. An electron or an atom, for example, may enjoy a microcosm of consciousness. If this is possible then everything has a consciousness (of varying levels) because everything consists of atoms and all atoms express a vibration, frequency and energy output.

The subject of consciousness has gone from simplicity historically, to extremely prodigious currently. The cause of this phenomenon is due to the popularity of thousands of documented cases of Near-Death Experiences (NDE) globally, which have literally had physicists' pole-dancing for attention.

American neurosurgeon, Dr Eben Alexander, in his acclaimed book, *'Proof of Heaven'*, describes his *'near death'* experience. During his journey, he was guided by a woman he'd never met before but he instantly recognised her (many people report meeting *'guides'* or *'teachers'* during a near death experience). However, Dr Alexander felt he'd known this woman for a long time. She guided him around his entire *'afterlife adventure.'* The chill factor is, Dr Alexander was adopted. He had no idea who his original birth family was. It was only later in life when he discovered his original birth family. They showed him a photograph of his sister, who had sadly passed away, so he didn't get to meet her. He instantly recognised the sister in the photo as the woman who had guided him during his *'afterlife adventure.'*

Another fascinating story is former Navy science officer, David Bennett who drowned for around twelve minutes. During this time, he had a *'life review'* and met people he recognized who were no longer part of his lifetime. He was also shown the future. He would get cancer and survive it. When he recovered, the doctor told him he had terminal cancer. He responded by saying, 'Thank you Doctor, I already know that, I'm going to survive it.' The doctor tried to correct him but Bennett had already seen he would survive. And he did.

It's in the reporting of new information like this where a reputable person is able to point to consciousness existing *'outside'* the brain; it therefore cannot be something imaginary, it has to be real. If during a near death event, everything one had been brought up to experience had already occurred, then it could be claimed, it was imagined. With so much documented research and clinical case studies in support, the biblical concept of *'Heaven'* is obviously a reality. Maybe not in pure Biblical terms but certainly, an afterlife exists.

If these NDE cases were mere hallucinations from the drugs administered by the medics then the patients couldn't have been declared dead by the medics because once the brain ceases to function, it's impossible to have any type of hallucination. This proves consciousness lives on indefinitely.

The majority of NDE cases follow a similar pattern, with the patient having left their body and idly witnessing the medical staff still around their inert body before their spiritual being is led away with the help of a Celestial presence and finally enjoying the presence of a higher spiritual consciousness of unconditional love.

Due to all these NDE cases, even the most hardened and sceptical worldly neuroscientists are now accepting: A Godly presence exists within us all and without, connecting the entire Universe with an omnipresent celestial divine energy force of unconditional love. Kind of like electro-magnetic energy – it cannot be seen but we know this energy exists all around us – ditto…!

Okay, it's a lot to digest and accept so, consider this simple analogy - think of a huge beach full of sea sand. This pile of sand, consisting of untold zillions of grains of sand en masse, represents the Universal Consciousness (God). However, each separate grain of sand represents a single Sentient Being, each with their own unique consciousness, but connected to the Universal Consciousness. Therefore, individually we are all a finite part of the Universal Consciousness, whom we call God, who is actually the sum of the Collective Consciousness of all life on earth and the Universe. This is what gives Universal Consciousness its power.

If we absorb the good from God (Universal Consciousness), our world moves forward in a positive direction, which is why positively addressing issues like Climate Change, animal farming, ocean and land pollution, over fishing, CO_2 emissions, wars, terrorism, etc., are so vitally important for the human race to urgently correct.

Obviously, when the world gets out of control and regresses, so do we, including everything on earth. It's a lot more complicated than this but this philosophy represents a logical and simple format. The issue here is trying to get the majority of life on earth into a positive state of mind because this is what accelerates our worldly spiritual growth and stabilises our world.

This can only be done if influential people like spiritual gurus, politicians, rock stars, sports stars, successful business moguls - people who have a mass following, are prepared to walk a path of light and love for the good of the world. A lot of people will then follow.

However, this is a little difficult when man (especially corrupt politicians) are liberally destroying forests, plants, animals, insects and marine life in mind boggling quantities while equally still destroying fellow man, for self-gain and greed. And we were given this world for free...?

They say Consciousness is like a computer without CPU. We cannot physically locate consciousness in the brain. Neuroscientists are of the opinion, consciousness exists all over the brain, becoming active whenever the billions of neurons start firing. We can accept though, the brain is a complex, functioning nerve centre, representing the epicentre of our life form, because everything that happens within our body, originates from the brain.

However, consciousness is not an intrinsic part of this machinery. For example – a television needs to tune in to an external signal in order to operate. If the brain represents a television, then the brain requires consciousness in order to function. The brain on its own is merely a lifeless receptacle. When you die, the brain no longer functions. It requires consciousness in order to function.

At birth we are born with a consciousness, which we inherit from our previous existence on the Other Side. As we grow and mature, our consciousness grows and matures. We all create our own unique, individual consciousness but we're still connected to the Universal Consciousness. We are therefore all ultimately Oneness with everything, electro-magnetically connected via subtle celestial vibrations.

For example - consider your relationship with your dog (a sentient being) and how intrinsically connected you are. Even though you are both completely different species, you can feel the 'love' connection, you know it exists, you know you're both connected. More on vibrations and how they guide and effect you in a later chapter...

Our senses are what feeds our consciousness. We need our senses in order to experience the outside world we live in. By its nature, consciousness requires you to be conscious of something.

If you lost all your senses, your consciousness would be limited to introspection. You would still be conscious, but you'd be limited to 'seeing' things that historically already exist in your mind, through introspection. Consciousness is therefore an individual's state of awareness of their environment, thoughts, feelings, sensations, memories; it is the executive-control system of the mind. The *'intelligence'*, for a simplified explanation.

It was Rene Descartes who said, *'I think, therefore I am'* essentially quantifying, *'proof of existence'*, based on the fact that anything capable of any form of thought, exists. Our relationship, connection or conduit with the Universal Consciousness is meditation and prayer. Remember, we're all a finite part of the Universal Consciousness so we're connected anyway. Unconditional love also binds all life together. Therefore, open your heart and mind to all creations and express heartfelt joy and love in everything you say or do. Alternatively, you'll continue seeking but never finding.

As much as Jesus, Buddha, Krishna, Muhammed or any other deity, are a finite part of God, manifested in flesh and blood but with a unique soul consisting of divine energy, so does all life on earth equally consist of divine energy and a unique soul and are therefore equally all a finite part of the Universal Consciousness. There are no exceptions or privileges for deities, exceptional humans, animals or any other life forms. It is what it is…

As already discussed, the realisation here is: If Universal Consciousness created everything, then Universal Consciousness is also within everything (the *'God Within'*), meaning, within all life on earth and the Universe. The Guru's say our spiritual destiny therefore is to overcome the trappings of our physical body and eventually exist in pure spirit eternally.

This takes some mental digestion but once you get your head around it and see the big picture, the realisation becomes incredibly lucid. The wonderful thing is – God is still creating…our world is still spinning…!

Hopefully this sheds some light on the initial question in this chapter of *'Who We Are…!'* It's an incredibly deep subject and therefore impossible for any of us to say we have the empirical truth on the subject matter, like so many religions claim, but thankfully due to the many *'Near Death Experiences'* encountered by so many individuals, we do have some guidance on this. In addition, there are exceptional clairvoyants/mediums worldwide who connect with the *'Other Side'* and all confirm the existence of a Universal Consciousness of divine unconditional love.

> *'An eye for an eye will only make the whole world blind.'*
> *Mahatma Gandhi*

We conclude this chapter with a wonderful story about the erudite Mahatma Gandhi when he was studying law at the University College of London. A Professor by the name of Peters, disliked Gandhi intensely and always displayed animosity towards him because he never lowered his head when addressing him. As expected, there were always arguments and confrontations. One day Professor Peters was having lunch in the University dining room when Gandhi came along with his tray and sat next to him. The Professor said, "Mr Gandhi, you do not understand. A pig and a bird do not sit together to eat." Gandhi looked at him as a parent would a rude child and calmly replied, "You do not have to worry, Professor. I'll fly away." He got up and moved to another table, leaving the Professor red with rage. Peters decided to take revenge on Gandhi's next test paper but Gandhi responded brilliantly to all questions. Unhappy and frustrated, Peters asked him the following question: "Mr. Gandhi, if you were walking down the street and found two packages. Within one was a bag of 'wisdom', in the other, 'money'. Which one would you take...?" Without hesitating, Gandhi responded, "The one with the money, of course." Professor Peters, smiling sarcastically, said, "I, in your place, would have taken the wisdom." Gandhi shrugged indifferently and responded, "Each one takes what he doesn't have." Professor Peters was speechless. So great was his anger, he wrote on Gandhi's exam sheet the word 'idiot' and handed it back to him. Gandhi took the exam sheet and sat down at his desk, smiling as he contemplated his next move. A few minutes later, Gandhi got up, went to the Professor and said to him in a dignified but cynically polite tone, "Professor Peters, you autographed my sheet but you didn't give me a grade...!"

Would love to have been there to witness this interchange

of dialogue. The arrogant Professor was obviously no match for Mr Gandhi. The moral of the story is, we all belong to the human race. The sooner we can overcome our differences, the sooner we'll advance spiritually.

Inner Self...

To understand life in more detail and discover further 'Who We Are', we need to get in touch with our inner self and understand how this works before we can connect more 'Life' dots together. The brain is the nerve centre of the inner self, so, this is the topic we look at next...

'It's the quality of our work, which is pleasing, not the quantity' - Mahatma Gandhi

The Brain

'An idea developed and put into action is more important than an idea existing only as an idea'
Buddha

The first time you observe an anatomy of the human brain, its many folds and overlapping structures can seem very confusing, you may wonder what they all mean. But just like the anatomy of any other organ or organism, the anatomy of the brain becomes much clearer and more meaningful when you examine it in light of the evolutionary processes that created it.

Probably the most popular model for understanding the structure of the brain in relation to its evolutionary history is the famous Triune brain theory, which was developed by Paul MacLean and became very influential in the 1960s. Over the years since, several elements of this model were revised in light of more recent neuroanatomical studies. Keeping this in mind, MacLean's original model distinguished three different brains, which appeared successively during evolution:

- The reptilian brain, the oldest of the three, controls the body's vital functions such as heart rate, breathing, body temperature and balance. Our reptilian brain includes the main structures found in a reptile's brain: the brainstem and the cerebellum. The reptilian brain is reliable but tends to be somewhat rigid and compulsive

- The limbic brain emerged in the first mammals. Controls behaviours of agreeable and disagreeable experiences, responsible for what we call emotions. The main structures of the limbic brain are the hippocampus, the amygdala, and the hypothalamus. The limbic brain is the seat of the value judgments we make, often subconsciously, which exert such a strong influence on our behaviour

- The neocortex, first assumed importance in primates, has two large cerebral hemispheres, which play a dominant role. These hemispheres are responsible for the development of human language, abstract thought, imagination and consciousness. The neocortex is flexible and has almost infinite learning abilities. The neocortex is also what enabled human cultures to develop

These three parts of the brain do not operate independently. They have numerous interconnections, which influence one another. The neural pathway from the limbic system to the cortex is especially well developed.

According to 'Scientific American', ever since the first mammals appeared more than 200 million years ago, the cerebral cortex has assumed greater importance compared to the brain's other, older structures. Because these structures had proven their effectiveness for meeting certain fundamental needs, there was no reason for them to disappear. Instead, time (evolution) has favoured a process of building expansions and additions to the brain, rather than rebuilding everything from the bottom up.

Scientists have also observed how the size of the neocortex has increased tremendously in primates, from the smallest monkeys, such as lemurs, to the great apes and human beings. Many scientists believe this growth in the primates' neocortex reflects the growing complexity of their social lives. Indeed, the ability to predict the behaviour of other individuals within a group seems to have attracted a large evolutionary advantage. Time obviously favoured the growth of the parts of the cortex responsible for social skills, i.e. language. These abilities were then improved as required. The increase in the folds of the cortex have also been a major factor in the evolution of the brain. These folds, enable a larger cortical surface area to fit inside the cranial vault, allowing for a better organisation of complex behaviours.

It is still common to hear animals discussed as if they were some inferior form of human beings, as if there were some kind of natural ladder on which human beings occupy the top rung. This is not what we see in nature.

Every evolutionary species has naturally developed independently. Rats, for example, are perfectly adapted to their environment. They are not in the process of extinction; they live in perfect harmony with their surroundings. All sentient beings meditate. Observe your domestic cat and you'll understand. The Egyptians nailed it...!

Our ignorance, when it comes to how intelligence arises from the brain, is accentuated by several observations. An adult male's brain is heavier than a female's brain. In the neocortex, the part of the forebrain responsible for perception, memory, language and reasoning, there is a disparity translating to 23 billion neurons for men versus 19 billion for women. However, no difference exists in the average IQ between the two genders.

The cranial capacity of old Homo Neanderthalensis, the proverbial caveman, was between 150cm to 200cm larger than modern humans. Yet despite their huge brain, Neanderthals became extinct around 35,000 to 40,000 years ago, a time when the smaller, more intelligent, Homo Sapiens shared the European environment with these giants. What's the point of having big brains if your small-brained cousins eventually outcompete you...?

Our lack of understanding of the multiplicity of causes that contribute to intelligence becomes even more apparent when we look outside the genus Homo. We observe how animals are capable of sophisticated behaviours, including sensory discrimination, meditation, learning, decision-making, planning and highly adaptive social behaviours.

Consider honeybees. They can recognise other bee faces, communicate the location and quality of food sources to their sisters via the waggle-dance and navigate complex mazes with the help of cues they store in short-term memory. A scent blown into a hive can trigger a return to the site where the bees previously encountered this odour, a type of associative memory that guides them back. This was made famous by Marcel Proust in his *'Remembrance of Things Past' (À la Recherche du Temps Perdu)*. The insect does all of this with fewer than one million neurons, weighing around one thousandth of a gram, less than one millionth the size of the human brain. Are we really a million times smarter...?

The prevailing rule of thumb holds, the bigger the animal, the bigger its brain. After all, a bigger creature has more skin that has to be innervated and more muscles to control and therefore requires a larger brain to service its body. By this measure, humans have a relative brain-to-body mass of about 2 percent.

Smugness is not in store, though. We are outclassed by shrews, molelike mammals, whose brain takes up about 10 percent of their entire body mass. Even some birds beat us on this measure. Humans still have so much to learn from nature and the animal kingdom.

People forever ask, what is it that distinguishes humans from all other animals, on the supposition that this one magical property would explain our evolutionary success;

the reason we can build vast cities, put people on the moon and so on. For a while it was assumed the secret ingredient in the human brain could be a particular type of neuron but we now know, not only great apes but also whales, dolphins and elephants have these neurons in their frontal cortex. So, it is not brain size, relative brain size or the absolute number of neurons that distinguishes us. Perhaps our wiring has become more streamlined, our metabolism more efficient, our synapses more sophisticated but how did we achieve this...?

As Charles Darwin construed, it is very likely a combination of all these factors, including many more that jointly, over the gradual course of evolution, made us adaptively distinct from other species, i.e. walking upright, speech, communication, etc.

We are indeed unique, but the important issue to recognise here is, so is every other life species, each in its own way, just as unique and just as necessary and vitally important to maintain the existence of life on earth. We are all sentient beings, all a divine part of the Universal Consciousness but we have yet to understand the sensitive existential vibrational connection existing between animals and 'The Other Side' because animal vibration frequencies are different to humans, some higher, some lower. It's complicated...

The real puzzle is, because we're all so different in character and behaviour, there's little evidence to show why some human brains are more developed in specific areas than others. With preference to areas specific, i.e. *'analytical'* or *'creative'*, we note how some individuals are able to easily excel over others. We have artists who are better than others and likewise we have mathematical wizards who are better than others. Why do those specific parts of the brain function better in some humans as opposed to others, considering all things equal...? This paradox brings us to the left versus right brain conundrum.

Left Brain – Right Brain...

The left versus right brain theory claims the left brain as the analytical dominant half and the right brain as the creative, dreamy half. The *'right brain-left brain theory'* originated in the work of Roger W. Sperry (1913–1994), who was awarded the Nobel Prize in 1981.

While studying the effects of epilepsy, Sperry discovered, by severing the corpus callosum, i.e. the structure that connects the two hemispheres of the brain, it reduced and even eliminated seizures, (as referenced in a study by Kalat, J.W. in 2009), because this prevented epileptic seizures crossing over from one hemisphere to the other. However, because the corpus callosum acts as a communication pathway between the left and right hemispheres, patients who had their corpus callosum severed, experienced changes in the way their brain handled information.

This led to multiple experiments conducted on split-brained people who had undergone surgery to the corpus callosum. The findings from the studies helped researchers map out the areas of the brain affected by the split. Sperry discovered, if the hemispheres were not connected, they functioned independently of one another. He found the hemispheres in human brains had different functions, i.e. the left hemisphere interpreted language but not the right. In a nutshell, the theory claimed, individuals who are active with their hands like craftsmen, artisans and so on were said to be left brain dominant whereas people who were able to create music, draw, paint or illustrate, act on the stage and so on, were more right brain dominant.

Generally, when people say, 'I am right-brained,' they usually base their statement on the following three assumptions: (Kalat, 2009)

- Different hemispheres are specialised for different functions
- We rely on our dominant hemisphere to process information
- The dominant hemisphere engaged will manifest in our thinking style (e.g. analytical or creative)

While the first assumption is scientifically supported, the other two have no scientific support, only theories. It's a fact, the two hemispheres are not mirror images of each other. It's also true, each hemisphere has its area of expertise. Experts also agree, certain types of tasks and thinking tend to be more associated with particular regions of the brain (also known as lateralisation). However, no one is fully right-brained or left-brained because the corpus callosum enables the two hemispheres to constantly exchange information.

Interesting to note - the right side of the brain essentially controls the left-hand side of the body while the left side of the brain controls the right-hand side of the body. This is for right-handed people.

What emerges from all this science is there are apparent independent practical left and right brain functions we use in everyday life, which we'll mindfully explore further for the purposes of meditation. You can then decide.

The Rubin Vase, Horse/Frog Profile Illusion...

 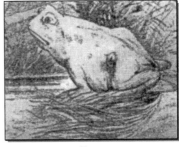

One   Two

At first glance, picture one, is either a vase or a glass. This is a typical instant left-brain pictorial reading. When asked to look at the image again and study it, the average person is able to determine, the image also contains two human profiles staring at each other. This is now a right brain creative function.

The same applies to the second image. At first glance it's a frog. When you have a second look, you can see the image is also a horse's head. Initially, you're unable to see both images at once, only one or the other. Unfortunately, our brain seldom ponders on the message the eyes have relayed to the brain, which then instantly makes a decision based on what was initially seen. Only when the information is recognised by the right brain is the double image noticed. The problem is the right brain is not an active brain like the left brain. It is slower in performance, more creative, which is why the left brain always gets to respond first.

A similar thing happens with speech. How many times has somebody said something and you've immediately replied and then been mad with yourself for having made the remark because it was stupid or sarcastic or rude...? Had you waited a moment; the right brain would have had time to analyse what was said. Your reply may have been completely different.

People have two ears and only one mouth. This means we should ideally listen more and talk less...!

Only when you become aware, are you able to focus and take control. If you consciously think about this every time someone talks to you; you'll be able to mentally block the active left side from immediately answering. The result has two wonderful benefits: You're forced to actually listen to what the other person is saying before you rudely cut in and answer (normally stupidly). The second is you'll mentally slowdown, which is a good thing because reflection is then possible when you slow it all down.

Here's an example: If you were asked to instantly respond to a word with the first thing that came into your mind and the word was *'black'*. Your immediate left-brain answer would more than likely have been *'white'*, which is the direct opposite and quite a normal answer. However, had you paused for a second or two before answering and mentally blocked your left brain and allowed your right brain to answer, you might have answered, *'rain clouds'* instead.

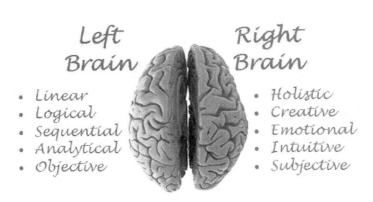

Left Brain
- Linear
- Logical
- Sequential
- Analytical
- Objective

Right Brain
- Holistic
- Creative
- Emotional
- Intuitive
- Subjective

The left brain is so dominant in most of us, we often don't get an opportunity to fully explore the right brain in everyday life. This is because our lives are so rushed and hectic, filled with left brain activities. Unfortunately, education and schooling curriculum's, focus almost entirely on the left brain whilst the other half of the brain is virtually neglected. This often results in the dreamer, the artist and the deep thinker (right brain dominant people) getting hopelessly lost in the schooling system. They leave school early due to frustration and therefore enter the real world largely uneducated.

Although the left brain is the more dominant cognitive power, our objective is to attain whole brain functioning or 'Hemispheric Synchronisation', which means training our minds to use both halves of the brain equally as possible because the results of accomplishing this means you'll be able to achieve higher intelligence levels, enhanced creativity and intuition, the ability to focus sharply, an advanced memory capacity and so on.

'The human brain has a memory capacity which is the equivalent of more than four terabytes on a hard drive'

Inside the Brain...

The brain's lobes basically control everything within our body and how we do things. They receive electrical currents from the nervous system and translate them into bio-chemical signals. We have incredibly sensitive chemical neurotransmitters for sending and receiving information between neurons. A natural decline in the function of certain neurotransmitters can lead to dementia and even depression.

We are however, only interested in our senses and how they feed the brain. All incoming information is received via our senses. The Thalamus receives this sensory information and relays it to the Cerebral Cortex. The

Cerebral Cortex sends information to the Thalamus, which then transmits the information to the respective parts of the brain and the brain stem.

The *eyes* send images to the Occipital lobes and the *ears* send sound information to the Parietal lobe. *Smell* or *scent* is controlled by the Olfactory Bulb, which is situated just under the Frontal lobe. The Parietal lobe is responsible for our *touch* sense and the Frontal lobe is the area of the brain responsible for *'taste,* which is the last of our five basic senses.

The Cerebellum (situated underneath the Cerebral Cortex) is responsible for balance as well as sending all sensory data received to the Cerebral Cortex. Yogi's bring intense awareness to this area for deep meditations. The Hippocampus is one of the most important parts of the brain. If you didn't have it, you wouldn't be able to remember anything. People with Alzheimer's disease lose all functioning of their Hippocampus.

Brainwaves...

Medical Science tells us the brain is an electrochemical organ, which basically means the brain is capable of generating distinctive brainwaves. This is caused by neurons in the brain stimulating electrical charges, which directly influence our meditations, thoughts, emotions, moods and even our senses.

Brainwaves are grouped into various categories and are active within all three levels of our consciousness. When any one of the brainwaves are active within the brain, they have an individual effect on how we behave, especially when it comes to the more relaxed right brain.

Brainwaves have been categorised because each group vibrates at a different resonance, i.e. a different frequency range. Neuron scientists measure them from the least active to the highest activity level.

The three most frequently used devices, to measure brainwave frequency patterns are: Functional Magnetic Resonance Imaging (FMRI); Magnetoencephalography (MEG); and Electroencephalographic (EEG). Of these methods, EEG is the most versatile and cost-efficient solution. All brainwaves run at different cycles or speeds. The slower the cycle, the deeper and more relaxed and powerful the brainwave becomes, which is what we experience when meditating.

1.) Beta Brainwaves...

When the brain is aroused and actively engaged in mental activities, which is for the majority of the average day, it generates Beta brainwaves. These are the most active brainwaves but are of relatively low amplitude. The frequency ranges from 15 to 40 cycles a second.

Beta is all about thinking, doing, acting, it's very busy. When Beta waves are present, the Conscious mind is capable of competently handling many functions simultaneously, whilst still actively functioning and making Conscious decisions. It is known as the *'gearbox'* of the mind. When Beta waves are active, we're like an angry bee, our mind flits at random; thoughts bounce off each other in their hurry to be recognized, each thought suddenly forgotten as we witness and adapt to new situations around us.

2.) Alpha Brainwaves...

Next are Alpha brainwaves, which are slower than Beta but higher in amplitude. Their frequency ranges from 9 to 14 cycles per second. Relaxing, painting, watching movies, listening to music, reading a book and meditating are all signs, highlighting Alpha brainwaves are present within the mind. In Alpha, we are more in touch with our senses and feelings, especially when meditating.

Alpha brainwaves are the abstract or creative brainwaves. When Alpha waves are present, the brain produces the bio-chemical Acetylcholine. This is what stimulates the brain to be creative. With Alpha waves, the mind becomes very good at receiving and analysing information in a calm and relaxed manner whilst still being alert. With Alpha, our metabolism slows down. We often drift off, see images, colours, and experience fantasies. We become aware of all the beautiful energy around us. We can easily get lost for a while once we're disconnected from our active Beta brain chatter.

3.) Theta Brainwaves...

Theta brainwaves follow, with even greater amplitude but

an even slower frequency. The frequency range is between 5 and 8 cycles a second. These are relatively slow brainwaves. Daydreaming, light sleep, dreams, mentally absorbing a beautiful garden, meditating, viewing a full moon or enjoying an exquisite painting, are all indications of Theta waves present. It can be a very creative and sometimes a spiritual experience (meditation). When Theta waves are present, people are frequently exposed to great ideas and historically, have made great discoveries.

It's that time when you are on the verge of sleep but still vaguely aware of what's going on around you. It almost feels like you are in two minds, experiencing light sleep activities whilst still being aware of any physical content like people talking, music on the radio, TV chatter and so on. It is technically called the *'hypnogogic'* state. It's also a state of meditation.

Theta waves are the *'semi awake'* or *'light sleep'* brainwaves. When Theta brainwaves are present, the brain produces the biochemical GABA, a natural relaxant that helps the brain to slow down and absorb information, especially when meditating. GABA is also used by the brain in the production of endorphins, like *'dopamine'*, which are the body's natural feel good chemicals.

We can easily activate Theta brainwaves during meditation. The Subconscious mind also reacts positively to repetitive affirmations when Theta brainwaves are present.

'Brilliant things usually happen in calm minds'

4.) Delta Brainwaves...

Delta is the fourth brainwave pattern. These brainwaves have the greatest amplitude and the slowest frequency. They typically range between 1.5 to 4 cycles per second. At death our brain waves are zero, so Delta is very deep. In a deep dreamless sleep, we can drop to as low as 2 to 3 cycles a second but any lower would be dangerous. We have no *'waking'* mental contact with this brainwave; it is that deep. Animals that go into hibernation for winter like bears, enjoy a deep sleep with only Delta brainwaves present. This is why Delta is referred to as the *'deep sleep'* brainwave. When the brain rests, these brainwaves become active and produce the biochemical Serotonin, which is like *'food for the brain'* as it nourishes the brain.

5.) Gamma Brainwaves...

These are the fastest brain waves. Although they can be hard to measure accurately, they tend to measure above 35Hz and can oscillate as fast as 100Hz. These super-fast brainwaves don't feature for long. They are rather short, sporadic, burst activity brainwaves in comparison to the other brainwaves, which have more specific functions.

Your brain tends to produce Gamma brainwaves when you're intensely focused or actively engaged in solving a problem. The energy in your body then exceeds your emotional tension, producing Gamma brainwaves.

You cannot enter into a Gamma brainwave state when you're physically tense. If you're tense, you lose focus.

You need to be energetic, but not tense. This same state is required for peak performance in a business context. When you're about to enter into a major meeting, you need to be energised but not tense. If you're tense, you won't be as clear, or focused, precise and optimized as you could be. People will read your vibe. Nervousness kills deals. You've got to be loose, flowing but energetic and totally in control of your senses. Set aside judgment and embrace pure perception so you're able to push to the limit of your perceptive capacity.

In this mode, everything is open, all of your senses absorb data effortlessly. You're able to engage non-judgmentally and effortlessly with what's happening around you. Your brain is completely free to engage fully in the performance. They say it's akin to being on the popular stimulant drug, Cocaine. Go Gamma Go...!

When your brain produces high levels of Gamma brainwaves, you tend to be happier and more receptive. You may also enjoy a higher intelligence quotient or IQ and increased concentration. If your brain consistently produces low levels of Gamma brainwaves, you may develop learning and memory problems.

Recap...

These are our everyday active brainwave patterns. As we progress in our mediation flow, there will be several references to these brainwaves. Take a minute to familiarise yourself with their functions.

When we go to bed and read or watch television, we still have active Beta waves present. As we start to get sleepy, the Beta waves are replaced with Alpha waves. As we fall asleep the Alpha waves are replaced with Theta waves and as we drop off into a deep sleep we slow right down. Delta waves then become active.

When we wake up, we go from Delta (deep sleep) into Theta (light sleep), into Alpha (awake but not quite with it) and then we become wide awake and are literally buzzing with Beta brainwaves. If we lie in for a bit and doze, we're in a drowsy mode (Alpha). We can then effortlessly slip back into Theta and sometimes even deeper into Delta.

When in Alpha or Theta mode, we often experience a flow of ideas because our creative juices have been stimulated, but we can just as easily lose it all by slipping deeper into Delta and falling fast asleep. It is important therefore to keep a notepad and pencil next to your bed. When you have those brief flashes of brilliance, quickly write them down or you'll lose them...!

A similar process happens in meditation. When we begin, the brainwaves are all busy Beta brainwaves. As we start to relax, the active Beta brainwaves are replaced with leisurelier Alpha brainwaves, which eventually slow right down as dreamy Theta brainwaves drift in.

In every day mode when Beta brainwaves are present, the mind responds immediately, will debate issues, will complete work issues and think in a language format.

Alpha and Theta waves then kick in and use this foundation of knowledge accumulated to explore and create, often increasing the knowledge base in the process but usually quietly exploring a creative angle, constantly refining, constantly searching, constantly creating, slowly processing the knowledge gained.

In the arts, using our Beta brainwaves, we learn how to paint, write, draw, etc., how many colours there are, types of materials available and so on. In Alpha, we take what we've learnt and we create. This is the Alpha strength, taking what has been learnt in Beta and simply utilising the knowledge to create a masterpiece.

Small children and animals function mainly in Alpha and Theta mode, whereas adults operate mostly in a Beta format. One is inclined to enter a more focused, expanded state of awareness (meditation) when brainwave patterns are mainly composed of Alpha. The act of smelling a rose for example and getting giddy on the scent is purely an Alpha thing but the act of seeing the rose; touching the rose; and then conveying that information to the brain is a Beta thing.

'A single human brain generates more electrical impulses in a day than all the telephones of the world combined'

TED...

In that now famous TED video that featured Neuron surgeon, Dr Jill Bolte Taylor, who suffered a stroke but was able to mentally analyse what was happening to her, she spoke about how her Conscious mind had shut down on her due to the stroke and her consciousness had involuntary moved over to her right brain. It's a fascinating video. One of the highlights was when she'd totally moved out of her Conscious mind and was aware of how she was experiencing Alpha brainwaves but could feel herself slipping deeper with Theta brainwaves becoming active although she was still capable of witnessing what was happening to her in the process.

In this state she experienced a complete out of body experience where she was able to witness the earth's geomagnetic energy field all around her. She described in detail how she couldn't seem to separate the energy between her arm and the wall. It was all merging into one.

This is not your everyday guru, making a bold statement (which they never do anyway!). This is an elite brain surgeon. There aren't that many in this world. They are above average, highly intelligent people. They may well be very left brain controlled and have libraries of knowledge to their credit but when these people have an ultra-right brain experience and want to share it with the world, you should listen because they know what they're talking about.

What can we learn from this...? Unfortunately, the majority of the world's population spends most of their time in their Conscious mind with Beta brainwaves present. If we could change this one thing globally and convince people to try and spend more time exploring their Subconscious mind in meditation, with Alpha or Theta brainwaves present, our world will become a planet of peace and harmony.

This is a lovely heartfelt story to end this chapter, about a student and his old teacher: A young man meets an old man in the park and asks, "Do you remember me...?"
The old man replies, "No, I don't remember you."
The young man says, "I was once one of your students."
The old man asks, "What do you do in life...?"
To which the young man answers, "Well, I used my intelligence carefully and became a teacher."
"Ah, good, like me hey...?" Replies the old man.
"Well, yes. In fact, I became a teacher because you inspired me to be like you." The old man, curious, asks the young man at what time he decided to become a teacher. And the young man tells him the following story: One day, a friend of mine, also a student, came in with a nice new watch. I decided I wanted it so I stole it. I took it out of his pocket. Shortly after, my friend noticed his watch was missing and immediately complained to our teacher, who was you. Then you said to the class, "A student's watch was stolen during class today. Whoever stole it, please return it." I didn't give it back because I didn't want to. Then you closed the door and told us all to stand up. You told us to close our eyes, because you would only look for the watch if we all had our eyes closed. So, we did and you went from pocket to pocket.

When you went through my pocket, you found the watch and took it. You kept searching everyone's pockets and when you were done you said, 'Open your eyes, we have the watch...!' You never said who stole the watch. That day you saved my dignity forever. It was the most shameful day of my life. But this is also the day I decided not to be a thief, or a bad person, ever again. You never even reprimanded me for my evil deed. You didn't take me aside and give me a moral lesson. But I received your message clearly and thanks to you, I understood what a real educator needs to do. "Do you remember this episode, professor...?"

"I remember the situation, the stolen watch, which I was looking for in everyone's pocket, but I don't remember you because I slipped over into my Alpha brainwave mode and also closed my eyes while searching."

What a wonderful teacher...love it...!

'Count your Life by Smiles, not Tears...!'
- John Lennon -

Mind States

'In Life there are only three Truths – The Truth; The Whole Truth; and Nothing but the Truth...!'

So, what are thoughts? Have you ever wondered how you process your thoughts...? The majority of our thoughts consist of sensations, feelings, emotions, impressions, ideas and so on, basically random issues we think of in our everyday life, based on information provided by our senses.

When we talk about thoughts, we are focusing on our consciousness, which is our cognitive ability. Neuroscience splits consciousness into three distinctive levels.

The Three Mind States...

- **The Conscious mind,** which is our active mind
- **The Subconscious mind,** which is a level deeper than the Conscious mind
- And finally, **the Unconscious mind,** which is a very deep level

Buddhist psychology claims there are as many as eighty-nine different mind states (which include different sleep states and altered states of consciousness in meditation) within all of us. We can reach some of these states in meditation or via hallucinogenic chemicals and plant stimulants but we are essentially only interested in the three primary states, with specific focus on the Conscious and the Subconscious minds because these are our everyday minds.

Sigmund Freud...

Famed psychoanalyst, Sigmund Freud, believed behaviour and personality were derived from the constant interaction of conflicting psychological forces, operating at three different levels of awareness in a vertical and hierarchical architecture of human consciousness. Freud likened these three levels of mind to an iceberg. The top of the iceberg you see above the water, represents the Conscious mind. The part of the iceberg submerged below the water but still visible, is the Subconscious. The bulk of the iceberg that lies unseen beneath the waterline represents the Unconscious. With each mind lying beneath the other, he believed they interacted across all three levels of awareness, each part playing an important role, influencing behaviour.

In order to understand the ins and outs of Freud's theory, it is necessary to first determine how each level of consciousness operates and cohesively interacts and the roles they play in shaping human behaviour and thought.

The Conscious Mind: Contains all thoughts, feelings and desires of which we are aware of at any given moment. Also expresses our mental processing, allowing us to think and talk rationally, including our memory, which is not always part of consciousness but can be retrieved and brought into awareness, on demand from the Subconscious.

Example: Being mindful in the present moment. Our everyday contact with the outside world. What you are thinking about right now. If you are aware of it then it is in the Conscious mind.

The Subconscious Mind: Contains information just below the surface of awareness. The Subconscious consists of anything that could potentially be brought into the Conscious mind. It can be retrieved with relative ease and usually can be thought of as memory or recollection.

Example: Think of your middle name. A similar example could be - what is your mother's birthday or when last did it rain or how long does it take to drive to the mall, etc.

The Unconscious: Contains thoughts, memories and desires, buried deep within, well below our Conscious and Subconscious awareness. Even though we are not aware of their existence, they exert great influence on our behaviour. According to Freud, all psychic energy originates in the Unconscious.

Example: The Unconscious mind is a reservoir of feelings, thoughts, urges and memories, outside of our Conscious awareness. The Unconscious also contains contents that are unacceptable or unpleasant, such as feelings of pain, anxiety, conflict, negative experiences from our past, which we've blocked out, or purposefully pushed out of our Subconscious. Memories and emotions that are too painful, embarrassing, shameful or too distressing to consciously face, are stored in the enormous reservoir making up the Unconscious mind.

The Freudian Slip...

One way to understand how the Conscious and Unconscious minds operate is to look at what is known as a slip of the tongue. Many of us have experienced what is commonly referred to as a *'Freudian Slip'*, at some point or another. These misstatements are believed to reveal underlying, Unconscious thoughts or feelings. Freud believed, while the Unconscious mind is largely inaccessible, the contents can sometimes bubble up unexpectedly, such as in dreams or a slip of the tongue.

An example of a Freudian Slip is a man who accidentally uses a former girlfriend's name when referring to a current girlfriend. While most of us may believe this to be a simple error, Freud believed the slip was a sudden intrusion of the Unconscious mind into the Conscious mind, often due to unresolved or repressed feelings from the past.

Conscious/Subconscious...

Freud or no Freud, whatever you're comfortable with is a good norm. All the consciousness theories accept a three-level consciousness tier in one way or another, we'll therefore stay with the standard Conscious; Subconscious and Unconscious levels and cover a basic inter-relationship structure for meditation, rather than a neuroscience analysis, because we are more interested in the awareness functions these three respective levels of consciousness share. Also, in relation to the left and right brain hemispheres.

The majority of our thoughts originate in the Conscious mind, which are sometimes then fed to the Subconscious mind, usually if there is a *'need to think about it'* required. Unfortunately, the majority of our thoughts are lost in the system because the mind can only process so much information at a time. We tend to completely overwhelm the mind with way too many needless thoughts. It's a human thing…!

Beware - the Conscious mind is home to the ego, which means this mind state doesn't always feed through the truth. The Subconscious readily accepts whatever information is given as fact and acts accordingly. Consequently, you need to take control of what information you accept. Our ego has a wonderful capacity to distort information, often for short term personal gain. The Subconscious is unaware the information has been distorted and therefore accepts the information as factual.

An imprint is made on the Subconscious and the brain then sets the wheels in motion, often with disastrous results. Talk about self-inflicted pain…!

If you think you're going to catch a cold because the weather has changed, then you probably will because this is what you'll imprint on your Subconscious mind. It's all because your senses, which are the information providers for the brain, don't have a sense of humour. Your senses pick up information and deliver the precise information directly to the brain for processing. Thus, be careful what you say and how you say it. Always try and keep it positive. If you consistently feed your Subconscious mind with thoughts of peace, harmony and good health, this powerful mind force will ensure your desire is fulfilled and more importantly, if you believe in it, it'll happen.

Our ego plays a huge part in our daily lives. It's extremely powerful and dominant. Our ego thrives on success. This is why we are so competitive in everything we do. We strive to succeed. We want to impress. We want to be the best no matter the cost or hurt caused to others. All because our ego is solely about self. Everything we do is usually reward stimulated. We are reward driven. Our actions are very often self-consciously done in order to seek a self-esteem reward or acclaim because this releases dopamine in the brain, which signals pleasure and success. With meditation and being mindfully aware, we can learn to let go of these self-imposed rewards.

Sometimes they are necessary but mostly they are

unnecessary. Again, a measure of balance needs to be applied because we want to love ourselves unconditionally and yet we also need to be aware of how we achieve success. Remember, we live in an environment of balance, so whomever we stand on or hurt in our quest for success, the damage we cause will be returned, normally with interest. It's a delicate balance because we need to control the dominancy factor of our ego whilst still allowing the Real You to develop materially and spiritually. And yet we cannot totally suppress our ego either as it is our ego that creates our character and our perceived image to the world, amongst other things.

The ego has difficulty remaining silent, always speaks out when it shouldn't. Always has to make a point. Loves to have the last word, especially female ego's...! As a sportsman, when you play a bad shot, you sometimes moan at yourself, talk to yourself, even have a full conversation. This is you (your spirit, the Real You) and your ego (thoughts) having a discussion. The mere fact there is a dialogue, proves two personalities exist within, otherwise there couldn't be a conversation.

'There is nothing more mindful, than realising you are not the voice in your mind, you are the one who hears it, for this is the Real You' - Michael Singer

It's quite normal for you (the Real You) to mentally compete with your ego. How many times do you argue with yourself...? It's not a Jekyll and Hyde situation with split personalities or schizophrenia; this is about you and your ego. The reality is; being human, we prefer to hide our true identity, our true feelings to the world. We rather blatantly exhibit a false identity, which is our ego.

Like all loud extremes, the ego is fragile. A simple thing like a hurt self-esteem or something a bit more serious like rejection or failure, is a bitter pill for the ego to swallow. It can cause dark moods, which sometimes linger. Being aware of it though, helps us manage it. Controlling our ego is probably one of our biggest challenges in life.

The Conscious mind demands constant stimulation, is the gatherer of knowledge, which the Subconscious converts to memory. The Conscious mind has parameters and boundaries. The Subconscious has no boundaries. The Conscious mind activates short term memory. The Subconscious activates long term memory because this mind has direct access to the Unconscious where all the long-term memory banks are stored. When reading this sentence, your short-term memory reads the words whereas your long-term memory recalls the meaning of the words.

The Conscious mind controls speech, numbers, analytical and logical thought processes, academic pursuits and the way in which we cognitively handle our daily working programs in a systematic and cohesive manner. The Conscious mind has more of a left-brain relationship whereas the Subconscious is more of a right brain fan.

However, as previously discussed, both of these mind states of consciousness, utilise the entire brain because various parts of the brain are used for specific functions, depending on the need or requirement, sometimes simultaneously, other times independently.

The Subconscious deals with the arts, music, abstract thought processes like meditation, colour recognition, imagination and intangible ideas. When it comes to listening to a song, the Conscious mind listens to the song and may try to remember the artists name. The Subconscious gets lost in the lyrics of the song. The Subconscious thinks more in pictures whereas the Conscious mind thinks more in logical and sequential thought patterns. It is the Subconscious that has all the deep answers and will even respond to suggestions. For example: If you are going to sleep at night and you instruct your Subconscious to wake you at a specific time in the morning, it will happen, if you believe it.

Do you drive a car with your Conscious mind or your Subconscious...? Well, that depends on how long you've been driving because when you first learnt to drive you probably drifted all over the road, slipped gears, left the hand-brake on, forgot to use the indicators when making a turn and so on. After a while you got so good you hardly thought about the mechanics of driving. How did this happen…? It's because the analytical Conscious mind is the mind that initially learns to drive. The Subconscious mind then takes over, (made an imprint on the

Subconscious). This is how driving a car eventually becomes effortless, something you do without thinking.

In life we often refer to this as being in our *'autopilot'* mode. It's a feeling that is similar to when you are in meditation and you've crossed over into your *'autopilot'* Subconscious mode. Alpha brainwaves are active, without any effort, or focused thought process, everything becomes extremely lucid.

Reading is normally a Conscious function whereas understanding is a Subconscious function, which makes reading a good dual mental function for simultaneous use of both minds. Try this exercise for speed reading: Open a book and run your finger down the left-hand side of the page at a speed faster than what you would normally read. Allow your eyes to follow your finger but peripherally look at the centre of the page as well. It's difficult at first (isn't everything new...?) but persevere and you'll find a few words will begin to stand out on each line as your finger runs down the page. These will be key words, which will convey sufficient meaning and understanding of the basic contents on the page. Reading the words down the page is a Conscious function but it is your Subconscious mind that has subliminally selected the key words and processed the information.

When a hypnotist hypnotises someone, they're able to override a person's busy Conscious mind and tap directly into their Subconscious. By doing this the hypnotist can virtually make the hypnotised person do practically anything and the person will have no recollection of it. If the hypnotist tells the person, he/she is paralysed, they will be paralysed until such time as the hypnotist snaps the person out of it and releases his/her hold. This is all about *'power of suggestion'*, which the Subconscious readily reacts to. This is powerful medicine because it means the Subconscious is very susceptible to suggestion, whereas the Conscious mind is too active to be influenced. It only really slows down when you go to sleep or you're able to *'still'* the Conscious mind via meditation or yoga techniques, whereas the Subconscious mind is always alert.

The Unconscious Mind...

This is our deep, inaccessible mind, where our memories and life history are stored. This mind state is only accessible via the Subconscious mind. In this elusive, bottomless mind state, we get to review and process the day's events while we are in a deep sleep. However, incidents of a high stress nature sometimes filter back, which then become active dreams in our REM (rapid eye movement) sleep.

Our Unconscious mind heals, flushes and banks daily accumulated information, allowing the rest of the conscious levels to operate in an uncluttered environment upon awaking to each new day, provided one has had sufficient down time or deep sleep.

The brain keeps time through a specific pattern of

chemical synthesis and the release of modulating chemicals such as melatonin and cortisol. In this sense, serotonin helps to regulate the onset of REM sleep during the night, creating a semblance of balance and ease of information flow between the three mind states.

Our three consciousness levels are a lot more complex than this simple explanation. This scenario only explains how they interact with each other and partially affect our mode of thinking. The more you meditate and slow life down, the more you'll discover, the world has so much more to offer and life is so much bigger than your ego's fanaticism on pure self. Controlling your ego is a major hurdle when meditating.

Having some knowledge will help you in life. Being mindfully aware is being prepared and being prepared means you get to control situations as they develop in life because you'll understand the influences and why they are happening and more importantly, you know they'll pass with time.

In the following chapter, we're going to look at a form of abstract communication in life and it's all about the vibes...

'Deja Poo - The feeling of having heard all this crap before...!'

Vibrations

'Respect means listening until everyone has been heard and understood, only then is there a possibility of Balance and Harmony. For this is the goal of Spirituality'
-Dave Chief, Grandfather of Red Dog-

We enjoy a range of intricate thought patterns, which are in effect, vibrations – even thought, generates a vibration. As already highlighted, these thought patterns resonate at various frequencies enabling us to tune in. All life forms are capable of generating vibrations, it's only the frequency levels that vary. Humans and animals for example, being higher up the chain in levels of consciousness, enjoy higher frequency vibrations than say insects or plants.

Everything in the Universe consists of energy, vibrating at various frequencies. Even things that appear solid, are made of vibrational energy fields and they all vibrate at unique frequencies; some even have rhythm. A table may look solid and still, but within the table are zillions of subatomic particles; atoms with buzzing electrons, protons and neutrons, vibrating with magnetic energy.

The relationship between energy, vibration and frequency is a perfect triangle, all three co-exist, you cannot have one without the other. If energy is present, it will have a frequency and a vibration. It's a synergistic relationship.

In life, we strive to attain higher, lighter vibrations because then we are happy, we are healthy. The lower the frequency, the denser our energy - resulting in deeper issues. Whereas, the higher the frequency of our vibration, the lighter the energy - we feel physically and emotionally strong. We experience greater personal power, clarity, peace, love and joy. Overall, our life takes on a positive quality. Resonating at a higher vibration can only be maintained if we don't succumb to the pull of lower vibrations and in a tasty world, it is not always going to be easy.

We cannot see vibrations but we can feel them and sense them. People live by the old saying *'seeing is believing'*. It's actually the reverse. Believing will make you see. Most people only choose to look at what they know and what they can see. They rely on their five senses, unable to accept; everything vibrates, even our thoughts and feelings.

Think of a mother hen for example, with her baby chics. As the mother scratches and digs around the yard in the sand and dirt for grubs, she emits a range of clucks and sounds, which her chics immediately respond to. She uses a certain series of clucks for *'danger'* and a different series of clucks for *'I've found food'* and so on. Clearly, there is a definite communication/language structure in progress between the mother and her chics (which proves consciousness exists in all animals). The clucks she emits are high or low, short or long, they're all different. Each series of clucks represents energy vibrations, expressed in wave formats. The vibration is the energy wave transporting the sound you hear. The frequency is the pitch. In this situation, you also have rhythm because of the pitch and then there is also sound, which now introduces modulation, which is about strength and tone. It gets complicated and these are just simple vibrations. It's the reading of them however, that takes a little understanding.

'If you wish to understand the Universe, think of Energy, Frequency and Vibration. These are your tools.' - Nikola Tesla

Water...

The late Japanese scientist, Masaru Emoto, conducted experiments on frozen water particles that produced hexagon crystals, using Magnetic Resonance Analysis technology (MRA) and high-speed photography to capture the results. He studied the scientific evidence of how the deep molecular structure in water transformed when exposed to human words, thoughts, sounds and intentions. His fascinating book, *'The Hidden Messages in Water'*, describes his innovative process.

In pure water, the crystals formed perfect hexagon

shapes. In normal chlorinated tap water, the crystals were distorted. This phenomenon intrigued Dr Emoto to experiment further so he played classical music to water samples prior to freezing and they produced perfect hexagon crystals. When he played heavy metal music, the vibrations caused the crystals to distort. He wrote words of love/gratitude and hatred/anger on pieces of paper and pasted them onto the water containers. Once again, love and gratitude vibrations produced perfect hexagon crystals whereas the anger and hatred words produced distorted crystals. This makes it difficult to deny a *'consciousness'* presence in water or the effect the vibrations had on the water. Plus, it also helps us to remember how incredibly important water is to our world. If our oceans stop moving and stand dormant due to pollution or man's interference, the oceans will die and so will earth.

Gigahertz (GHz) is a frequency unit that measures the number of wave cycles per second. Hertz (Hz) refers to the number of cycles per second with periodic one-second intervals. One GHz equals one billion cycles per second whereas one MHz equals one million cycles per second and one Hz equals one cycle per second. GHz is used to study electromagnetic spectrums, including computing and radio transmissions.

The *'sound'* to *'water'* phenomenon may also be due to the *'resonance wave cycles'* of water's reaction to various musical sounds. Water resonates at a deep 22.235GHz, which is really powerful. However, music resonation to water would really depend on the type of instruments and their respective volumes. So, certain modes of music will create perfect hexagon crystals when water is exposed to the music while other music may distort the crystals because the resonation doesn't sync.

What does this mean...? According to *'Science & Sound'*, water has the ability to absorb, similar to a paper towel or a sponge. If you spill a liquid, you clean it up by wiping a wet sponge over the spill. The sponge absorbs the liquid. The same thing happens to sound. When sound travels through a medium such as water, it's absorbed, caught by the molecules within the medium. The medium actually converts some of the acoustic vibrations of the soundwave into heat when the molecules of the medium start vibrating. The molecules are at rest before the soundwave comes through. In order for them to start vibrating, the sound must be powerful enough to overcome the viscosity of the medium through which the sound is propagating.

Therefore, a mix of music with various sound frequencies, played to water, will obviously produce different hexagonal water crystals when frozen. It's still fascinating though that water has the ability to react accordingly when exposed to alternate vibrations. Similar to sound, with water's unique absorption qualities and deep molecular structure, water also has the ability to heal. The medical world, constantly call for humans to drink at least eight glasses of water a day. This is because water has the ability to absorb body toxins and cleanse our system in the process.

Note: Drinking chlorinated tap water or super refined bottled water from the local supermarket will not have the same absorbing qualities as pure water. You need to catch rain water in a bucket and drink it or consume water from mountain streams or similar to really get medical benefits of consequence. Wildlife, the insect world, plant life, etc., all rely on the magical healing and absorbing properties of clear water.

Over the last decade, science developed a *'resonance theory of consciousness'*, suggesting resonance (another word for synchronised vibrations), is at the heart of all physical reality in general. Vibrations, are therefore key mechanisms behind all life consciousness.

Taking this a step further, everything in our Universe is constantly in motion, vibrating, even objects appearing to be stationary are in fact vibrating, oscillating, resonating at various frequencies. Resonance is a type of motion, characterised by oscillations between two entities, i.e. protons and electrons. All matter therefore consists of vibrations of various underlying magnetic fields and frequencies, which constitute the basic mechanism for all physical interactions to occur.

Spirit forms, from the *'Other Side'* (in the Spirit World), vibrate at a higher frequency, which is why we cannot see them. If spirits or angels wish to make themselves visible to us, they have to lower their vibration frequency to our level.

As already mentioned, if we felt the need to describe energy in a visual format, we'd picture it in a wave format because this is how energy behaves. Similar to radio waves, these are waves that cannot be seen by the naked eye. Energy has to move in a wave format (up and down pattern) because that is how energy's forward momentum is generated. If energy moved in a straight line it wouldn't go anywhere. It's the up and down wave pattern format that generates the rhythm and thus, creates energy's momentum, simply called, vibrations.

We can see light energy, which actually consists of tiny balls called photons that make up the energy waves in the light. It was James Clerk Maxwell, who discovered light as an electro-magnetic wave. Sound also moves in waves, which is yet another form of energy.

With regards to human vibrations, thinking is a form of energy, measured in frequencies, which we commonly refer to as 'Vibes'. You've heard the saying, 'I could feel the vibe'. This is your intuitive sense tuning into the surrounding human vibrations, which function in an explosion of colours and frequencies, enabling us to simply dial in, again like a radio transmitter, but we get to do it mentally. Anybody can learn to 'tune in' and pick up vibes. We can change our perception by merely changing our frequency. Our thoughts make up our personal world, so by thinking positive and harmonious thoughts, we create a pleasant disposition for ourselves.

Vibrations are often quite specific. We actually do it automatically. How many times have you made eye contact with a member of the opposite sex...? You send vibes out; she/he picks them up and sends back similar vibrations in return. It's the same when you encounter a road rage situation. You sit in your car and glare at each other. These are *'bad vibes'* or intentions you're transferring to each other. Your vibrations reach out and resonate with the other person's vibrations. You're communicating without talking, you are communicating by vibration, via waves of kinetic energy.

Another example: you're sitting next to someone and you're both having a conversation. You're talking and listening as you receive a reply. What is happening while you're talking is all your focus and therefore your concentrated cognitive energy is on the person you're talking to, immediately linking you together. Your vibrations, (your energy) and their energy, connect. Now suddenly a third person walks over, sits down next to you and joins in the conversation. Immediately, your vibrations link with theirs as this new person joins your invisible magnetic web.

Every time you speak or even think, you send out new vibrations. If you so much as point your finger to mentally reinforce a point you are trying to make, you throw out vibrations. Our brain understands this and involuntarily uses these vibration links to translate messages and information.

Due to the balance effect of the polarity in life, whatever it is you're seeking could also be seeking you. Plus, you need to be aware of the negative forces at play, which work just as effectively. When someone is talking to you, watch their behaviour. This is what their real vibrations are telling you because behaviour is controlled by thought, which works on vibrations and sometimes vibes communicate so much louder than words. Alternatively, look directly into their eyes. You're able to see everything the person does with their body.

If you are on a long-distance telephone call with someone, besides your vocal vibrations, there are also *'thought vibrations'* transferred between the two of you. You cannot see one another but you are able to mentally connect via your vibrations. These energy vibrations don't necessarily travel back and forth down the telephone line like your voice does. The fact you are both communicating is sufficient for the vibrations to tap into the same frequency. They resonate, magnetically connecting both of you instantly, no matter how far apart you are or where you are.

Have you ever witnessed how a pride of lion's hunt? The planning, the strategy, their technique, absolute stealth, the high concentration levels and their alert mental telepathy. They use low frequency thought vibrations and body language to communicate. It's incredible to observe.

Mankind has exchanged energy vibrations since they learned to communicate. Take for example a group of people sitting together in a discussion. They each feed off the energy of the one who is currently talking. However, it's how they feed off the energy that is the key. If they look down on the person who is talking, they disturb the magnetic flow because they're suddenly introducing negative energy. Whereas, if they mentally support the person talking with positive energy, everyone in the group gains.

If one gets into an argument with another person, the person with the strongest energy usually wins. In the process, they draw energy from the defeated person, leaving the person physically and mentally drained. And it doesn't only affect humans and animals. Basic life forms like plants don't have eyes to see or ears to hear but it has been scientifically proven, they too have vibrations. Plants respond to sunlight and even music. When placed under shade, plants grow towards the light. When placed near music, they bend towards it when the music is harmonious and away from it when the music is discordant. People talk to flowers, vegetables and trees, showering them with love. In response, the plants enjoy a bountiful growth compared to similar shrubs that weren't shown any love. Plants are able to sense their environment. They respond efficiently to insect attacks and are even capable of movement, to a limited extent.

It doesn't stop here. Take for example a painting. The

painting consists of the energy from the painter that went into the painting. It also consists of the energy of the canvas it was painted on, the energy of the framework made by whoever put it together and then there is the subtle energy of the actual beauty of the painting itself. In addition, every time someone stops and admires the painting, the painting absorbs energy from that person until it begins to gain an actual presence that can be felt. Some more than others, which is why you may feel like you're magnetically drawn to some paintings as opposed to others in the same room.

Findhorn...

There's the amazing story of Findhorn, which is quite incredible. It goes back to the early sixties and probably started even earlier but it only became famous in the sixties. It all began with an extraordinary Scottish community on the Morey Firth where people verbally and mentally communicated with plants and vegetables with spectacular results. Their gardens experienced phenomenal growth. In addition, they discovered the 'little folk', which are small, angelic forms or sentient beings operating on a higher frequency to humans, virtually unseen except to the clairvoyant at Findhorn, who communicated with these garden fairies.

At Findhorn, they grow forty-pound cabbages, roses bloom in the snow, nothing is impossible and it all started in an old caravan site with a rubbish dump as their garden, which they transformed into an oasis of spiritual communion and a veritable Garden of Eden. Absolutely astonishing...!

In Paul Hawken's book on Findhorn, he recounts the story of when he was talking to Leonard the one gardener, who had to remove some of the local bushes to make way for the garden. Leonard first went and explained to the bushes what he had to do with them and when the time came to remove them he could easily remove them from the ground with one hand, almost as if they had released their hold on life whereas when he tried to remove similar bushes he hadn't spoken to, they wouldn't budge.

At Findhorn, putting a plant into a pot is like putting a plant in jail. Plant life only does really well when it has the freedom of the earth, exposed to its many natural nutrients as well as the elements, like the sun for growth, the wind for spreading their seeds and the rain for pure water.

The Foundation and Community of Findhorn were founded on the principles of being still, listening to the wisdom, which is in all of us and acting from this deep place of unity with all parts of life. The transformation of barren sand dunes into a vibrant international community with beautiful gardens, attests to the power of these principles. Every material object they acquired came from God manifestations.

They believe purely and solely in the *Law of Manifestation*. Peter Caddy, the founder member explains:

- You are what you think
- You become what you think
- What you think then becomes reality

He relates the story of how they needed a Greenhouse and asked for it, meditated on it and thought about it constantly but it failed to manifest. The more he thought about it he suddenly realised his request hadn't been specific enough so he asked God for a Greenhouse but this time he supplied the specs, the material and everything about the Greenhouse in great detail. The Greenhouse arrived a week later.

Thousands of people throughout the world have visited Findhorn to share in the magic. It's still a thriving communal centre and still visited by seekers from all over the world. Irwin Thompson launched a sister centre in America, called *'Lindisfarne'*. People go there to soak up the wonderful energy and experience the magic.

This is all polarized energy that you cannot see or define but it exists. Everything on this earth, including non-life, has its own energy identity and energy field because everything, as disclosed in a previous chapter, consists of atoms. The more you spend time understanding this, the more you'll begin to experience it, absorb it and grow with it. The 60's Hippies were onto it way back when they claimed – *'It's all about the vibes man...!'*

'Your energy speaks volumes'

Affirmations...

Affirmations are also vibrations, the more you repeat them the stronger they become. Affirmations are about *'Power of Suggestion'* or what hypnotists refer to as *'Brainwashing the Subconscious Mind'*.

They have been used since the beginning of time for motivation and mind conditioning. The basic concept consists of repeating a series of positive assertions or statements to create an imprint on the Subconscious mind.

For affirmations to be effective, your emotions and feelings need to be aligned with what you wish for. It's not enough to merely ask for something if you don't truly have sincere emotions and feelings in harmony with your wish. You need to fall in love with what you desire in order to be in the correct vibrational zone. Act what you feel. If you ask for money through prayer, meditation or just by wanting it, it will not help if your emotions and feelings are programmed from your youth to think you don't deserve to be rich, or you cannot handle being rich, etc. If you grew up in a family where your parents said: 'Do you think I am made of money, we can't afford that...!', then most likely your Subconscious is programmed to believe this, hence your inner feelings and emotions will not be aligned with your wish, which means it will take some initial conditioning to get a positive imprint firmly established on your Subconscious.

One method to accomplish this is by recording your affirmation, put the recording on repeat, use a pair of headphones and go to sleep with the affirmation repeating endlessly into your Subconscious.

By applying repetitive and positive affirmations every day, you can re-program your Subconscious mind with new beliefs, provided they are real and have significant meaning to you. Always talk to your Subconscious in the present tense. The Subconscious mind doesn't understand time because it doesn't exist. When you use positive affirmations, be sure to phrase them in the now. For example, don't repeat an affirmation that says, 'I am getting fit and healthy.' Rather say, 'I am fit and healthy.' By using the word *'getting'* means you are not healthy, you are only *'getting'* healthy. You need to be very specific and to the point.

Don't focus on the problem you want to release. Focus on what you want to obtain. The Subconscious doesn't understand negation. If you repeat an affirmation like, 'Help me to stop smoking.' This is too abstract. Rather phrase your affirmation with, 'I have stopped smoking.' Use sensory based language, without abstraction. The Subconscious cannot discern non realities or abstract goals. The more specific you can be about what you want to create, the stronger the vibration and the actual imprint made on the Subconscious mind.

Using affirmations takes practice. Like anything in life, the more you use positive affirmations to imprint your Subconscious mind, the better you'll get at achieving your objectives. It's all about shaping your mind. The world is then your oyster. The best time for affirmations is when you are on the verge of sleep at night or first thing in the morning when you wake up because this is when you still have Alpha brainwaves present. In this state, you have direct access to your Subconscious mind, which is far more receptive to affirmations than the Conscious mind.

The Human Aura...

Surrounding the body is a shimmering light termed the Aura. It is fed from an iridescent cord of light, extending up the spine, out the crown of the head, re-entering the body at the belly button in a never-ending cycle. When a person dies, a common saying is, his/her *'Light'* has gone out. This *'life cord of light'* is the light they are referring to. This may sound a little arty farty but it's real.

The Auric light surrounding the body is made up of seven subtle layers of energy vibrations. These vibrations are in colour and they change according to our moods and how we act, think, talk and feel. The frequency of these vibrations is too high for the naked eye to see but you can develop your intuitive skills to the point where you'll be able to *'see'* with time. Animals, with their acute senses are able to detect Auras. This is how they read people and other animals. Although animals can pick up fear or love intuitively, they're also able to read your Aura, instantly determining if you are friend or foe. In Africa, out on the plains, buck will often ignore a pride of lions who may stroll nearby whereas at other times they'll flee for their lives. This is because they can 'see' or 'read' what mood the pride is in, from their Aura's.

To get a minimal glimpse of your Aura, sit in a naturally lit room with just the sun coming in from an open window. Join your fingertips lightly together in front of you and hold the position for a few seconds. Slowly release your finger-tips. As your fingertips withdraw from each other you should be able to see a reflection stretching between the fingertips. Go back and forwards slowly with your fingertips and you'll see it more clearly. This is your Aura's vibration you're playing with. There is a photography process called 'Kirlian Photography' that can photograph the energy emanating from our bodies. Actually, energy radiates from everything because everything has a living frequency of energy.

Your Aura is also known as the presence that defines your personal space. This can be felt immediately when someone comes too close to you and both your Aura's connect. It's like an electric shock. It's worse if the person still comes even closer and completely gets into your personal space. In other words, they get way too close. Both your Aura's immediately conflict. You instantly feel uncomfortable and either step back or you instinctively push the offending person out of your space.

An Aura's Emotive Colours...

Listed below are the general emotive colours of the subtle

energy bodies within a person's Aura, with a brief interpretation of each.

Red

This colour indicates you are tired, at a low ebb and irritable or even angry. You've heard the saying, "I saw red...!" when someone is angry.

Orange

This colour indicates you're feeling emotional or distraught. Something or someone has upset you.

Yellow

This colour is associated with mental activity and concentration. You may exude a soft yellow glow when tasked with a lot of mental action.

Green

A green Auric light is known to be calming, soothing and relaxing and therefore has many positive attributes.

Blue

Healers often have a blue colour in their Aura. Blue is the ideal colour to work with if you need to give or receive healing energy.

Indigo

An Indigo Auric light is connected with psychic abilities. Someone who is surrounded with an indigo glow will also have good intuitive powers.

Violet

This is a spiritual colour. If you are currently walking a strong spiritual path then your Aura will contain a lot of violet.

Brown

A brown Auric light indicates a practical person, one who enjoys solving practical solutions to life's problems. One who is strongly grounded, dependable and capable. The colour brown is an earth colour.

Black

Black is the absence of light. It can indicate depression and a lack of spiritual direction. People with black Aura's are inclined to be hyper sensitive and negatively motivated.

White

This colour indicates purity. It is the colour of pure spiritual energy. There are very few people who achieve this level in their lifetime but it is one that we should all be striving for.

Silver

Silver has a reflecting quality, associated with humour and harmony. Comedians and people who enjoy engaging in witty repartee usually have this colour Aura.

Gold

Gold is associated with success. People with a gold Auric light are often extroverted and have a positive outlook on life. This colour indicates confidence and inspiration, which is all linked to success.

How Does This Help Us...?

Let's have a look at an example: If we know a person's general Auric colour is brown but also shows clouds of red, which is a fairly common character trait, then we know this person is a well-grounded kind of person, meaning they are practical, dependable and will get the job done. However, the red cloud indicates this person will also be quick to anger, have a short fuse and intolerance to fools.

Had the person been surrounded by say blue clouds as opposed to red clouds then although they are well grounded (brown aura) they also have strong healing abilities. If the person had a predominantly black Aura then this person has issues with life, more than likely walks the dark side. He/she is not to be trusted, doesn't value or respect you or any other form of life in general and has no spiritual direction.

Having specific Aura colours is linked directly to our vibrations and our senses. This helps us when meditating to mentally tune into the energy surrounding us. By doing this we are able to change our existing mood patterns. When your ego is in full swing, your aura reflects brightly. The opposite applies for when you're in a negative mood. Whenever you have an adrenaline rush, your aura reacts accordingly.

For example: If you come home after a particularly bad day, you're angry and frustrated (red Aura) and therefore decide to meditate to try and console yourself. You go to your usual quiet place and settle down but find you have a problem concentrating due to interruptive thought patterns resulting from events that occurred earlier during the day. To get rid of this angry red cloud, visualise a calming green light, which has the power to suffuse the situation, leaving you feeling serene and relaxed when you conclude your meditation session. Using one's Aura to detect moods and even sickness can benefit us in everyday applications.

The following is a wonderful story, illustrating how moods affect our personality. It's about this guy who gets home from work, he's very tired, it's been a long day, he's not in a particularly good mood. He reclines in his favourite chair, pours a single malt, picks up the paper and starts to read. His young son comes into the room and pesters him, wants his attention, hasn't seen him all day. The father gets angry, irritated. On the page in front of him is a picture of a globe of the world. He hastily tears the picture out and cuts it up into little pieces. He smiles smugly and hands it to the young kid along with a sheet of paper and a glue stick.

"See if you can stick that together son and make the world whole again." He smirks, knowing the task he's given his son will occupy him for a long time. To his amazement his son comes back to him in only a few minutes with the completed picture of the globe stuck down on the sheet of paper.

"How did you do that so quickly boy...?" He gasps.

"Was easy Dad," his son replies, "on the back of the picture of the world was a picture of a person. All I had to do was get the person right and the world automatically came right...!"

Aren't children the best things in life…? They do make our world good and are a powerful enough motivation to make us want to hurry home every day. Children only get one childhood. It's up to us to ensure they enjoy every minute of it. It's even better if we get to enjoy it with them and it's all about interpreting the vibes and sharing our vibrations.

Children are so open, so innocent, they readily tell it like it is. Reading young vibrations is easy if you're in tune with your kids because once you have children in your life; everything you do thereafter is ultimately about your children.

Try and give your attention and energy to your children because without it, life will be challenging for them. Isn't this a big enough incentive to want to maintain a consistently spiritual Auric light…?

In the following chapter we look at our senses, how we utilise them and how they assist us through life…

'A body's Aura says what words cannot'
Martha Graham

Our Senses

It matters not how long you have forgotten, only how soon you remember - Buddha

Whenever our senses pick up information, it's instantly delivered to the brain. The receptacles we have, as in: hands, ears, mouth, nose and eyes are merely intricate and complex body parts, designed to receive information. They don't represent what our senses are. They're merely the instruments, the receivers.

We have five basic senses, which we use on a daily basis and two esoteric senses. The five basic senses are fairly limited in comparison to most animal's senses but our Creator enabled us to have sufficient of each in order to navigate our way through life. Our five basic senses are:

- Sight
- Hearing/Sound
- Touch
- Smell
- And taste

It is claimed, should you lose one of your senses, the others become considerably enhanced. If we're able to enhance our senses via the loss of one sense then ideally, we should be able, with practice, to enhance all our senses over time without losing any.

Basically, our senses make the best of what resources we have available. We therefore sometimes use manufactured add-ons to supplement our five basic senses. For example: If we want to see clearly into the distance, with our limited vision we can't accomplish this but if we use man-made binoculars with high intensity magnified lenses then we can easily achieve this. So, what we lack in depth or intensity in our senses, we more than make up for in intelligence because we're able to produce *'tools'* and *'aids'* to supplement our five basic senses and considerably enhance them at will. Although our human senses are fairly limited, they are still truly quite remarkable. A human with normal functioning senses can:

- Feel on the face the slightest breeze or change in the wind
- Distinguish between a mass of colours even though some of them are almost identical
- Differentiate between many odours in the air even though they are similar
- We have between 5,000 and 10,000 taste buds on the tongue that help us determine specific tastes
- We can hear a distinctive sound and even gauge its direction

Not bad going for our five basic senses although somewhat mild compared to other mammals, like our animal friends but still pretty impressive. Although, one of our best senses is still common sense...!

Our eyes however are quite astonishing. We have in excess of two million working parts in our eyes and the ability to process around thirty-six thousand bits of information every hour. Extraordinary...!

Unfortunately, the majority of us experience only our five basic senses on a daily basis. We tend to live in a five sensory mode, denying ourselves the right to enjoy our other two senses as they are somewhat elusive.

The first of these additional two senses is our Sixth Sense, which we refer to as *'Intuition'*. We use this sense to *'tune-in'* to what's happening around us, almost like a radar. We use it to determine good or bad in people, sense danger or read emotions/vibrations in others. We use this sense without realising it, will call on it Subconsciously whenever we need to.

The other esoteric sense is our seventh sense, which the mystics refer to as our *'Spiritual'* or *'Universal'* sense. This sense is more accessible in meditation, prayer or light sleep. Taking cognisance of the above, our seven senses are:

- Smell
- Touch
- Sight
- Hearing/Sound

- Taste
- Intuition
- Spiritual

A brief overview of each follows:

1.) Smell...

Smell is a wonderful sense. Unfortunately, we are able to smell obnoxious smells before we smell beautiful scents. Still, on a summer's day venturing outdoors, inhaling deeply and capturing the wonderful scents of flowers or freshly cut lawn, rain that has just begun to fall, the keen salty smell of the ocean or the many myriad pollens of fragrances carried on the wind, represent just a few of the absolute pleasures of this sense.

In addition, all life has a distinct personal scent. This is how animals recognise us. From an intuitive point of view, with development and awareness, we are capable of even smelling some intangibles, like fear or someone's presence as they enter a room. It is our sense of smell that conveys to the brain what is *in the air* and all around us at any one time.

This sense also has the power to bring joy to the brain (releasing dopamine), like when we smell aromas that are indeed enjoyable, such as flora, food, etc.

2.) Touch...

People communicate with their *touch* sense. It's often seen as an intimate form of communication. To touch another person is a direct transfer of positive energy. When touched in return, you receive energy. The energy connection is complete when you physically touch, which is why the effect is so electric.

Touch is also about *'feeling'*. To feel an object, this sense tunes into the object's vibrational frequency, giving you a clear message of what the object is, what it's made of, its weight, its shape, its texture, its size and so on. Mentally you can visualise what the object is and what it looks like just by feeling it. You don't have to see it.

Human touch is provided by microscopic sensory receptors, which are actually specialised end tips of nerve cells, in the skin.

3.) Sight...

Humans enjoy varying degrees of sight depending on their creative ability. Artists may see objects in colours whereas an architect may view the same object in a third dimensional form. Both people will however assume, what they have seen is all there is to be seen. Similarly, when we visualise something in our mind's eye that is not physically there, our interpretation is different to the next person's. These are normal human traits but it's the detail provided by each person that is fascinating because it describes to us how they saw it.

On a daily basis we are bombarded by visual messages, ranging from neon lights, advertising hoardings to television and computer screens. There's no end to it. We see, we hear and we absorb. In fact, it becomes too much for the Conscious mind to engage, so most of it gets lost in thought but anything that appeals to us, mentally sticks. It's a continuous cycle.

This results in us hoarding countless images in a memory bank within the Unconscious mind, which we automatically accumulate on a daily basis. From this formidable database we are able to recognise an object whenever we see it again, even though it may be several years later.

Sight allows for the easy transference of all visual information directly to the brain. However, because there is so much sensory input available in this area, we have come to rely on this sense to form our first impressions and only then do we make our mind up. We tend to do this naturally. Psychologists teach us to never *'judge a book by its cover'* but we always do and we do it on first sight. This sense is so powerful our brain immediately accepts and believes everything it receives.

Note: Because the two eyes are set apart, each eye sees a slightly different view of an object. In the visual centres of the brain, the views are compared, which helps us to judge an object's distance.

4.) Hearing/Sound...

Listening to a symphony in an acoustically sound proofed theatre or having a top of the range sound system playing beautiful melancholy music or even sitting on the beach and listening to the sound of the waves or listening to the sound of the wind as it feathers through tall leafy trees, are just some of the more beautiful sounds we can tune into with this sense.

Sound can also describe danger. Harsh noises like the screech of motorcar tyres or gunshots invoke a whole bunch of different emotions in us. These noises are irritating and at times, offensive. We tend to move away from unpleasant noises but are eagerly drawn towards pleasant sounds.

It's also easy to fall into a pattern of 'hearing' people based on how they sound rather than what they are saying. Some humans sound more convincing than others. They have the 'gift of the gab' so to speak. It's a common, lazy human fault but the problem is also due to all the mind clutter, which tends to make us lose focus. It's only when we accept this and really begin to tune in, we are able to use this valuable sense correctly and develop it accordingly, to experience the full enjoyment it offers.

Buddha said, "When you have really learnt to listen, you'll be able to hear: a flower grow; a pin drop; the slightest breath of wind...!"

Sometimes we just need to learn how and when to 'shut up' even though it is so tempting to have our say. Musicians will tell you to listen with your inner ear. This means to really listen you need to capture the source of the sound. The average person listens to a song and is inclined to sing along. However, for musicians, they're listening, they're involved and grooving with the particular song but they're listening with far deeper intent. They go into analytical mode, focusing on the independent instruments, the chord structure, the scale mode, the key, the arrangement and the intricate way in which the producer has blended the mix. Musicians are always intrigued by what contributes to a particular song because they want to know how to play the song, get that solo or funky lick down. They like to crawl into the songwriter's headspace. Even if they have to check it out on 'You Tube', the magnetic pull to get to know the respective song intimately, warts and all, is interminably strong. They mentally connect with the sound source.

'Happy is the hearing man; unhappy is the speaking man'
RW Emerson

5.) Taste...

In order for humans to ingest food it first needs to get past our sensitive taste sensors. This has ensured this sense to be one of the body's strongest defence mechanisms. When we taste something, the sensation is radiated directly to the brain. An instant decision is then made. We either like it or we dislike it. This sense is very direct. With taste, you get to decide immediately. We may convince ourselves to try unpalatable foods, but if it doesn't taste pleasant, we won't have any desire to consume it. This is one sense the brain listens to without question. Our taste sense does have so much more to offer though.

When you bite into a firm peach and that rush of flavour fills your mouth and rolls around your tongue, it teases you into immediately taking another bite so you can experience the same sensation again and again. For this reason, taste is often referred to as the *'Teaser'* sense.

Taste has the distinct ability to instantly convey to the mind exactly what has gone into the mouth and also to describe in detail what all the tasty sensations are that go with it. The four major taste receptors are: sweet; sour; bitter; and salty. There is however an additional taste receptor called *'Unami'*. This one is all about how much we enjoy a specific taste. It's when we crave a certain food.

Note: With all five basic senses, the more you become aware of them, the better you'll be at enhancing their capabilities. So many people today take for granted what their senses do for them on a daily basis. They are in fact completely oblivious most of the time. Only when you relax, are mindful for a minute and mentally accept that your senses are the main information providers for the brain, will you start experiencing and exploring whatever it is your five senses are sensing in the moment.

However, those who restrict themselves only to their five basic senses are not going to develop any further than what their five basic senses have to offer. It is necessary therefore to explore both the *'Intuitive'* and *'Spiritual'* senses as well.

'Philosophy is common sense with big words'

6.) Intuition...

This sense is well known as the elusive *'Sixth Sense'*, the sense that conveys extra sensory powers, allowing the beholder to mentally resonate with surrounding vibrations at random. Intuition defies all realms of logic, yet it is intuition that allows us to go beyond our five senses. Intuition offers a huge step forward as we then get an opportunity to explore within the intangible Subconscious.

With a bit of practice, your intuition can pick up vibrations. In addition, your intuition is the sense that enables you to hear that *'little inner voice'* (your Spirit Guide), if you care to listen and ignore your ego for once. Some people refer to it as their *'gut feel'*.

When it comes to our intuitive sense, often what we sense becomes sufficient evidence for us to make our next decision, sometimes good but unfortunately, sometimes really bad. For example: We have this inert ability (intuition) to sense when someone likes us or alternatively dislikes us. We pick this up initially by looking at the other person. Using our other senses, we'll then listen to how the person talks, check how they are dressed, note their presence and so on, thereby making up our mind fairly quickly and logically whether we feel threatened by this person or if we feel reasonably connected, even comfortable but it is our intuition that makes that final decision.

When you come into the presence of people and you

sense their energies and their thoughts, the same is true for the energies you project for others to sense about you, so be careful.

The issue at stake here is: How are we able to sometimes get it right and other times get it so wrong and then we end up getting hurt, led down the path, deceived, etc. Why can't we zero in and get it right every time like an animal does…?

It's because we haven't sufficiently developed our intuitive sense and then we act rashly, usually because it suits us. We also need to learn to control our emotions and not let them control us because they have a huge effect on how we read a situation. The problem is, our senses are real. The information we receive from our senses is exactly as it is. They don't have the ability to lie, they cannot bluff. There is no deceit or treachery; they are a very exacting vibration.

Intuition can also trigger flashes of inspiration, ideas, songs, art, concepts and so on. The creative arena is very much a part of your intuitive sense. As you increase spending time in meditation, so your intuition and spiritual senses will develop.

Get creative…!

7.) Spiritual...

This is an abstract sense. The sages refer to it as *'awakening the greatness within'*. With regular meditation and prayer, you'll gain access into this incredible arena – the God

Within. However, one needs to constantly develop their sensory powers to really appreciate this sense. Initially, you need to accept:

- Your Spiritual sense exists
- You have faith, God is indeed within you
- You are comfortable and happy with this fact
- You are celestially connected to the Universal Consciousness (God)

Once you accept and believe this with all sincerity, every time you pray, this sense will open doors you never knew existed. Walking a true spiritual path and regular sincere prayer, will keep this channel open, putting you in touch with your spiritual self – your God within.

Using Our Senses...

Senses in the animal kingdom are on another level. A mother seal can identify her pup from amongst thousands of identical looking pups just by scent. Think about that...! Did you know dolphins are so smart, within a few hours of captivity they can train people to stand on the edge of the pool and throw them fish...?

Okay, that's a joke but dolphins are warm blooded mammals. They enjoy a high level of intelligence and superior senses. A dolphin hunts fish using a sophisticated sonar system. Cats hunt at night because they can see in the dark while bats 'see' in the dark using an echo system. Animals, insects and birdlife have an onboard GPS. They're all able tune into Earth's Geomagnetic field in order to circumnavigate their way around. Dogs can hear our heartbeats and sync in with them. From this, they can tell how stressed or how calm we are from our heartbeat. In Japan, they have goldfish who play underwater soccer with a ball. Netflix have a documentary called, 'The Hidden Lives of Pets'. It's a fascinating insight into animal intelligence. Definitely worth a watch. These Sentient Beings enjoy advanced senses, way beyond a human's reach.

We use our senses for everything. We are completely reliant on the input received. Senses are after all is said and done, our way of understanding what is happening around us. We use our senses to formulate what it is we want to say, how we feel or how we act. Take time out to develop them, especially the two abstract sixth and seventh senses.

In the following chapter we look at our *'emotions'* and how they affect our balance in life…

We are all ultimately one with everything.
Sadly, it's our beliefs that separate us'

Emotions

'Peace comes from within. Do not seek it without'
- Buddha -

Emotions are stimulated by our thoughts. When we express our emotions, several of our senses are usually invoked. The more senses implicated, the more powerful the emotion experienced, meaning - we actually make our own emotions.

We're essentially talking here about emotions like anger, fear, resentment, hatred, happiness, humour and love to name just a few. They are created via our basic senses from a cognitive reaction. This is why they are so powerful and have such a strong mental effect on us. Some emotions like *'empathy'* for example are even more *'out there'* and are therefore more difficult to comprehend.

Empathy is not sympathy. Empathy represents many things but a prime example would be when you're able to mentally *'feel'* another person's pain or anguish. Without realising it, you cognitively connect with the other person, briefly allowing both of you to share a mental reaction.

For example: You're walking along the side of the road on the pavement. A mother and her child are walking towards you. The child is bouncing a ball. Suddenly the child loses control of the ball and it bounces out into the road in front of an oncoming car. The child immediately chases it. The mother screams, glances at you for a millisecond and then manages to reach out and somehow pull the child to safety while you stare in abject horror and anticipation. Glued to the spot, you cannot move. For a brief moment both you and the mother mentally connect, your vibrations resonate on the same frequency. You both share in the pain and terror of what could have potentially happened.

These are deep emotions. Let's have a closer look at why these emotions are so powerful and have such an effect on us. As already discussed, emotions are linked to our senses. Our senses convey messages to the brain. The brain then creates an appropriate reaction or in this case, an emotion. In the above example, both you and the mother's eyes saw (sense) what was about to happen, anticipated the anguished result (emotion), instantly relayed the identical information to the brain and the brain reacted accordingly.

In this situation, it was the frequencies that were in sync. Emotions carry their own frequencies. The frequency of anger or danger often triggers higher frequencies. One can almost feel the vibrations re the above scenario without even being there. As both parties witnessed the above scene unfolding with the child running into the road, another element was happening simultaneously. This was the *'empathy'* element. As both parties mentally visualised what could have potentially happened, their frequencies resonated.

Pascal Fries, a German neurophysiologist, claims, it's all about neuronal synchronisation, which in terms of shared electrical oscillation rates, allows for the smooth communication between neurons and groups of neurons, capable of resonating over vast distances with other similar neurons vibrating on the same frequency. This is what typically happened in the above example with the child running into the road. Neuronal synchronisation, applies to all life forms.

'Resonance is a truly Universal phenomenon, at the heart of what seems like mysterious outer worldly forces controlling the balance on earth' - Michael Young

Our emotions are characteristically unpredictable. We don't have a lot of control over them because we tend to react irrationally, instead of calmly pausing to think about it, before instantly responding or reacting to a situation. Emotions are not a given virtue like our senses. Everybody's emotions are vastly different, creating large scale neuronal activity across the brain when expressed.

Those who have done a stint in the military are taught throughout their comprehensive training to ignore their emotions. When the trainees eventually go to war, they are genuinely torn by the vicious conflict of war. At times, they seek raw revenge for a lost comrade even though emotionally, they would normally have preferred a nobler justice; they suffer pride and patriotism tinged with shame, complicity, betrayal and finally guilt. Racked with fear before their first deployment, they worry about killing a human being. After their first kill, their elated emotions create a neural block as they self-accept a mode of *'kill or be killed'*. Their training kicks in and they become mindless killers. When they finally return home, many of them are scarred for life. Some become hunters and murder innocent animals to feed their bloodlust when all they are striving to do is to try and overcome their shame and regain their once simple emotions of love and trust and happiness. It can take many years for war-torn soldiers to fully recover the effects of a harsh war, awash with intrinsically deep emotional twists and turns and vivid, invasive personal memories.

People with high emotional levels find it problematic to calm down, reflect, seek within and get balanced. Life is a lot more fun when you can let go of unnecessary stress and recurring high emotional disorders, which are mostly self-inflicted but obviously it's difficult to deal with if you've experienced a troubled past.

It's like desire. In life, we're often motivated by desire to a large extent. The more we desire something the more we want it until it becomes an obsession, stimulating our emotions in the process.

The reality is, it's actually our emotions that enhance our desires, which eventually become obsessions. Once we have the object of our desire, the obsession and our heightened emotions dissipate, in fact they disappear completely. It's almost like it was all about the challenge. As soon as we've conquered it and own it, we no longer desire it.

Again, it's only when we become aware of our emotions and how they affect us that we're able to get a grip on addictions like desires and realise, we probably didn't need the object of our desire anyway as it would have become just another anchor, something we'd have to sell at a later date because we'd no longer have a need for it.

Communication...

When it comes to emotions and how intense they can be, one of the reasons we enjoy such enhanced emotions is because we have the ability to communicate. Communication is one of the reasons why humans have evolved so successfully. Due to our ability to communicate, our emotions have become ultra-sensitive. What would any of our emotions be without our vocal ability...? Love without words...? Anger without shouting...? Laughter without sound...? And so on. Granted, we'd still have emotions but they'd be played right down without us having the ability to express them vocally with so much tone, passion and angst.

Communication has many levels but only one goal, which is shared understanding. We choose our words and the pitch carefully in order to communicate the right mood and effect to describe our feelings, ideas and thoughts. The tone of our voice tends to convey a lot more than mere words though. Be aware therefore of what you say and how you say it because it is likely to be said back to you in the same manner...!

The average adult human language has a comfortable base of around four thousand words. Without communication, human emotions would be rather dull and boring instead of vibrant and rich in colour, full of meaning and expression, with the ability to bring excitement, laughter and vigour into our daily lives.

'Don't judge anyone unless you've walked a mile in their shoes because then it won't really matter, they'll be a mile away and you'll still have their shoes...!' - Billy Connolly

Human Behaviours...

Psychologists accept, humans are complex individuals, with multifaceted behaviour patterns. However, for simplicity, they can be divided up into *'the Takers'* and *'the Givers'*, with four basic overall character traits, as follows:

1.) Predator
2.) Worker
3.) Creator
4.) Artist

The Predator – As in the animal kingdom, this left brain thinking human is top dog, i.e. – leaders; ruthless CEO's of major companies; military people; police; security; politicians; etc. Their choice of sport is Boxing; Martial Arts; Rugby; etc. Awesome to have these guys in your corner when things get a little messy but the (balance) other side is, they willingly prey on the weak; always get their own way regardless of the hurt caused to others; and generally, adopt a low esteem attitude towards everyone. They waste not want not and therefore seldom have close friends, or associates in business because the spotlight is always only on them. They belong to the *'Takers'* of this world, not the *'Givers'*. Marriage and religion are for personal gain only. Physically, they are not necessarily huge, powerful people. They are usually, lean but well built, in perfect shape, i.e. – the eagle, lion or tiger. They can also be as small as a rat or spider and equally as deadly.

The Worker – This is your blue-collar worker, the engine of any nation. Essentially, they are Earth people, mostly overweight or large in statue. Plumbers, electricians, carpenters, builders, farmers, etc. They are well grounded, left brain thinking, happy people that get the job done. They are very popular with loads of friends, a safe marriage and strong religious morals. They willingly participate in any sport, normally for the exercise rather than a fanatical desire to win. They are compassionate towards each other, animals and Mother Earth and normally live a balanced life between work and play. The other side (balance) is these people lack personal direction in life, i.e. they need to be led to be successful. They belong to the *'Givers'* in society, will usually stand against the *'Takers'* of this world. In the animal kingdom, they would be the Rhino, the Elephant, the Buffalo, the Beaver, etc.

The Creator – This is your scientist; palaeontologist; academic teacher; professor; engineer; programmer; IT specialist; etc. The people who create and advance human society as we know it. Without these incredible people, we'd all still be cruising in the dark ages...! They are not really into sport but will participate in fitness routines like cycling; walking, swimming; judo; etc., which keeps them trim. They prefer to walk a personal spiritual path rather than belong to a formal registered religion. Friends are normally associates they work with. They are avid readers and appreciate cooking and entertaining dinners. The other side (balance) is these people live a closet lifestyle. They prefer their own space so they will normally choose to avoid crowds and busy lifestyles. They are *'Givers'* not *'Takers'*. In the animal kingdom, they would be the gentler animals.

The Artist – This is the creative, right brain thinking, slow minded, dreamy musician; writer; artist; sculptor; poet;

etc., who really isn't overly concerned re the world, politics, or what's happening next door. They exist in their own creative bubble, follow a personal spiritual path and close friendship. They are not into active sports, preferring yoga workouts; surfing; tennis; golf; - social sports rather than overly competitive sports. The other side (balance) is these people are seldom successful in the business arena or wedlock as they find it difficult to commit to anything long term. They are *'Givers'* not *'Takers'*. In fact, they will give you their coat off their back on a cold day. They are almost fanatical about animals with constant fears for their welfare. Usually, the more eccentric they are, the more creative they are. In the animal kingdom, they are also the gentler animals but mostly the weirder ones…!

This is a simple extrapolation of human behaviours. There is a ton of info re this topic with many psychologists injecting their personal interpretations, which vary from simple to extremely complex. In the spiritual world, the Guru's seem to prefer the unpretentious, *'Givers'* and *'Takers'* model.

Everyday Emotions...
What follows are a few everyday emotions and how they affect us:

Fear...
Fear is one of the *'Big Five'*, also known as the four fingers

and the thumb. The four fingers are: Power; Wealth; Fame; and Love with Fear as the thumb. The Sages believe these five pillars are 'Life' integrated. If you have Power, then Wealth will follow and with Wealth comes Fame, which can lead to Love. They don't necessarily have to follow in that pattern, they can follow any alternative pattern and they'll work. If you have Wealth then Power will follow and so on. Fear however, is the one opposite (the thumb) because if you achieve the other four fingers, you'll constantly have 'fear' (the thumb) of losing one or all of them...!

A lot of fear situations are actually a delusion of the mind, merely a negative thought we allow to creep in. We sometimes mentally see things that aren't there. This is the negative ego intervening because the ego is scared of failure. The ego only wants to win in order to boost self-esteem so it creates negative vibrations, which we call fear, to prevent us from doing things in case we fail. Always bear in mind, people or issues can only hurt you if you let them. Once you accept this, you'll know it's just your ego reacting.

It's okay to be scared, everyone has their scare moments. The motivation is not to fight fear, rather accept the initial fear and let it pass through. Easier said than done but if you slow down and mentally absorb what is happening, you can control your fear. Slow deep breaths will help with any situation. By doing this, you're able to re-focus and make good decisions.

It's not always about *'flight or fight'*. There are usually alternatives to most fear situations but if *'flight or fight'* are your only options then at least by controlling your breathing you get a chance to assess the situation and make the right choice.

Fear comes in many guises. It doesn't need to be a violent situation. You can have fear of spiders, various predator animals, heights, small spaces, huge waves and so on. It's all fear and it impacts the same; the adrenalin kicks in, senses are heightened, nerves are tense. Take a step back, re-focus, get your breathing under control and assess the situation before making any rash decisions. Once you get into a routine of handling stress in this quiet attentive manner, you'll soon gain confidence in dealing with any stress situation.

Anger...

There are many *'anger'* situations we could explore but we'll use a simple scenario here like when someone says something derogative to you and you take immediate offence. This would usually be a remark made to you of a personal nature that bruises your ego and lowers your self-esteem. Basically, whatever someone says to you should never be sufficient to affect you and propel you to express your emotions, unless you mentally allow it to. This is what generally happens:

- You initially feel hurt about what was said

- You mentally generate an emotion (anger/rage) the more you think about it
- You react by saying something, thereby unloading your rage verbally
- You defend your action with a reaction, which can continue indefinitely until you run out of steam or realise how silly you've been and you end it

These reactions represent the four stages of most anger situations. To prevent this from happening you need to mentally cut it off at stage one and re-store the balance.

How do we achieve this...? If you are aware answering a rebuke is going to lead to a heated debate or worse (a physical encounter), rather choose to ignore the situation but you can only do this if you are mentally aware of the consequences that will inevitably follow. This is not implying you become a passive doormat; this is more about avoiding direct conflict for the sake of it. Granted, there will be times when everyone will be called to stand up and those times are inevitable but if you're mentally in control, you get to choose to either ignore a situation or make a stand.

The consequences of replying are always worse for both parties because these situations generate way too much negative energy, which mentally upsets your balance and corrupts all your thoughts going forward until such time as you can offload them and move on.

Being human, it's difficult to ignore anything, let alone

a direct personal remark but the long-term advantages are worth it. Rather ignore the remark, observe it, learn from it and move on because maybe they were right. There had to be a reason for them to have made the remark in the first place.

If you are able to do this once, the next time it happens, it will be so much easier to control and you'll be mentally prepared for it, plus the other person will be the loser; he/she will carry the negative energy, not you. Sometimes it's not worth raising your voice and upsetting your balance.

It was Gandhi who advocated peaceful revolution. In the face of a charging British Police force on horseback, Gandhi requested his followers to sit down and eventually to lie down. This completely perplexed the British Police. They didn't know how to handle the situation. Had Gandhi and his followers stood their ground they would have been punished, which is what had happened to them previously when they'd chosen to stand firm.

*'If you are patient in one moment of anger,
you can escape many days of sorrow'*

How about a love couple who have just had a loud and proud argument...? One cannot ignore the raw energy of anger as opposed to the strong vibrations of love, which are more healing, steady, soothing. If you shout or emit a harsh sound with the attached emotion of anger, it has the potential of inflicting instant damage to the person you are shouting at, i.e. a bruised self-esteem/ego. Such sounds at close range can be upsetting. However, when one is in a state of anger, the negative energy expressed is of a high frequency but often lacking in substance. Anger therefore, usually ends up reverting back to the person who created the sound.

Anger and Art - creativity connects with our own existential fury. Aggression is a vital feature of most poignant art. If it weren't for the internal angst, past hurt or old love scars in a lot of artists, their art would fail to tell the story as vividly and vibrantly, as a lot of art does. The same goes for musicians and many other expressions of creativity. Anger emotions are readily exposed in an artists' output, normally the louder or intensely, the better...!

Humour...

'The most wasted days of our lives are those in which we did not laugh...!' - Sebastien Chamfort

We don't necessarily laugh because we're happy, we are happy when we laugh. Humour is one of the best healing emotions we have, automatically increasing our vibration frequencies. As a child, we laugh over three hundred times a day whereas as an adult we sadly laugh only about fifteen times a day and yet everyone understands what having a sense of humour is all about.

Humour is the one emotion that usually ends up

making life palatable when sometimes little else does. It's humour that allows us to go beyond our other emotions, enabling us to express ourselves completely through joy and laughter. It's often been said, a good bellyaching laugh is food for the soul.

The true joy of humour is it positively escalates an emotional high (brain releases dopamine) beyond all else and is therefore extremely enjoyable. It's a human's ability to appreciate humour and share it, making this emotion one of the most valued human feelings. Humour has the ability to open up your receptive abilities and stimulate insight into your higher self. It's also a wonderful cleansing and healing vitality plus it's a powerful energy booster for the soul. Nothing gets you down if you are able to laugh at a situation, plus it's infectious, when you laugh, everyone around you also laughs.

Taking yourself seriously can present a huge obstacle in life. This is an ego thing. Unfortunately, when it comes to the ego, there is no laughter. The ego focuses only on the self and feels vulnerable when threatened. This can be avoided if you laugh often.

Although laughter is indeed incredibly medicinal, it doesn't mean you need to giggle incessantly at anything and everything like an idiot because we have enough of those in this world already. Walk your 'Life' path with bliss, laugh and love it.

Love...
'All you need is love – Love is all you need' - John Lennon

Creating a strong field of love positively affects those both near and afar. A *'love'* vibration carries enormous strength. Some people stare down the barrel of life forever and never find true love but when your heart is filled with pure love, you'll never experience loneliness. Love is an attraction; it attracts people towards each other. Love fills your life with joy. Scientists claim, no less than twelve sensory parts of the brain are collectively stimulated when you express heartfelt love. This powerful emotion releases feel-good chemicals such as dopamine, oxytocin, adrenaline and vasopressin, leaving you feeling mentally intoxicated.

The common sign or logo for love is a heart because your heart Chakra is the energy centre for love. When you are consumed with true love, the emotion is so powerful it completely envelopes you. To really experience a life filled with love you need to increase your inner feeling of love. Then share this inner love with those around you because filling your life with pure love is an incredibly powerful emotion that will continually uplift you.

Love is also about trust. Trust and love are symbiotic. The one intrinsically goes with the other. It's not a dualism or a yin and yang thing, it's more about co-operation. When you really love someone, you trust them. It's about trusting and being trusted. Respect is the other leg of the triangle of love. You need to love and respect yourself before you can learn to love and respect another.

If you don't know love then you cannot love or respect

yourself and you will have problems loving and respecting others. Those who have experienced only hurt and pain in their lives will often desire to hurt and inflict pain on others. This is a never-ending vicious circle. If you feel you are currently part of this circle, you need to break free at your earliest opportunity.

Love is without doubt the strongest form of vibrational energy in our Universe. God has unconditional love for everything. Dogs have unconditional love for their humans. A mother has unconditional love for her child. Parents have unconditional love for their children. Powerful stuff…!

And it's the same with animals. Walk up to a mother lioness with cubs and try stroking her cute little felines. You better have good insurance…! Once a bond of love has been formed, it's very strong. As a parent, you instinctively feel this passion, this unconditional love you have for your children. If you can genuinely feel this love then you should be able to understand God's love and know within, you are a part of this love. If you spread this unconditional love across to your neighbours and all other life forms, especially God's very own, like the animals and the environment, then know in your heart, life's *'Balance'* will ensure unconditional love is returned to you in abundance. This is a guarantee.

Receiving love always makes you feel a better person, spiritually advances you and completely energises you. It's that absolute happy feeling you get when you truly know you are loved. It doesn't matter who it is, the feeling is the same. It's all about the love and being loved. Absorb the energy. Spread it around. It's infectious and the world needs love. Thought infused with love is all-powerful. The magnetic attraction of love as an energy force is so strong it can be felt across the world. Two lovers separated, living on either side of the world, will still be mentally connected by the energy force of their love.

These are examples of strong magnetic bonds of love. Lesser bonds of love are for example, your love of a specific personal item like a watch or similar (attachments) or something as simple as your love for certain clothes, which make you feel good about yourself. Learn to love. Learn to give and receive love. The rewards are huge and when you are able to truly love, it will change your perspective on life.

Each time you act out of real spontaneous love and overcome your fears, you advance that much closer to realising your full potential and accepting with pride, your true self. This is where you want to be.

Roses have always been associated with love, especially red roses. There's an old saying about the thorn amongst the roses but the real perspective is, it's not a bed of roses containing a few thorns but rather a few thorns that have managed to produce a magnificent rose, meaning: Even when ugly thorns experience love, they produce beauty. Be thankful thorns have roses because this proves, even the bad still have good in them…!

Happiness...

Real happiness starts within. Self-worth should always be worth more to you than material wealth or social status, regardless of what society you come from. In yoga, standing on your head is uncomfortable but it stimulates glands in the brain, which creates happiness. No matter how bad it may seem at times, there will always be those worse off than you. It is said, if we all had to deposit our bad baggage in a designated place and we had to suddenly witness the extent of everyone else's bad baggage, we'd hastily retrieve our meagre pile of baggage and be very happy. By simply modifying our behaviour appropriately, we begin creating causes for infinite happiness in our daily lives, instead of endless suffering. We need to see ourselves in terms of who we are rather than what we have.

Happiness is one of the good emotions in our daily arsenal. We need to try and generate as much happiness as possible in our lives. If you're currently doing things that make you feel unhappy, stop doing them. Move on. If you want to know how fortunate you really are, consider, over one billion people in this world will go to sleep tonight without having eaten today.

By focusing only on what is bad in your life you are essentially blocking what is currently good in your life. This is because when you focus only on the bad in your life you attract more of the same. Whereas when you focus on the good things in your life, you equally attract more of the same. What would you rather have…?

Find your balance. Be happy…!

'All Life Forms have two main desires in life – Survival and Procreation. Tread lightly...!'

Re-Cap...

The following chapter, *The Game of Life,* plus the next two chapters, *Life Is...* & *The Simple Life,* are what really constitute the essence of this book. The previous chapters were all about arming you with the tools (the knowledge) to play this wonderful Life game. Now we get to explore this multifaceted game, warts and all, hopefully simplify some of Life's complexities and overcome many of the challenges, whilst still appreciating the wonderful opportunities available. Knowledge is everything...!

There are many tools we've explored in the preceding chapters but some of the more salient points are as follows:

- We strive for *'Balance',* in life, defined by energy forces of opposites that exist, i.e. direct cause and effect
- Magnetism is a *'dynamo'* force of energy, ubiquitous throughout the Universe, creating cosmic magnetic fields on planets, earth, moons and even asteroids
- Earth has its own Geomagnetic energy field, causing all magnetic needles to point due North.
- Earth has an atmosphere, which protects earth and all life on earth from the sun's radiation.
- The Schumann resonance of 7.83Hz., facilitates a deep synergy coupling for all life, subtly connecting with earth's Geomagnetic energy field
- Man-made electro-magnetic energy (radiation) is harmful to all life on earth
- By simply re-balancing our body frequencies, we have the power to improve our health

- We have five brainwave frequencies – Gamma, Beta, Alpha, Theta and Delta. Each brainwave pattern dictates our behaviour, moods, emotions, etc.
- We have three consciousness levels that affect everything we say, think or do. They are the Conscious; Subconscious and the Unconscious
- We have an active left-brain hemisphere and a dreamy, creative right-brain hemisphere
- We have seven senses – sight; sound; touch; taste; smell; intuition; and spiritual
- Everything throughout the Universe, consists of atoms
- Energy, frequency and vibrations have a synergistic relationship
- We have an Auric light surrounding our body
- We are spiritual beings consisting of divine energy existing in a human body
- We are surrounded by vibrations, with patience and our intuition, we can learn to read them
- God represents Universal Consciousness, an omnipresent Celestial Divine Spirit of unconditional love
- We're all a definitive part of the Universal Consciousness
- The Universal Consciousness represents the Collective Consciousness of all life
- God is within us and within everything we see, hear, taste, smell or touch
- All Life Forms are sentient beings, sharing emotions, unique characters and a soul
- Love is the sincerest form of vibrational energy and the most powerful emotion we have
- Our senses are our way of understanding what is happening around us

Part Two

The Game of Life

'We are stardust, we are golden, we are billion-year-old carbon and we've got to get ourselves back to the garden...!'
- Joni Mitchell -

This sums it up quite nicely and it could all be left here, but being human we never seem to leave anything alone because in essence we consist of this electrifying mass of divine energy trapped in a human body but still caught up in life's slippery slopes of desire, greed, torpor, sloth and everything else that constantly challenges and tempts us on this wonderful planet called earth. In fact, most of us don't even know we need to get ourselves back to the garden and some of us don't even care because let's face it, the good life is just so damn tasty...!

Bob Dylan wrote a beautiful song called: *'Like a Rolling Stone...'*

'How does it feel
To be on your own
No direction home
A complete unknown
Jus' like a rolling stone...'

We are so easily tempted to take the wrong path through life, knowing full well it leads nowhere. We happily hop, skip and jump like a rolling stone, quite content, getting up every morning and aimlessly ploughing through yet another calendar day. Another dollar, another day and so it continues.

Derek Sivers says, *'A new day begins when I wake up. Nothing changes at that moment. A new year begins when there's a memorable change in my life. Not January 1st. Nothing for me changes on January 1st. I can understand using moments like January 1st as coordinators, so cultures and computers can agree on how to reference time. Shouldn't our personal markers and celebrations rather happen at personally meaningful times…? The year really begins when you move to a new home, start school, quit a job, have a big breakup, have a baby, quit a bad habit, start a new project or whatever. These are the real memorable turning points; where one day is different than the day before. These are the meaningful markers of time, your real new year. This isn't selfish. You know your friends and family well enough to acknowledge their special days. The day I most want to celebrate someone's life has nothing to do with the calendar day they were born. The 14th of February is not when I celebrate my romantic relationship. To force these celebrations on Universal dates disconnects them from the meaning they're supposed to celebrate. It's thoughtless. Celebrate personally meaningful markers. Ignore arbitrary calendar dates. The best days of your life are not planned. They just happen.'*

And it happens to all of us, even academics and those who are supposed to know. The best days of your life are in fact every single day because if you make every day count then you are getting the best out of what life has to offer. Embrace the fact that every day is a bonus. Every morning you wake up, you get to enjoy yet another incredible life adventure. It's a mind thing. It's about living in the moment and enjoying every second. When you get to view life from this perspective, your outlook on life changes. You begin thinking positively, obstacles are merely there to be overcome, all part of the adventure. There is no destination, it's all about now. Right now. This moment. Life is…

Sadly, a lot of us live in a selfish bubble, surrounding ourselves with whatever we've achieved in life. We gallantly boast our triumphs and conquests, desperate to prove how great we are. School reunions, locker room banter and similar, are perfect examples of *'pissing contest'* arenas, where we verbally lord over friends and peers. We commit these acts in order to emboss our personal CV's so we may achieve yet more fame, more money, more power and so the cycle continues. It's all about me, me, me…ego…!

One day though, we sit back and mindfully realise we've matured; life has somehow slipped us by. The *'life'* adventure, which was once so exciting, is now looking a little bleak. The children have grown up and moved on, the pace of business has lost its desire and physically we just don't cut it anymore, we have way too many aches and pains.

Realisation finally sets in; we sit and ponder our future. What is going to happen to us in our latter years...? Will we end up in one of those old age homes because we can no longer look after ourselves, stuck in a lonely single room for the rest of our days, communicating with people of a similar age and disposition who drool, can't hear you, repeatedly pass obnoxious wind without warning, gabble on incessantly and incoherently about their famed youth and exaggerated achievements and so on.

Your eyes mist up as you realise this is probably it. No-one in your family really wants to bathe you every day, wipe your butt and spoon feed you, so it's off to one of those nicely packaged retirement homes where you'll wait out the rest of your days in total boredom, staring endlessly at a blank wall – *'Aarrrggghhhh..!'*

Let's not go there anymore because it doesn't have to be that way. Going forwards, we'll rather keep it positive. Making a change in life though is ultimately your decision and it's a decision you need to personally endorse. It is however, a two-pronged decision because to do this securely you need to make physical changes as well as spiritual changes.

Change is also about getting balance into your life and making good choices. Let's begin by having a look at the physical changes necessary. The physical changes may consist of a whole new life program. To make it work, it needs to become part of your everyday lifestyle because the new you, is hopefully forever.

To begin, if you're overweight, then consciously commit to losing weight. Join a gym and firm up, start a long-term exercise program, even if it's only walking, try joining a yoga class or similar. The activity list you can do is in fact extensive. The main thing is to get active and maintain a regular exercise program. Basically, it's all about getting your body in tune because that in itself is a big step towards being happy. Surrounding yourself with positive vibrations makes life a lot easier to manage and having a strong healthy body will go a long way to promoting a positive mental attitude. Health is really everything because without your health, you have nothing.

Try and avoid eating animals, fish, poultry and dairy. Not only is it unnecessary, it's way too heavy for your complicated digestive system. Eat more salads, beans, lentils, nuts, pasta, legumes, rye bread, fresh vegetables (preferably raw – make smoothies) and fresh fruit. Drink a lot of fresh water every day. Cut out nicotine and alcohol abuse. Exclude high sugar content foods, pastries, white breads, high cholesterol-based foods and so on.

Yup...you've heard it all before...! Fact is, it works and there's just way too much medical proof to substantiate it. One of the major causes of many forms of sickness has to do with the digestive system, i.e. the gut and its powerful immune system. Get this right and you eliminate a large chunk of potential ills and getting this right is all about eating right. It's a discipline but if you put your mind to it, you can do it.

During our time on earth, we eat every single day, sometimes several times a day. For some people, eating is a means to survival, for others, it's a preoccupation. They plan their entire day around this obsession. Life becomes a feeding frenzy. To put it rather bluntly, whatever goes into your mouth has to eventually come out the other end and according to the medical gurus, the sooner the better. Be careful what you eat. Get it right...it's worth it...!

Spiritual Changes...

So, working out regularly and eating correctly is great for the physical side but what about the spiritual side...? The other leg of our balanced triangle, what changes are you prepared to make here...? We need a healthy and well-developed spiritual mind as much as we need a healthy body in order to really enjoy life on earth. The Gurus have a saying - Eat to fuel your body, not feed your emotions...!

The New You...

To begin your new journey, you can start by *clearing out the cupboard*. This means getting rid of your old way of thinking, which is about letting go of any lingering hatred, guilt, rage, greed, gossip, fears, negative vibrations/energy, basically clearing out your past and saying goodbye to it, forever. Those past imprints and impressions you left on various objects or people in your life, no longer exist.

'Don't worry about tomorrow; tomorrow will care for itself'

Whatever happened yesterday, cannot be undone. It's the past. Get over it. Whatever is going to happen to you tomorrow, you don't know so don't worry about it. You may not even see tomorrow, which is rather pessimistic but its reality, so rather focus on what's going on in your life right now because this is what affects you going forward. Stephen Stills, in his early days with Buffalo Springfield, quoted the break-up of the band was because - *'We'd lost the ability to stay in the moment.'* Sound familiar…?

To help overcome your past, take a sheet of paper and write everything down you consider to be either bad or issues that may have hurt you in your past. Include: names, places, people, every hang-up, every negative issue you can think of because what we are going to do now is to subjectively cleanse your mind. Once you've written everything down, put your piece (or pieces) of paper in a metal bin and set them on fire. While they're burning you can say this affirmation (or similar) repeatedly: *'Ashes to ashes; dust to dust; this is my past; Dear Lord, in you I now trust. Please forgive me for any pain I may have caused for I am now free. Before you, is the new me...!'*

Repeat this affirmation continually until your papers have completely burnt out. Select a stick or a rod and stamp those burnt pieces of paper until the ashes turn to dust. Continue repeating the affirmation. Now hold the metal bin up high in front of you, turn it upside down and commit this ash dust to the wind. Continue repeating the affirmation until you can no longer see the dust.

So, what's happened here...? Well maybe you realised it or maybe you didn't but you have just conducted a funeral for your past. It's over. It's behind you. Now you can go forward and for this new adventure, you begin with a new affirmation: *'Hello new world, from here onwards, this is the new me and I'm walking tall and I'm walking free because whatever happened yesterday or previously, no longer concerns me...!'*

Repeat this continually. You can do the entire ritual a couple of times if you have serious hang-ups to mentally off-load. This may sound like a hocus-pocus magic thing but by using these affirmations you're able to condition and convince your Subconscious mind, you are serious about letting go of your past. By using affirmations in conjunction with a practical application like the burning of the papers, you are focusing all your positive energy into one arrow, aiming it straight at the subject. In the process, you stamp an impression on your Subconscious mind. Your *'power of suggestion'* to rid yourself of your past, convinces your Subconscious. You're finally free. You've convinced yourself. And the cruncher is: If you seriously believe in it, it will happen and you shouldn't have a problem believing because it concerns you and this is what is real.

Once you've got your past out of the way and you're comfortable with it, you can now start on a daily affirmation to begin thinking positively. When you lie in bed in the morning, having just woken up and you're still collecting your thoughts together, think of something you need to accomplish for the new day. You can even write it down the night before and leave it on your bedside table. It can be a spiritual motivation or a material issue but it must be real and within your reach. Something like: 'I want to fly today' isn't within your reach. You weren't designed to fly. You don't have wings so don't be silly. You could begin with something like: *I am in control of my Life and I will: (insert whatever it is you want to achieve for the day...)'*

When you wake up every morning, this is the first thing you are going to tell yourself. It's an everyday affirmation. Repeat it with conviction because with enough conviction you will imprint your desire. This is why you need to repeat affirmations.

Pick Up & Move On...

By tuning into your Subconscious you can convince this deep mind state to do almost anything. Not convinced...? How often has a situation like this happened to you...?

You're busy with a task and it's not working out. You curse, you complain, you get extremely worked up and frustrated, which only increases as you accumulate more and more negative energy. Regrettably, the situation deteriorates the more you attack the problem. The bad news is, from then on, the rest of your day spirals because the accrued negative energy completely dominates your thoughts. Your ego completely takes over and the anger and frustration only increase.

It doesn't have to be like this though. Here's a solution. We call it the *'Pick Up & Move On'* solution, which emanates from the game of golf. This is because in the game of golf there is a wonderful life lesson to be learned. Golf at the best of times is an extremely humbling game. It's a very exact and precise game. When you strike the ball, you only have to be one degree off. This is all it takes to miss the fairway and drive your ball into the bush or miss a Par saving putt.

In golf, you have a small leeway in the standard *'Better Ball'* game. You get two extra shots over Par to still compete. Every hole is rated as either a three, four or five Par, which is the number of strokes you have at your disposal to sink the ball and make a Par. Having an allowance of two additional shots means you still have two chances to at least score a point. After that you have to *'Pick up your ball and Move on'*. At the next hole, you start fresh, which means you get to go for Par all over again. You have a new hole and a new beginning. It's a wonderful game with a valuable life lesson to learn.

'The only time my prayers are never answered is on the golf course' - Billy Graham

Let us now apply this golf rule to our earlier scenario where the task you were doing wasn't working out. Rather, *'Pick up and Move on'*, meaning – instead of getting worked up and frustrated, walk away and leave it for a while, leave it for a day if necessary. Better still, sleep on it.

When you do this, this is what happens: When you were involved in the project, it was your Conscious mind in control. By walking away, you immediately released the problem from your busy Conscious mind. Why...? Because your Conscious mind then instantly re-focuses on whatever it is, you're going to do next. The new activity will completely override whatever it was you were busy with previously. The initial project is temporarily forgotten. In the meantime, your relaxed Subconscious mind has picked up the problem. By originally committing yourself to the project in the first place you stamped an imprint on your Subconscious.

While you continue with your day doing other things in your Conscious mode, without you realising it, your Subconscious continues thinking about the problem. This is what happens when you get to *'sleep on it'*. Now and again throughout the day, your Subconscious will interrupt your busy Conscious mind (normally when you're having a quiet moment) and you'll get little flashes of the earlier problem you experienced with maybe a few solutions thrown in. You may even bump into someone you know during the day who has knowledge or experience of the same problem. Your intuition will immediately interrupt and subliminally get you to connect with this person and discuss the problem. More solutions are provided.

Result: You go back to the problem later or the following day and all of a sudden, the problem is no longer such a problem. You get to solve it without any frustration, leaving you wondering why you initially got yourself so worked up over nothing. This is how the system works and it works for everybody. It's only once we understand, are we able to Pick up and Move on...!

Image...

Your image represents what you project. It's not the Real You. We hide the Real You and as already mentioned, only project what we want the world to see via our image, which is ultimately our ego. We also have the ability to very quickly adapt according to the situation at hand.

For example: When we're with Christian people, we tend to think Christian thoughts and act accordingly. Whereas when we're with intellectual people, we tend to think intellectual thoughts. The same is true in the presence of good or evil, strong or weak, positive or negative people.

Our image is so important to us and it's all because of our entertaining ego. The problem is, the minute we present a false image in front of people who know us, they quickly see through it and once they do, we lose face. Life can then get complicated. The Real You is all inward, the ego is all outward. The following is a brief representation:

Persona: This is your image, how you project yourself, what people see when they first meet you. The way you dress, talk, act and so on. It's what you want people to think you represent. Whether you are fat or thin, short or tall, missing limbs, whatever, it's what everyone physically sees.

Psyche: This is the spiritual Real You, your spirit energy, your inner beauty. It's what radiates within. People cannot see this image. Neither do they often get to learn about this private and personal image.

What can we learn from this…? It's about discipline and being aware of who we really are and acting accordingly. Being mindful allows us the freedom to choose how we want to be seen and what image we really want to project, ignoring for once our powerful dominant ego, choosing to rather present ourselves as real people without our false ego image dominating. This is when little steps become big steps…!

Equality...

Some religions, governments and especially Unions, believe we were all born equal and we should strive for equality in life. This is obviously not possible because as already mentioned, we all exist on various levels of consciousness. In life, there will always be the rich and the poor, the haves and the have not's, the spiritually advanced and the atheists and so on. This is the way society rolls.

'You cannot multiply wealth by dividing it' – Dr. Adrian Rogers

The following simple analogy to describe equality using politics as an example, illustrates why we will never all be equal in life. An economics professor at a local college made a statement to his class that he'd never failed a single student but had once failed an entire class. The class insisted Socialism worked. No-one is poor and no-one is rich, a great equaliser. The professor then said, 'Okay, we'll use this class as an experiment to prove Socialism can never work. All grades will be averaged, everyone will receive the same grade." The class all agreed.

After the first test, the grades were averaged and everyone got a 'C'. The students who studied hard were upset and the students who barely studied were very happy. As the second test rolled around, the students who had put in no effort, studied even less and the students who had previously studied hard, decided they also wanted a free ride so they studied very little. The second test average was an 'E', no-one was happy. When the third test rolled around, the average was an 'F'. From there on, the scores never increased as bickering, blame and name calling resulted in hard feelings because no-one wanted to study for the benefit of anyone else. As expected, all the students ended up failing dismally.

The professor explained to the class, "Socialism would also ultimately fail because when the reward is great, the effort to succeed is great but when a government removes the reward, no-one is inspired to succeed." He said, "You cannot legislate the poor into freedom by legislating the wealthy out of freedom. What one person receives without working for, another person must work for without receiving. The government therefore cannot give to anybody anything the government doesn't first take from somebody else. Ultimately when half of the people get the idea they don't have to work because the other half is going to take care of them and when the other half gets the idea it does no good to work because somebody else is going to get what they work for, that is about the end of any nation.

'When the sun rises, it rises for everyone'

It's a strong story, we'll always be different, it's what characterises us as individuals and makes us interesting as a species. Some of us will work hard and give of our best at everything we do, others will look for the easy way out. All part of what we call, *'The Game of Life…!'*

Energy flow...
To block negative energy from entering your body, fold

your arms across your chest. This simple body movement has the effect of closing your Aura. You not only stop energy from entering your body, you also prevent energy from leaving your body. Most people do it naturally as soon as they're put into a defensive position.

When doing this, slow down your breathing as it will help keep you grounded. Conversely when you throw your arms wide open, you open up your Aura and willingly accept and transfer energy. When communicating with someone, speak in a calm and harmonious voice. This sets your tone and helps convey to people, you are balanced and totally in control.

The east has a cool tradition called *'Feng Shui'* meaning, *'wind-water'*. This is about keeping one's energy light and balanced so it flows freely, unimpeded. The idea is to use the surrounding energy forces to harmonise individuals with their environment. For example, because the world spins on its axis from west to east, use this energy projection to your advantage by positioning your bed in line with the directional flow of the earth. Alternatively, use the earth's Geomagnetic energy flow as your line.

This all makes for good logic. People in the east strive to create perfect conditions for the Universe to flow through them. Then it's about maintaining the balance and keeping it light. An appropriate mental image for life's naturally ordained flow is that of water, which is physically effortless in its action. It isn't necessarily still, nor is it passive, for it flows logically around obstacles culminating in a given destination, regardless of the obstacles it has to navigate. This is effortless action. Water uses gravity and the natural contours of the landscape, instead of forcing issues, to reach a destination. Water can never be anything but effortless and yet it is quietly ever so powerful.

What does this mean…? It's all about rolling with the punches, accepting change, taking what life dishes out regardless, which can be difficult but it's far better than constantly opposing everything and trying to enforce your life path, to go your way. Preferably, go with the flow…!

One should never determinedly make rigid long-term plans either because they're often just a figment of your imagination. You have no idea what tomorrow brings. Life evolves naturally and always when you least expect it, issues happen, sometimes good and sometimes bad.

The sages have an interesting life philosophy. They say fish don't swim, they ride the ocean's current and birds don't fly, they ride the wind, meaning don't stress trying to control your life's destiny. Accept that everything will happen anyway. Live in the moment and enjoy every moment as it happens, as it unfolds. This permits you to take advantage of opportunities as they occur. So, allow life to take you harmoniously on your preordained life path. You're going that way anyway, why fight it and create mountains you cannot always climb.

The celebrated American actor, Morgan Freeman, says he started acting at the age of eight years old when he was part of a school play. Once the play was over and he'd experienced the spotlights, the stage and the audience's warm reception, he knew from that day on, he wanted to be an actor. This humble man went from nothing special in Memphis, where he was born, to a leading actor in Hollywood, famous throughout the world. He claims, he just knew from that first school play, acting was his destiny. He went with the flow.

People from the east and the west tend to think differently about life. In the west it's all about setting specific goals; working towards progress and perfection; controlling life and stroking the ego, constantly evolving whereas in the east it's about letting go of the dominant ego and control; it's more about seeking inner peace and relinquishing material possessions. The west leans towards furthering material progress whereas the east seeks to further spiritual progress. Just saying...

The Three Life Platforms...

According to the Tibetan Guru's, the three platforms to enlightenment are:

- Acceptance
- Forgiveness
- and Peace

Acceptance means accepting your deal in life. Whatever life throws at you, accept it, don't fight it. It's part of your journey. Forgiveness means forgiving all those who wronged you. What you resist, creates conflict. What you accept and forgive, sets you free, which brings you peace.

Peace is the ultimate reward, which will lead to unconditional love and eventually, fulfilment. The more you discipline yourself to accept and forgive; peace and love will be your custom. Your vibrations will magnetically attract love vibrations from those around you. Renunciation will follow as you seek to get even lighter.

In spiritual union, renunciation is an abandonment of the pursuit of material comforts and desires, in the interests of achieving a deeper spiritual enlightenment. You get to decide how 'light' you wish to go in life.

There are those who choose to believe we're all here, just hanging in, waiting for the world to end. God will one day let go his mighty reign, collect his loyal earth followers and depart with them to another world. If you're not one of his devotees then you won't be allowed on the bus so you may as well live life to the extreme. The problem with this theory is, people are once again awarding God with human desires and emotions based on their own imperfections. Fact is, God is not human so that's probably not going to happen.

We need to know why we're doing whatever it is we're doing and optimise on every opportunity. For a practical example, let's say you want to achieve fame, or create a masterpiece of art, or make as much wealth as possible, or you are driven by business with the given highs and lows and the responsibility and control of employees or you seek a spiritual route. Whatever it is, at the end of the day, most of us seek peace of mind, some personal freedom, with sufficient funds to maintain a relatively comfortable zone of existence. Ultimately, you never want to have a boss again or be dependent on others for your lifestyle.

If we look at a *'Hollywood'* situation for example, the majority of the wealthiest people in Hollywood are the ones you've never heard of. Whereas, the movie stars, porn stars and other Hollywood hogs, have careers that exist solely for fame. An actor or Director or Producer is judged on his/her last movie. The fall rate is therefore high, whereas the private entrepreneurs optimise their careers solely for profit.

What can we learn from this...? It really depends on what you want out of life. To begin, you need to know what drives you the most and then focus all your energy on your chosen path. If for example its fame, then choose the movie star route but if it's for wealth, choose the investor route. If you're lucky, fame can produce wealth as well, then you've achieved both goals but this seldom happens. It is more for the chosen few in society so, choose what feels right to you.

Everybody has their own set of values in life and will often judge you according to their values and either respect you or look down on you. This should never concern you if you are focused on what you aim to achieve in life. Maybe you'll prefer an easier route; work on the rigs for three months and then go to Bali, chill out and surf for three months and so on, plus you'll have the ability and freedom to live wherever you want because you'll have very few possessions to anchor you.

This might not seem like a very challenging life path but you will achieve inner peace and happiness with very little stress. However, there'll be no long-term wealth and definitely no fame. It really depends on you and who you are and what you want in life. It's all about attaining inner peace and balance.

In South Africa, a country on the tip of Africa, they are blessed with the might of Africa's big five wildlife: Lion, Leopard, Buffalo, Elephant and Rhino.

All these indigenous wild animals are contained within huge Game Parks where they are protected against poachers and hunters. Further up North is Botswana and Zimbabwe where people often go to see the magnificent Victoria Falls (the largest in the world). This is rated as one of the most powerful energy centres in Africa. It's a divine place with perfect conditions to simply let go and enjoy the moment.

To witness the falls in all its glory is spectacular, in fact it's beyond spectacular. There aren't words to describe it. You have to see it to understand the sheer power, the awesome energy, the incredible volume of water and the overwhelming size of it all. The best time to go is on a full moon, which significantly boosts the energy levels. Spend a few days just chilling and absorb all the abundant energy. You will find inner peace.

People come to Africa to feel the spirit of adventure, experience the heat, smell the indigenous bush, hug the massive trees and soak up the wonderful energy on offer. They also come to see the animals in their natural habitat, which always leaves a profound mental imprint. You have an opportunity to feel wonderfully balanced, find your centre and become one with nature because all of a sudden, you're a part of it all.

Being out there in the wild, under the hot sun, connecting with the animals, definitely brings it all home. You'll quickly discard your mental baggage, your desire for possessions, your petty hates and whatever else, in favour of peace and serenity.

'If I've ever experienced magic, it's being in Africa...!'

Elephants...

If you do a game walk and observe elephants, you'll get to learn a bit about them. They're either left or right-handed, respond to love like a dog, are very playful, sometimes cheeky. They have a mischievous sense of humour, are very sensitive, quick to anger if upset and will defend their herd to the death when threatened. They have amazing memories, grieve like humans over the loss of a herd member, display incredible mothering skills and have a deep cognitive and emotional intelligence.

There is a famous elephant in Taiwan called 'SUDA'. She paints self-portraits of herself in stick form and even signs her name. You can call it up on You Tube, lovely to witness. It takes an entire elephant herd to raise just one calf. They all care for the little ones because gestation takes almost two years, so their young are very precious. A single herd is led by a Matriarch. There is strict order. The herd is a tight cohesive unit. Man is not easily accepted in their environment, considering humans hunt/poach, steal their young for zoos/circuses and private Game Parks, etc., illegally export their ivory to China and the eastern countries and so on. It is despicable what mankind has done and is still doing to these magnificent animals who display deeper social emotions than even humans.

Elephants are the real 'kings' in the animal world. They have no predators other than man and occasionally lions, who will attack an isolated sick or old elephant or they'll prey on unprotected young calves. Elephants eventually die at around sixty to seventy years old when their teeth fall out and they can no longer eat. They are the most amazing animals with an abundance of beautiful energy. Sadly, their numbers are dwindling at a rapid rate as demand from the east for their ivory increases. Poachers are quick to respond for financial gain throughout Africa. Around 40,000 elephants are murdered every year. It is difficult to comprehend how any sensible human could be a part of this terrible slaughter. If you feel the need to get involved then please log onto any of the many elephant sites for anti-poaching, donations, welfare, rehabilitation centres, etc.

The late Lawrence Anthony, who owned a Game Reserve in South Africa, was known as *'The Elephant Whisperer'*, a title he earned when he saved two elephant herds destined for culling because of farm destruction they had caused. At his own expense, Anthony transported the herds to his private Game Reserve in Zululand and cared for them. Initially the Matriarch of the herds wanted nothing to do with him but eventually accepted this passionate human and welcomed him into the herd.

Years later when Lawrence Anthony died, both herds travelled from their far away locations, through the wild Zululand veldt to Anthony's house. Neither of the herds had been near his house for over a year. Back in the day, the herds used to raid his garden and drink from his swimming pool. Both herds took up sentry at the garden wall of the house and stayed for two days in silent respect for this great man who had done so much for them. None of the local wildlife experts could explain how the elephants knew Anthony had passed away.

If we are God's caretakers of Mother Earth then we need to make a globally concerted effort to protect our wildlife, all of our wildlife, especially Africa's elephants and rhinos because with man's insatiable greed, there won't be any left.

When you go up North and experience the real Africa, get down and get dirty. Smell that dry earth, listen to the raw, poignant cry of the fish eagle and witness the animals in their natural habitat. It's wild. Explore and you will find yourself. This is what going with the flow is all about. You'll feel so balanced and centred after an African experience. Definitely good medicine...!

'We need so little in life and yet we ask for so much'
- Kiko Michel -

Man, the Gatherer...

Man, by nature is a gatherer. We tend to gather information from everyone we meet, including humour, certain idiosyncrasies, speech patterns and even annoying habits. We glean information and either hold onto it, if it has appeal or we let it go. This is how we build our character, constantly evolving as it develops. We mentally grow and gather knowledge from meeting new people, travelling and getting involved in *'people'* activities.

Society today is very *'hero'* driven. Our heroes are always the action guys. We tend to place way too much value on aggression and hubris, which is portrayed daily in movies, television, magazines and the media. Everywhere we look, our media heroes are bad role models. We need to acknowledge this and prevent it from affecting our way of thinking, especially with our youth. Rather difficult in an angst driven society where the strongest and the loudest always seem to win.

There is a saying, 'Crowded elevators smell different to midgets.' Tough on the midgets but this is really because mankind has a natural desire to succeed in life. Mankind desires growth. We always want to go higher. Like a tree that grows taller than other trees to enjoy more sun, so we strive to constantly outwit, out run and over achieve against everyone else. We live these selfish lives wanting only more. What's in it for me…!

As we mindfully re-focus, we get over this paranoia. We become more aware of our mind, our true self and our hidden potential. If we take time out to tune in to what's happening around us and within us, opportunities start opening up, the world suddenly looks a better place and so it becomes reality for every day following. You soon realise, you and you alone have the power to change things in your life for the better.

'The best time for new beginnings is now...!'

I Am...

In society we are faced with endless rules that seem to govern our every move. When you realise the rules are put in place to create harmony among the masses, you then begin to work with the rules and not against them. It's like the game of soccer, only when you learn to pass the ball, are you a team and it takes an entire team to win a game.

In essence, as already mentioned, it's about slowing down the pace of life. Once you can accomplish this, you'll observe things you somehow never noticed before, possibly because you were always in too much of a hurry. When this happens, you'll begin to see things for what they really are and be captivated by the beauty, the ingenuity, the wonderful presence of everything around you.

One day you'll look up and see the Universe out in space and it'll suddenly hit you, God is indeed everywhere and in everything. The sheer magnificence of God and what God has created on earth and within the entire Universe will leave you in awe, totally gobsmacked. You'll wonder how you could have failed to notice all of this before. You'll start asking questions like: 'Did I think the earth just happened...and the entire Universe with its perfect magnetic structure just fell into place...? How did I not see all this...? Was I so caught up in my day to day life of gossip and work and routine and shallow friends and whatever else that I somehow missed all this incredible perfection around me...everyday...?'

Being aware allows you to walk confidently through your fears into the unknown, knowing the *'Balance in Life'* can work for you and is not always against you.

There's an old story about a mystic who was explaining his dualistic behaviour to a student. He said, 'I feel like I have two dogs living inside of me, one good and one bad and they're always fighting.' When the student asked which dog usually wins, the mystic replied, 'The one I feed the most...!' Be careful which one you feed...!

When you feel right with life, material possessions lose their value but friendships and family increase tenfold in value. The constant life challenging fear of never having enough, dissipates as you learn to overcome your greed, your ego and your material fears of uncertainty. Your desire to watch the news on television and read the newspapers to discover how bad the world is around you, also loses interest.

It's not that you no longer care; it's more about you no longer have that desperate *'need to know everything'* attitude because clogging your mind with unnecessary information creates needless mental anchors in life.

Peter Vosloo, a retired English school teacher, often proofreads manuscripts for grammatical corrections and so on. He was always fairly extroverted and didactical in his approach to everything, probably a carry-over from his teaching persona…! Anyway, one morning, he took his cup of tea and sat down in his garden to enjoy the early morning sun. However, this time he mindfully experienced phenomena in the garden. He watched a snail make its way slowly across the step, in front of him. He saw a grasshopper and for the first time noticed its interesting colours. He watched a trail of ants crawl up the wall in military precision, he could hear the crickets clicking their legs, heard the myriad of bird songs and even the rustling of the tree tops around him. He became intrigued, observing in total wonder and awe, the perfection of the plants and flowers in his garden, the magnificence of the beautiful trees. He began to feel all the wonderful energy around him. He suddenly burst out laughing as he realised, he'd had a little *'mindfulness'* experience.

This is what happens when you let go and enjoy the wonder and freedom of the Subconscious mind. Peter has now taken up meditation and yoga with enthusiasm. He's relaxed and at peace with himself, says he's become very aware of all the abundant life energy and he loves it. It's opened up a whole new life experience for him.

James Dent once said: 'A perfect summer's day is when the sun is shining, a slight breeze is blowing, the birds are all singing...and the lawnmower is broken...!' He should have added, 'and the beers are cold...!' because life is also about having fun. We never really know where we're going until we actually get there and that's the most exciting thing about life - the unknown. How boring would it be if we knew...?

Eating Right...

As previously mentioned, consuming the right food is crucial to maintaining a strong, healthy body. We tend to choose foods that are commercial rather than selecting foods that are healthy for us and this is where the bad habits begin. One must be conscious in the moment and learn to listen to the body, which initially takes a bit of effort. Listening to the body is a matter of feeling it within. It sounds a little wacky but if you get into a routine of listening to your body, getting in tune with the respective vibrations of your body, it resonates quite naturally. Basically, if something doesn't taste good, let it go. This is your body telling you, warning you.

One must also take note of how the body responds to certain foods. Discomfort, feeling low, constipated, diarrhoea, agitated or nauseated after eating is more than likely a sign the body is being challenged. You also need to take cognisance of your food allergies. Don't aggravate them. Your body has an inherent intelligence. Every cell within your body is ingenious in its form and function with a complete blueprint requirement in order to function correctly and maintain a healthy physical structure.

Some people follow strict belief systems based upon their religious affiliation. Spiritually, this is perceived to be controlling and therefore unacceptable because forcing everyone to follow what may only be healthy to a small percentage of the flock, while the remainder go under nourished, is obviously not right or fair.

'Real Food is Grown – not Born'

Animals...

With regards to eating animal flesh, your goal should ideally be to avoid judging anyone, even though the majority of humans have a difficult time with animal cruelty and the feasting of animal flesh, it's really all about personal choice.

Understandably, once you've seen the light, it's difficult to comprehend how others fail to see, which causes a deep internal conflict within, knowing full well, everyone is aware of the terrible suffering endured by animals, considering they are also sentient beings with a soul. Your personal desire is always to set all animals free, safe from human cruelty. Unfortunately, this is a challenge we all have to face because we need to learn to respect the rights of others who have yet to see.

Personally, strive for a higher love in that all human life will one day get the bigger picture, set all animals free and no longer consume them. The right way to change people's perceptions is to lead by example, people will eventually follow...

Animals, like all other sentient beings, deserve all the love and respect we can possibly afford them. We all need to live on this earth together in co-existence. We are not here to dominate any species. Rather, we are here to learn from all species, share and co-exist, in balance with nature. Sadly, we have not learned this. It's a simple lesson of kindness, decency and respect, for all life species on our incredible planet.

To conclude this chapter on a lighter note, this is a story about a young couple who moved into a new neighbourhood. The following morning while they're eating breakfast, the young woman notices her neighbour hanging up the washing outside.

"That laundry is not very clean," she remarks to her husband, "she doesn't know how to wash correctly. Perhaps she needs better laundry soap." Her husband looks on, remains silent. Every time the neighbour hangs her washing out to dry, the young woman makes the same comments. About a month later, the woman is surprised to see a nice clean wash on the line so she turns to her husband and says, "Look honey, she's finally learned how to wash correctly. I wonder who taught her." The husband replies candidly, "Actually, I got up early this morning and cleaned our windows."

What we see when watching others depends on the purity of the window through which we look and we really do need to look at ourselves more often. There is an axiom that goes: 'Only when you are doing what you really want to do, what you truly love doing, will you find deep contentment and satisfaction in life.' Sometimes we have to earn that satisfaction in life, provided we do so without harming anyone.

Remember, we came into this world with nothing and we'll leave with nothing. We cannot escape this fact. While we're on this earth plane, we need to surround ourselves with happiness. Enjoy your material possessions but don't let them imprison you. What would life be without God's incredible creations to view through a window…?

Your world is only a reflection of yourself. If you can accept this, then cool off finding fault with everything. Attend to yourself; set yourself right mentally and emotionally, for when you change your inner self, the rest will follow accordingly. Feel the cold wind on your face and learn to love it…!

Life Is...

*'The way I see it, if you want the rainbow,
You gotta put up with the rain'*
- Dolly Parton -

Life is sometimes so simple and yet other times it's so difficult, it tests us to the limit. For example: deciphering common axioms, i.e. what is the difference between a human being and being human...? How many of us will take time out to try and understand this...?

- **Human Being** - like any other being; busy in four basic living activities of life - eating, sleeping, mating and defending. This is common amongst all beings with little difference in quality or quantity
- **Being Human** - the responsibility of aspiring and achieving self-realisation, expressing one's humanity

The following is a nice little parable that explains this variable so beautifully: Once a group of pigeons lived on an elevated structure of an ancient temple. When the Hindu festivals were planned, the temple management body decided to renovate the temple, so the pigeons had to find an alternative place to roost. They found a nearby church and moved across but there were already pigeons living there. The existing pigeons however accepted the new arrivals and they all lived happily together. Before Christmas arrived, the church management decided to renovate the church so all the pigeons had to relocate once again. They found a nearby Mosque. All the pigeons flew across to the Mosque and once again had to adjust with the existing pigeons who lived on the Mosque. After some time, the Mosque authorities decided to renovate the Mosque so once again the pigeons had to relocate. They couldn't find any place to settle except in the nearby trees in the natural surroundings. Time passed and all the pigeons lived peacefully on the trees.

One day, below a tree on which the pigeons were sitting, communal clashes erupted amongst the Hindus, Christians and Muslims. A baby pigeon witnessing the chaos, asked her mother, "Why are they fighting...?" The mother pigeon replied, "They are human beings. The Hindus are from the temples, the Christians are from the church and the Muslims are from the Mosque." The baby pigeon asked, "Why is it the human beings are divided when they are all human beings because we are called pigeons, regardless of whether we live on a temple, a church or a Mosque." The mother replied, "We birds have understood well the concept of communal harmony and how to live together. Whereas, human beings have yet to learn the art of Being Human."

Weirdly enough, we may all be human but only a few of us practice being human. We even tend to talk and treat each other inhuman most of the time. As already mentioned, it's all about how we play this Game called Life. What follows are some *'Real Life'* everyday situations.

Although success comes with hard work, it's also associated with failure. This is because in order to succeed you may be faced with countless challenges, which means you might fail a few times before you finally succeed. It takes hard work; it isn't the Universe that's against you. It's about getting off your butt and making it happen, being out there, involved, making decisions and cognitive choices.

We live in a society where pizza gets to your house faster than the police. If you sit back and think you'll do it all later because right now you need to enjoy yourself then you need a reality check. Rather be proactive. Make the right call, get your hands dirty and just do it. Comes a time when you learn to accept, you have to enjoy the light as well as the bulb...!

You know the saying: 'Burn the candles, use the nice sheets, break out the good cutlery and crockery often, wear the fancy lingerie, don't save anything for a special occasion because every day is special and realise, now and again, when it comes to things like chocolate, resistance is futile...!

Politicians often start out with great intentions to serve their nation but often get misled by the power at their disposal and end up taking from the nation instead. This can happen to anybody in this situation. Be aware, if you are in a position of power or authority, don't abuse it. They say politicians and diapers have only one thing in common: They should both be changed regularly and for the same reason...!

The time comes though when you need to actually stand tall and take an honest look at your life. Face reality and make some conscious decisions regarding your future. Stop caring what others think and start focusing on what matters to you. With regards to the 'others', never presume for one minute everybody is 'full of it' and refuses to make changes in their lives. Try and believe in the good in all people. It may just take a little motivation for you to see it.

The early bird might get the worm, but it's the second mouse that gets the cheese. You don't always have to be first in the queue for everything. Reflection and a little thought are a good thing. Less is often better than more. Some are born to rule while others are born to be fools but you can be a leader if you choose because every box has a lid. There is a perfect partner, a perfect career and a perfect path for every one of us plus there'll be many interesting 'Life' opportunities to consider and equally, many 'Life' challenges to face and overcome. This is why we refer to life as a game. You get opportunities and you get challenges. Sometimes you can even make opportunities from your challenges and you'll certainly get faced with more challenges whenever you make use of an opportunity.

In this world there are two kinds of wealthy people: Those who originally had nothing, built an empire through hard work and continued working at it and then there are those who inherited their wealth. If you take the money away from the first kind, they're like fishermen, they'll start over and build another empire but if the second kind lose their money, they seldom come back and re-build to their former glory.

In the past, it was always the strong (the jocks) who got all the good jobs, made all the decisions, got the best girls and so on. Today it's changed. Geeks and Nerds now have all the say. They design computer software programs that earn them mountains of money. Their brains do all the talking. They hold all the top positions in companies and they steer those companies to huge financial success. Women are in love with their power and follow them everywhere. Who would have ever thought the meek and mild would come to the fore…!

Fact is, things change continually and they always will. Maintaining a harmonious balance in life with regards to relationships and those around you, therefore is essential.

As previously mentioned, refrain from judging others as judging is possibly the single biggest cause of conflict in people. It's not in your power to mentally alter them or adjust their way of thinking. The only thing you can do is to lead by example if you really want to instigate change in someone's life.

What can we learn from all this…? We build our lives; we don't just inherit our lives. This is the *'bones'* of the *'Game of Life'*. We come to the earth plane with a life path, to learn and build our lives. We overcome challenges and we move on, wiser and stronger. Every time we do this, we absorb wonderful new energy. Once we realise this and accept it then the idea of constantly building our lives becomes natural to us. We lose our fears about the future and what's going to happen tomorrow. With time, we realise, there isn't a tomorrow. Every morning we wake up, it's always today. And it's going to be a good day…!

On an average day, an average person runs about sixty thousand thoughts through his/her mind. However, ninety-five percent of those thoughts are the same thoughts that ran through his/her mind the previous day and the majority of them were negative…!

When it comes to words there are no surprises either. Women say around seven thousand words a day whereas men only say around two thousand words a day. Never lend your cell phone to a woman…!

The late Henri Nouwen told a lovely story about John and Sandy. They'd always lived in complete harmony.

"We've never had an argument before," says John, "let's at least just have a little squabble like other people do." "But how do we start an argument...?" Sandy asks innocently.

"It's very simple," replies John, "I take this stone and say, it's mine and then you say, no, it's mine. Then we have an argument...!" John sits down, picks up the stone, turns to Sandy and says, "This stone is mine...!" Sandy looks at him, lays her hand gently on his arm and says, "Well, if it's yours, then you have it."

Nice simple *'let go'* story. Life can be simple if you're prepared to let go now and again. As we progress in life it's often the little things that come into play on a daily basis that constantly test us and test us, they most certainly will do because no debt in our Universe goes unpaid, including the good debts. It all comes down to how we deal with these issues, for this is what makes us better people. Sometimes it's all about letting the other person have the stone. Maybe they needed it more than you did. People may doubt what you say, but they'll usually believe what you do.

Verve...

Doing well in sport, or even a hobby or project is a mindset. What this means is to approach the sport/hobby with the right energy. Having a negative mindset or even doubt can work against you. How do we remain positive...?

First of all, you need to really love and enjoy the particular activity you're doing. You must be able to thrive on the energy released from scoring that goal, or sinking that putt, or creating a work of art and so on. If you genuinely love what you're doing, it immediately overcomes most of your hurdles because you're already going with the flow. Secondly, you need to get in the zone. You do this by completely relaxing and getting your mind focused on the present. Think now, this instant. Release, don't tense. Breathe in slowly, deeply, hold it, slowly exhale. Tensing up restricts the flow of energy through your body and prevents you from enjoying yourself.

Getting in the zone also means you need to try and tune in or resonate with the energy of the respective sport or activity. Finally, you need a confident attitude. This is paramount. For example: If it's a game you're playing and you really love the game, chances are you'll be positive anyway. Having a good attitude is also about how you play the game. This means treating the game or sport as a game and not a life or death situation, with a win at all costs type attitude. Lighten up, it is after all only a game and you're doing it for fun. If you lose, it's no big deal. Mentally, let it go immediately. Don't let it get to you. This is a Conscious ego thing that will try and upset you. Be aware of it. Acknowledge it and move on. It works.

Great minds discuss ideas
Average minds discuss each other'

Gossip...

This is what happens when you listen to gossip. When you listen to someone else talking, you immediately absorb their vibrations via your senses. If you're receiving positive vibrations then it's not a problem but if its gossip you're listening to, then it's normally negative information you're picking up. This will stay with you and grow within you like a cancer, which means you'll carry those negative vibrations around with you until such time as you finally unload them and this will definitely have an effect on your attitude towards life. You know what happens to a computer when it picks up a virus...? The virus soon destroys the entire system. When people gossip, rather walk away.

Alcohol...

'If you can lie on the ground without hanging on, you're not drunk' - Billy Connolly

People often resort to drink because they're feeling down. Problem is, this means they're already in a negative vibration mode. As they consume more alcohol, their vibrations become steadily tainted. They start to lose control of their actions and their cognitive. The Conscious mind goes into confusion allowing the ego to lose all discipline. They mouth off at anything and everything. The Subconscious mind gets a little stimulated but is also confused because there's no direction coming from the Conscious mind.

This is why alcohol normally affects your speech first and then your eyesight, your balance and most of your voluntary muscles. The more alcohol you consume the worse it gets. Eventually, the Conscious mind practically shuts down completely, making it difficult for you to even walk. Anyone coming into direct contact with you immediately picks up these heavy vibrations clouding your cognitive ability. It's definitely not a good thing, considering your objective in life is to reach for higher, lighter, positive vibrations.

The following is a lovely tongue in cheek extract from the American television sitcom *'Cheers'*. It's rather old but very funny and quite appropriate here. Cliff Calvin was explaining the *'Buffalo Theory'* to his buddy Norm while they were sitting together at the Cheers bar, dusting the froth off a few cold ones.

Here's how it went: "Well ya see Norm, it's like this, a herd of buffalo can only move as fast as the slowest buffalo and when the herd is hunted, it is the slowest and weakest ones at the back that are knocked off first. This natural selection is good for the herd as a whole because the general speed and health of the whole group keeps improving by the regular trimming of the weakest members. In much the same way, the human brain can only operate as fast as the slowest brain cells. An excessive intake of alcohol, as we know, kills brain cells, but naturally it attacks the slowest and weakest brain cells first. In this way, regular consumption of beer eliminates the weaker brain cells, making the brain a faster and more efficient machine. That's why you always feel smarter after a few beers...!"

Mind Over Body...

The mind is so incredibly powerful. It has complete control over the body. If you convince yourself someone can burn you with a simple stick, you'll feel the actual burn even though it was a harmless stick. This is the power of mind over body, also known as *'The Placebo Effect'*. Imprint the Subconscious and you'll believe it.

While we often think of our bodies and minds as two distinct entities, it turns out they are much more entwined than we might assume. Researchers are continually finding evidence; the brain has a distinct power to manipulate the body's physiology. The mind/body connection can work in our favour or detriment, depending on our knowledge of a situation and our ability to control our thoughts.

Judging by their ability to meditate for hours on end, abstaining from food for days and their vows of silence, most us would agree, Tibetan Monks have better control over their minds and bodies than the average person. Still, what's particularly amazing is some of them can control physiological processes, such as blood pressure and body temperature, feats many medical doctors find astounding.

In one of the most notable exhibits of their skills, a group of Tibetan monks allowed physicians to monitor their bodily changes as they engaged in a meditative yoga technique known as 'g *Tum-mo*'. During the process the monks were cloaked in wet, cold sheets and placed in a 40degree Fahrenheit room. In such conditions, the average person would likely experience uncontrollable shivering and soon suffer hypothermia. However, through deep concentration, the monks were able to generate body heat. Within minutes the researchers noticed steam rising from the sheets covering the monks. Within an hour, the sheets were completely dry. Although the display was fascinating to the doctors, for the monks it was an ordinary occurrence. New monks use 'g *Tum-mo*' as a way to improve their meditative strength and often hold contests to see who can dry the most sheets in one night. The Buddhists claim the heat they generate is a by-product of meditation, since it takes energy to reach a state of alternate reality, a place unaffected by our everyday world.

Many athletes claim it helps them to perform better when they mentally play through an impending game or sporting activity, prior to stepping on the field or court. While we might assume, doing so is a mental pictorial exercise enabling them to focus more on the game, there may be other tangible changes happening inside the body.

Take, for example, Air Force Colonel George Hall who was locked in a small, dark North Vietnamese prison for seven years. While most would lose their minds in such circumstances, Hall went to his happy place, so to speak, by mentally playing golf, every day of his imprisonment. His visualizations were extremely in-depth and included everything from driving the ball off the tee, raking the sand traps, feeling the wind and of course sinking the ball into the put. Regardless of being weak and many pounds lighter than before his capture, one of the first things Hall wanted to do after his release was play a legitimate round of golf. He was invited to the Greater New Orleans Open where he astoundingly shot a 76. When a member of the press suggested his performance was a case of beginner's luck, Hall replied, "Luck, I never three-putted a green in the last five years…!" Despite his physical deterioration and not stepping on a course in over seven years, his body had developed muscle memory, based simply on his imaginings.

Jack Schwarz a Dutch Jewish writer, also lived in horrific conditions in a Nazi concentration camp during World War II. Like so many others, he was beaten, starved and tortured beyond what most of us can comprehend. To cope with his situation, he began the practice of meditation and prayer, which he developed to the point where he could block out the pain of his torment and subsequently withstand his situation. After his release, Schwarz continued his mind over matter practice and occasionally demonstrated his skills by putting a long sailmaker's needle through his arm without injury. He also displayed his ability to regulate his body's blood flow by causing the puncture hole in his arm to bleed or stop bleeding at will.

Schwarz was studied by researchers at the Menninger Foundation. They found he could indeed control many of his bodily processes with only his mind. Men of few words are usually the best men...!

Furthermore, through an electroencephalograph machine, they determined his brain had different electrical activity compared to most other test subjects. According to Schwarz, he could also see people's Auras, which allowed him to gauge their physical, emotional, spiritual and mental conditions.

Undoubtedly, it's difficult to keep a positive attitude when you're facing a life-threatening disease. However, based on a variety of medical studies, doing so can mean the difference between living and dying. For example, in 1989, Dr David Spiegel of Stanford University, conducted a study on 86 women with late stage breast cancer. Half of the women received standard medical care while the other half were given weekly support sessions in addition to the standard medical care. During the sessions the women shared their feelings, talked with other patients and generally had a positive outlet where they could cope with their illness. At the end of the study, the women in the support group lived twice as long as those not in the group.

In recent years, David Seidler, writer of 'The King's Speech,' claimed to have eliminated his cancer through meditation and imagination. After battling bladder cancer for years and only two weeks away from surgery, Seidler decided to see if he could get rid of the cancer through his imagination. He admittedly thought the idea was a little wacko but by that point he figured he had nothing to lose.

So, he spent the two weeks leading up to his surgery envisioning a clean, cream-coloured, healthy bladder. When Seidler went in for his pre-surgery biopsy, the doctor was stunned to find a distinct lack of cancer. He even sent the biopsy to four different labs for testing but it was clear.

Although the mind has the power to heal, it can also destroy. Always use it positively. You have the power to make a current illness worse by constantly worrying about it. Alternatively, you can heal it by thinking positive healing thoughts, controlled via your breathing patterns. Use it, don't abuse it…!

Growing Old...

'Papa was a rolling stone
Wherever he laid his head was his home
And when he died, all he left us was alone'...
-Temptations-

'Time has a way of moving quickly, catching you unaware of the passing years. It seems just yesterday, I was young, married and embarking on my new life with my soulmate. Yet in a way, it seems like eons ago and now I sit and ponder what happened to all the years. I know I lived them, I have glimpses of how it was back then, including all my hopes and dreams.

But here it is, reality, the 'back nine' of my life, caught me completely by surprise. How did I arrive here so quickly...? Where did the years go and what happened to my youth...? We were always untouchable, invincible, independent, innocent, secure...?

I remember seeing older people through the years and thinking, those older people are years away from me. I was still cruising the 'first hole' back then. The dreaded 'back nine' was eons away. Old was for 'old' people. I never began to imagine what it would be like. Suddenly, here it is. Reality check...!

My friends are retired, have all turned grey. They move slower. I notice all the older people now, they're my friends. Some are in better or worse shape than me but I notice the great change. My friends are not like the ones I so clearly remember, who were once young and vibrant.

Fact is, our golden age is indeed upon us. We are now those older folks we used to see and never thought we'd become. A lot of friends are even missing. Each day now, I find that taking a nap is not a treat anymore, it's mandatory, cause if I don't take a nap of my own free will, I fall asleep where I sit...!

I enter into this new season of life unprepared for all the aches and pains, failing eyesight, loss of hearing and strength and the ability to do things I wish I'd done but never did. I'm however mentally secure knowing that when this adventure comes to an end, a new adventure begins.

I have regrets. There are many things I wish I hadn't done; plus, many things I should have done. In fact, there are many things I'm glad I did do. It's called living the life. From here on, I intend living only in the moment, enjoying every fleeting second. This, I will do...!

If you're not on the 'back nine' yet, let me remind you, it arrives faster than you think. Whatever you'd like to accomplish in your life, do it...! Don't put things off too long. Life goes by so quickly. You have no guarantee you'll see all the seasons of your life. Live for today and above all, say all the things you want your loved ones to remember, confident they'll appreciate and love you for everything you've done for them and most of all, done with them, in all the years past.

Life is a gift. Sadly, we only realise this much later in life. The way you live your life is your gift to those who come after you, so live it well, with respect and dignity. Trust me, it is health that is real wealth, not pieces of gold and silver.

Going out is good but coming home is somehow, always better. Your own bed and your own toilet mean everything to you. Old is good in some things: Old Songs, old movies and best of all, old friends...! It's not what you gather, it's what you scatter that defines what kind of life you've lived. Your kids are slowly but surely becoming you. However, your Grandchildren are simply perfect. They don't judge you; they really love you...!

Finally, today is the oldest you've ever been, yet the youngest you'll ever be. Enjoy this simple day while it lasts and never regret growing older, it is a privilege denied to many...!'
J Tossard

One great thing about growing old, (there aren't many,

but it sure beats the alternative – dying young...!) is that spiritually the mind is far more receptive. We are spiritually more active and even pro-active in our latter years. As we progress in life, we pass on what we've learnt to our youth who then develop the concepts and expand on them. This is how mankind evolves. We cannot see this experience we call 'Life' but we're all aware we are alive and we experience this every second of every day, which is why we shouldn't waste time judging others or worrying about what happened yesterday when we still have so much to do today.

Physically, as you grow older the body begins to slowly reduce in size, which is mainly due to hydration of the discs between the vertebras. This is also due to bad posture over the years, which is why practicing yoga on a daily basis is so good. (Yoga promotes strength in the axial skeleton). With time, the body's entire bone structure eventually stops growing and reduces in size as the core bones lose density. The body also loses muscle density, which slowly evolves to fat as the body slows down. The mind's ability to recall is impaired but not the mind's ability to create or store information. However, although the body stops growing and slowly weakens as muscles relax, the ears and nose continue growing, which is why older people always have those rather distinctively large ears and noses...! This doesn't enhance their basic senses in any way but their intuition is heightened the older they become.

'The body may grow old but the mind never grows old
It only gets wiser!' - Mahatma Gandhi

In fact, the most spiritually productive years in one's life can be from over the age of sixty, health depending of course. This is due to having a more relaxed mind, which we should all be able to enjoy. You are only as old as your thoughts and therefore as young as you think you are. You can make your life on this planet as pleasant as possible, even in old age. Happiness and keeping healthy is something you can choose in advance and you do this by staying healthy because every day is a gift. As long as you can open your eyes and focus on each new day, you'll take pleasure in all the happy memories you've been privileged to enjoy throughout your earth time because old age is ultimately like a bank account, you withdraw in later life what you deposited along the way.

'Growing old is about focusing on what you have,
instead of what you don't have'

In the east old age is revered, even sacred. The aged pass the torch and impart their wisdom. Whereas in the west, old age is regarded as someone who is past it and has now sadly become *'spare'* baggage. Unfortunately, age is also against one in the workplace, which is such a pity. Employers only see grey hair and a withered body instead of a vast magical chest of experience and wisdom. When old employees leave a company, they are seldom replaced. A huge life force goes with them.

The following is a wonderful story about age and youth: One day a very old poodle dog was busy chasing butterflies in the African bush. Before long, he wandered too far in and got hopelessly lost. He walked around in circles until he suddenly noticed a young leopard heading rather rapidly in his direction with the intention of having him for lunch. The old poodle thought to himself, 'Wow, now I'm in trouble...!' He looked around furtively and noticed some old bones lying nearby on the ground so he immediately settled down and chewed on the bones with his back to the approaching leopard. As the leopard was about to leap on him, the old poodle exclaimed loudly, "Wow, that was one delicious leopard! I wonder if there are any more around here...!" Hearing this, the young leopard halted his attack in mid-strike. With a look of terror on his face, he slunk away into the trees. "Whew, that was a close one, that old poodle nearly got me...!" He wheezed. Meanwhile, a monkey who'd been watching the whole scene from a nearby tree, figured he could put this knowledge to good use and trade it for protection from the leopard. Determinedly, he swung off the tree and chased after the young leopard but the old poodle saw him go and figured something was up so he followed him. The monkey soon caught up with the leopard, spilt the beans and struck a safety deal for himself for the future with the leopard. The young leopard was furious at being made a fool of. He said to the monkey, "Hop on my back and you'll see what I'm going to do to that conniving canine...!" The old poodle watched the leopard approaching with the monkey on his back. "Now what am I going to do...?" He exclaimed feverishly. Instead of running, the wise old dog sat down with his back to his attackers, pretending he hadn't seen them. Just when they got close enough, the old poodle chortled loudly, "Where's that damn monkey...? I sent him off an hour ago to bring me another leopard...!"

Moral of the story: You can't beat experience and true experience comes with age. The following is a light-hearted reflection on being old and how to enjoy it:

- After loving my parents, my siblings, my spouse, my children and my friends, I have now started loving myself

- I have realised that I am not 'Atlas'. The world does not rest on my shoulders

- I have stopped bargaining with vegetable & fruit vendors. A few pennies more is not going to break me, but it might help the poor fellow save for his daughter's school fees

- I always leave the waitress a tip. The extra money might bring a smile to her face. She is toiling much harder for a living than I am

- I stopped telling the elderly that they've already told me that story so many times. If the story makes them walk down memory lane and relive their past with joy, so be it...

- I have learned not to correct people even when I know they are wrong. The onus of making everyone perfect is not on me. Peace is more precious than perfection
- I give compliments freely & generously. Compliments are a mood enhancer not only for the recipient, but also for me
- I have learned not to bother about a crease or a spot on my shirt. Personality speaks louder than appearances
- I walk away from people who don't value me. They might not know my worth, but I do...
- I remain cool when someone plays dirty to outrun me in the rat race. I am not a rat and neither am I in any race
- I am learning not to be embarrassed by my emotions. It's my emotions that make me human. I will sometimes cry if I want to, some memories are sad...
- I have learned that it's better to drop the ego than to break a relationship. My ego will keep me aloof, whereas with relationships, I will never be alone
- I have learned to live each day as if it's my last. After all, it might well be my last
- No matter how talented, wealthy or intelligent you are, how you treat animals tells me all I need to know about you

- I'm responsible for my own happiness. Happiness is a choice; you can be happy any time you want to...!
- Smile, for you are indeed privileged to have successfully reached this stage in life – so many didn't...!

Trees...

Humans have always had an affinity with trees. Maybe it's a tree's ability to provide shade from the hot, baking African sun or maybe it's just the superior element of strength they project. Whatever it is, we love trees. A tree is a living entity, a sentient being with an Aura, a soul and a massive dose of wonderful energy. They react the same way as plants do to human affection, which we explored in an earlier chapter, but they have so much more to offer. In the U.S.A. there are forests of Redwood trees. Some of the trees are over two thousand years old. Their birth would have roughly coincided with the same time Jesus walked the earth in the Middle East. These monster trees are truly majestic to witness. Sadly, the loggers are cutting them down for production, which has caused a major public outcry but still the carnage of these incredible trees continues, as it does to trees elsewhere around the world.

Due to the overbearing size of trees and their long lifespan, trees have the ability to store an abundance of energy. Grouped together in a forest or wood their energy is nothing short of grandiose. Taking long walks through forests and woods has a very positive effect on the psyche because you get to absorb the surrounding existential energy projected from the trees.

Forests and woods are often referred to as *'energy centres'* on earth. Similar to our bodies having energy centres like Chakra's, where energy concentrates and accumulates, earth also has powerful points or energy centres. When this energy is harnessed correctly it can be used to positively influence all life on earth with growth and development. Findhorn is a prime example of an energy centre. If your intuitive sense is sufficiently developed, you'll feel this energy, whenever you walk through or cross over any of earth's many energy centres and they're not all in forests. Some exist around waterfalls like Victoria Falls in Botswana, Niagara Falls in Ontario, Canada or Stonehenge, in Britain.

Trees also provide oxygen and have a specific smell. It's more than just that woody smell. It's a smell unique to trees. Next time you go into a wooded plantation, stop for a moment and breathe deeply, you'll smell it. The air is always fresh and vibrant when you're around big trees. You feel a lot more grounded and in control.

Various trees have been known to have different effects on people. In Patrice Bouchardon's book, *'The Healing Energies of Trees'* he talks about certain species of trees that made him feel rested whereas others made him feel energised. He also provides methods that enable one to sense the life force of trees and to access a tree's energy for healing and spiritual development. He further postulates, each species of tree contains an energy field, some of them capable of resonating with our human energy fields. It's all about the vibes...!

This is easy to accept because if you sit down and study a huge tree and focus in your senses, you'll soon notice the perfection of its leaves and the many shades of green, the gnarled and twisted roots, the tremendous girth of its powerful boughs and the way it dances in the wind. With time and practice your intuition will enhance your awareness of the tree's energy and its extraordinary powerful vibrations. You may even see its Aura outline.

Trees constantly compete for height against other trees to get more sun. They make music with their leaves when they rustle, even in the slightest breeze. There's a specific feel to the bark, sometimes rough sometimes smooth and when you look up and try to see the very top branch, you begin to wonder how long the tree took to grow way up there and the many stories forever untold, behind its fascinating life history, plus every tree is unique.

Although trees' vibration frequencies may vary, one can still absorb all the wonderful positive energy they release. The older and bigger a tree is, the more energy it has to offer. Trees are affectionately known as the *'Guardians of Nature'* or the *'Lungs of Planet Earth...!'*

Clean Out...

When walking a *'Life'* path, it's wise to do regular housekeeping in order to get rid of old vibrations and negative vibrations. Some people prefer to go for either a good body massage, partake in a sport, do a session of yoga, listen to music, paint or play an instrument, use Salt lamps and so on. It all works.

With a massage, you not only feel good about yourself when you emerge but you're completely relaxed and focused, plus during the massage you very quickly drift off into your Subconscious, which in itself is very calming and soothing. The smell of camphor oils and eucalyptus plus the calming sensation and emotions of the masseur as they work their skilled, strong hands over your body (especially the feet) relaxes you to the point where it becomes very easy to let go. A lot of people fall asleep. Those more aware, use this opportunity to explore their senses and go into a deep meditation.

With sport, for example, surfing - the cleansing of the ocean plus the feeling you experience (they say only a surfer knows the feeling – well its true...!), which is kind of like being able to walk on water, puts you on cloud nine. You feel relaxed and refreshed after a stimulating surf. It's also an excellent physical workout. With yoga you get to stretch and arc your body into insane positions, which requires a lot of physical effort and focus, leaving you completely relaxed afterwards. Yoga teaches you to surrender and receive, enhancing stillness, balance and alignment to your sometimes, twisted body.

By playing an instrument you get so caught up in the

music, you very quickly activate Alpha and even Theta brainwaves in the Subconscious, enabling you to mentally soar as the music takes you on a fantasy journey. Some people love to dance. Play good dance music really loud and just let go. Dance your heart out. There are wonderful healing properties like endorphins, released in the brain when you let go completely like this, plus it's a good physical workout.

You can also take a Himalayan Salt bath or use a Salt Stone lamp to balance the *'ions'* around you. As already covered in a previous chapter, we are constantly radiated with man-made artificial electro-magnetic energy waves, caused by electronic devices such as computers, televisions, cell phones and so on. These devices emit harmful energised waves (*Electro-Magnetic Frequencies)* or EMF's. They promote illness due to the frequencies constantly overlapping our natural 7.83Hz frequency. The consequence of this continual exposure directly interferes with our central nervous system and our immune system. These extreme artificial frequencies also interfere with the natural development of our cells and contribute to the accumulation of free radicals.

Salt Crystals emit a neutralising vibration frequency of around 8Hz into the immediate environment and so restore our balance. Using a Salt Crystal Lamp next to a high frequency electronic device for example, will step-down harmful EMFs and bring them into resonance.

In life we need these calming activities to reduce our

stress levels and restore balance in our sometimes, complicated lives.

Hippy's...

In the late 60's and early 70's the hippy cult movement evolved all over the world, known as the *'Hippy Counter Culture'* where everyone could tune in, turn on and drop out. For most of us from this era, it was where we initially learnt to live in the now, cherishing each moment, surrounded by love, peace and harmony.

It was essentially a bohemian lifestyle, a Utopian society, living an uncluttered, *'giving'* life as opposed to the existing *'taking'* life we were all used to. We had many, many really happy times. It was a huge part of our youth, a culture that will stay with us in memory forevermore. The characters that crossed our paths, the music festivals and the personal musical jam sessions with one another, the journey, the families or tribes, living together in perfect harmony, will never be forgotten. This was our happy place and anyone who was there, still feels it's vibe today. Hippy communes sprang up everywhere, throughout the world, comprising male and female, black and white youth, all living together in harmony. Normally an old house, where the rent was affordable or preferably on part of a derelict farm, out of the public view, was the ideal setting.

In South Africa, Cape Town was the equivalent of what San Francisco was to the USA, i.e. the cosmic centre of the hippy cult movement. In Cape Town, an area, stretching from the upper Gardens across to Woodstock, mirrored Haight-Ashbury in San Francisco. The British counter-culture or underground scene was also linked to the hippy and subculture of the USA. Its primary focus was around Ladbroke Grove and Notting Hill in London. Australia, New Zealand, Canada and several major European countries, all had their hippy communes with their youth tuning in, turning on and dropping out.

There's a familiar saying among today's baby boomers; if you can remember the 60's then you weren't really there...! Besides the soft drugs, which were omnipresent, people were once again finding themselves in art and music. *'The Hobbit'* and *'The Lord of the Rings'* were designated reading material at the time. Tolkien enjoyed royalty status as did Dr Timothy Leary, a Harvard Professor, who had experimented liberally with Psilocybin, a popular hallucinogenic drug of the day. Leary was an American psychologist, renowned for his strong advocacy of psychedelic drugs. Opinions of Leary were polarised, ranging from bold oracle to media slut but he was without doubt the hero of American consciousness at the time and was seen as a genius by the rebelling youth of the 60's. The Moody Blues, a popular progressive rock band in the UK, immortalised Leary in one of their songs.

Hippies were essentially anti the stuffy nose, didactical and authoritarian approach of ruling government ministers, including *'control freak'* parents. Freedom was the definitive path, which is what everyone was ultimately seeking; essentially to break free from the rut, the disciplines and the strict social order of everything. Little did we realise just how profound and spiritually deep we all were. Peace, harmony, love, flowers in our hair and the most incredible music and art ever produced, literally changed the world.

It only lasted about ten years but for a while the world shimmered, love flowed in abundance, people of all races and creed accepted each other without question or repose. In the USA, Bob Dylan turned poetry into music and turned on the world. Donovan and Cat Stevens did the same in the UK. The Beatles completely revolutionised music as we knew it and in the process, revolutionised the entire world.

A war existed between the law and the hippy's, with many hippy's being arrested and spending time in jail for smoking marijuana and dropping acid (LSD), which was completely unjust as they all ended up with criminal records, which impacted seriously on their future careers in life.

Sadly, all things eventually reach full circle. Hard addictive drugs like cocaine, heroin, morphine, various amphetamines, speed, ecstasy and an assorted cocktail of other mind-bending drugs replaced the harmless marijuana and acid drugs, which signalled the end of the era. The hard drugs caused the loss of young lives.

It was time for the hippy era to move on. People grew up, got married, had children and shouldered new responsibilities. The music too was replaced by two revolutionary genres. The first was Punk Rock, a hard, angry sound, associated with violence and hubris and the second was Disco dance music exacerbated by movies like *'Grease'* and *'Staying Alive'* featuring a young John Travolta who was at the axis of the Disco revolution, along with groups like the *'Bee Gee'* brothers, plus others.

The closing of the Hippy epoch was sadly the *'balance'* that had to follow. All things must pass in life. There couldn't be the one without the other.

Change...

'The world changes. Fashions change. Fads change. Some people don't. You learned things that were true back then, now they're false. You got successful doing things one way, now that way is moot. You still consider yourself an expert but that expertise has expired. You dug so deep into something, you lost perspective and didn't realise the landscape had changed. Sometimes, it's just a change in situation. The strategy that got you to where you are is different from the strategy that will get you to where you want to be next. The solution for all of these is 'Unlearning'. From 1997-2008 I was so deep in my little world of CDBaby, I lost all perspective. I learned so much about the music business and spoke like an expert about it for years, until I finally realised, the world had changed. What I was saying wasn't true anymore.

From that point, when asked for my opinion about the music business, I'd say, "I don't know." I know my old opinions are wrong, I don't trust them anymore. That's when I realised it was time for unlearning and relearning. In my case, it coincided with selling my company. I've decided to stay out of music until I can revert with a new perspective. It hurts to go from feeling like an expert to feeling like an idiot but it's crucial to go through the pain, or I'll never grow. This is a modern situation that's here to stay. Technology will keep changing the world ever faster. We have to keep unlearning what we knew and relearning anew' - Derek Sivers

Change is about accepting. It's also about adapting to the new. In Africa, there is an incredible lizard species called a chameleon. It can change its body colour, which is kind of like its Aura, in order to blend in with the immediate surroundings, making it difficult for enemies to detect it.

Most humans try to blend in, others love to stand out in a crowd. We all have different Aura's, which change according to our moods, situations or the people we mix with. We're no different to chameleons.

As *'Derek Sivers'* says, we need to learn to unlearn and then relearn for this is how we'll adapt to the constantly evolving changes affecting us throughout life. The problem is, technology accelerates at such a speed, if you don't keep up, you're very quickly left behind.

We live in a modern and demanding world, don't fight it, rather find your balance in life and go with the flow.

Change is like a holiday. Many people are afraid of change when there's nothing to really be afraid of. It's like turning the page of an exciting book, you want to know what's coming next...!

"Be the change you wish to see in the world"

The Simple Life

'When you forgive, you heal - When you let go, you grow'

This is a wonderful life story that goes something like this: A professor stood before his philosophy class with some items in front of him. When the class began, he picked up a large, empty glass jar and started to fill it with golf balls. He then asked the students if the jar was full. They agreed, it was indeed full. The professor then picked up a box of pebbles and poured them into the jar. He shook the jar lightly. The pebbles rolled into the open areas between the golf balls. He then asked the students again if the jar was full. They agreed it was. Next, the professor picked up a box of sand and poured it into the jar. Of course, the sand filled up everything else. He asked once more if the jar was full. The students responded with a unanimous "Yes...!" The professor then produced a cup of coffee powder from under the table and poured the contents into the jar, effectively filling the empty space left between the sand. The students roared with laughter.

"Now", said the professor, as the laughter subsided, "I want you to understand; this jar represents your life. The golf balls are the important things - spirituality, family, health, friends, wisdom and knowledge. These are the things, if everything else was lost and only they remained, your life would still be full. The pebbles represent the things that matter like your job, house and car. The sand is everything else, the small stuff." The professor paused and took a breath, "However, had you put the sand into the jar first there would be no room for the pebbles or the golf balls. Well, the same goes for life. If you spend all your time and energy on the small stuff, you'll never have room for the things that are important in your life. So, take care of the golf balls first. These are the things that really matter. Set your priorities positively because the rest is just sand." One of the students raised her hand and inquired what the coffee represented. The professor smiled. "I'm glad you asked. It just goes to show, no matter how full your life may seem, there's always room for a cup of coffee with a friend...!"

Okay, it's just a story but the moral is justified. It is the 'golf balls' that help to build character in life. These are the building blocks, which will inevitably advance you on your life path. Everything else is a bonus. You're no good to anyone if you're no good to yourself.

Jesus said: 'Live in the world but not of the world', meaning we are born into this world; we live our life according to our pre-ordained plan and when our time is up, we leave this earth. We will never be *'of'* this world because we are not part of Mother Earth or Mother Nature, the entities that make up this world. We are merely passengers. You know the adage, 'He who is not busy being born is busy slowly dying...!' We are born into this life; we will live it and we will pass on and leave this life.

Roots...

Early on in life someone usually inspires you. It could be your parents, an older brother or sister, even a close friend who may have been a year or two older than you. It's normally someone who is senior to you, someone who had a huge influence on your life. Someone you respected, listened to and took guidance from. It can also be a combination of several people. This is because when you're young, you're extremely susceptible to absorbing vibrations, any vibrations. Anyone who inspires you, naturally makes an impact on you. As you grow older, you begin making your own decisions in life. You stop randomly accepting other people's energy. Their influence on you therefore dissipates as you develop and mature. You however still retain many of those personality influences you absorbed earlier in life because they made an imprint on you, so you'll always be able to recall those situations, even when you're much older.

All these past experiences are what helped shape you as a person, built your character and prepared you for your life journey. Your roots are important building blocks in life. This is about where you were born and spent your youth. Later in life, you probably moved, relocated due to marriage or career or opportunities. You may even have emigrated to a foreign country. Over time you settled in and adapted to the new scenario but your roots will still be where you were born and spent your youth. No matter how much you try and become like those around you in your new town or country you'll never forget where you came from.

Why...? Mainly because your early lifestyle represents your culture, your family, friends, customs and so on. You'll never really completely let go of your roots because this is where you initially experienced life. For better or worse, it will remain a part of you for the rest of your life. Having solid roots in life helps keep you grounded, focused and in control.

'When roots are deep, there is no reason to fear the wind'

Building Bridges...

This is not the big construction type bridge over rivers we're referring to; this is more about building solid relationships, friendships and spiritual adventures in life. You've heard the saying, *'don't burn your bridges'*. Building bridges happens every time you meet someone in life because you get to learn from that person. Sometimes it's you who is doing the teaching but even from teaching comes learning.

The world is full of so many colourful characters, if we care to take time to listen to all the people that cross our paths we can learn and experience so much and this is just from listening. With some of those people you will also form a lasting relationship and then you'll get to learn a whole lot more. This also applies when you join a new company or a group, be it a project group or a group of friends or a club or similar, you get to meet new people and learn a whole bunch of new stuff. Life becomes interesting. New bridges are built and so the cycle continues. The warning is, when you leave those friendships, associations, companies and so on, ensure you leave harmoniously. Don't burn the bridges you have managed to build because it all comes back to maintaining a balance in life. You can be sure you'll need those bridges sometime in the future and if you burnt them when you left then you're going to have a problem relying on them again. This is because you met those people or joined that company and built that bridge for a reason. This is how life works. It wasn't just a coincidence. You needed to meet those people in order to gain knowledge to prepare you for what is still to come.

Building bridges should be fun anyway. Make sure you keep them open. You never know when you'll need them. The Guru's say – *'In life, we build bridges, not walls…!'*

Tragedy...

We have a life that is about choices and this is what's

interesting about life. We also have challenges and opportunities and many other issues that are guaranteed to pop up when we least expect them. It's all part of the ride. Unfortunately, just when everything is going perfectly, tragedy strikes. You lose a loved one to the *'Other Side'*. It feels like your world has abruptly ended; completely knocks you back a whole bunch. "What have I done to deserve this...?" You cry out in vain; you're devastated.

Unfortunately, it happens to everybody. These are harsh challenges to overcome. The emotional challenges in life are always the toughest. Sadly, you can't continue on your path until such time as you are able to accept what has happened. To help you get through this, you need to allow yourself time to grieve. This is natural and it's a good mental cleansing process. Remembering loved ones lost is also respectful to those who have passed on. We want to remember them. They had an impact on our lives when they were still with us and we'll cherish them in our memories for a long time to come.

Eventually though, you have to wash away the pain. You can do this with a simple affirmation to thank your loved one, who has passed over, for their time spent with you and wish them spiritual harmony on the other side. With time the affirmation will help you deal with your loss. This works equally well for a pet who has crossed over.

The famous *Kübler-Ross Model* defines five stages of

grief:

- **Denial** - You are in a state of shock and absolute denial. It is difficult for you to accept what has happened
- **Anger** - Anger is a necessary stage of the healing process. Be willing to feel your anger, even though it may seem endless. It will eventually dissipate and the healing process can then begin
- **Guilt** – you feel guilty because you never spent enough time with your loved one or you didn't do this or didn't do that. It's okay to feel guilty, it will pass
- **Depression** – a dark cloud enters your life. You feel as if the entire world is against you. This depressive stage of grief passes when you finally accept the reality
- **Acceptance** – finally accepting the reality, your loved one has physically gone and recognising this new reality is now a permanent reality

These five stages represent a framework for helping to cope with the loss. They are merely tools to help us frame and identify what we may be feeling at every stage. By recognising each of these five stages, we get to monitor our progress, which ultimately helps us to successfully navigate our way through this sensitive journey.

Remembering those who have passed, requires more focus on love rather than pain, i.e. it's about remembering the good times as opposed to the bad or difficult times. We naturally feel better about ourselves by focusing on the good times. This helps us move forward in a way that honours our loved ones. Know within, your loved one hasn't died; they've merely left their earthly body. Their spirit lives on indefinitely. They've completed their work on earth. Their time has now come to move on. It was their ordained plan they made prior to re-entering this life cycle and they have now fulfilled it. It will happen to each and every one of us. If you grieve too long, you may hold them back from progressing spiritually on the other side.

Another good cleansing method to overcome tragedy and raise your spirits, is personal journal writing. This represents a private and emotive flow from your mind and heart onto paper or your computer screen. You can speak your mind in absolute detail, remembering all the wonderful times you shared together. The finite detail you express is all yours so it doesn't matter how deep you go. In fact, the deeper the better because it all contributes to the overall cleansing. Regular journal writing in this manner can be extremely beneficial to your emotional health.

Music is another sincere way to lift your spirits, no matter how negative or low you may be feeling. Throw some music on the sound system and kick back for a while. It works wonders for the soul. If you can play an instrument, all the better. Music is receptive, going straight to the Subconscious mind. This is why listening to music is so relaxing. We all know how certain songs have an instant effect on us, able to trigger off emotions and invoke memories. That's the beauty of music. Listening to good music not only relaxes you, it changes your whole Aura colour and your mood for the better.

It was the famous guitarist, Carlos Santana who said: *"Sound and tone are everything. Sound waves, resonance, vibrations...these are our tools. With these tools we get to give people chills and guitars allow us to do that Subconsciously; we don't even have to think about it...!"*

It is difficult to overcome tragedy. It doesn't matter if it's a loved one or a household pet, the love you have nurtured cannot be extinguished or replaced but the passing does represent the closing of a chapter or event in your life. You have to move on. Only you will know when you're ready to accept and continue on your path.

Hoarding...

The wise men from the east claim negativity is often a result of owning too much. They say unless you reduce your needs in life, you'll never be personally fulfilled because you'll always be concerned about all your possessions and whether they're currently devaluing, or being abused, stolen and so on. The answer here is to regularly have a good tidy up. The rule is simple: If you haven't used an object or an article for a while, get rid of it. Dump everything you don't use. Give it away. Don't hoard. Guaranteed, there are others out there who will be able to use whatever it is you're throwing out plus giving has a wonderful cleansing vibration attached to it. Let it go...

The famous British Tornado bomber pilot, John Peters was one of the initial pilots to be shot down over Iraq during the Gulf war and taken prisoner. Peters and his navigator, John Nichol went through hell from their captors, stripped of all dignity, constantly subjected to severe near-death beatings, starved and kept in isolation, neither of them knew day from night as they suffered a constant barrage of abuse.

When finally rescued, Peters said he behaved like a selfish squirrel, hoarding everything he could find. Having being deprived of everything, he couldn't stop himself even if he didn't need the object. He just wanted to surround himself with possessions he could constantly feel, touch, smell, taste, to the point where he felt as if his senses had gone into overload mode. It took him a while to wind down and let go.

This is an extreme case of hoarding but you get the point. When you don't naturally give of your own free will, you quite easily become a hoarder and becoming a hoarder means you'll never get to appreciate the gift of giving and what a natural high it is.

Career Path...

When you're young, choosing a career can be a difficult decision. Be wise. From the very beginning, your objective should always be to aim only for the highest possible position within the career of your choice. For example, if you choose to join an Airline, don't settle for a steward's job on a passenger airliner just because you want to see the world. Your sights should be on becoming the Captain of a 747jet airliner or similar. Likewise, if you want to join a production engineering company, your desire should be to become the CEO, not just a worker.

There's a saying – 'you should always aim for the moon because even if you miss, you'll still land among the stars', meaning always aim for the top position because then your focus and all your energy will be on achieving. Whether you make it to the top or not doesn't matter. Guaranteed, by aiming for the top you'll get a lot further than simply arriving at a specific job to merely take every day as it comes. By constantly visualising yourself in the top position you'll imprint your Subconscious. This will set your course correctly. Bear in mind - life is a like a game of chess, every move counts...!

How do we know what career to choose...? You'll know instinctively when the right career opportunity arises because your intuition will lead you. For example, if you're very creative, you'll naturally be drawn into that environment. The creative energy flowing from you will point you in the right direction, even though you may not realise it. You'll probably begin by meeting and mixing with like-minded people. You might then secure a job in the creative industry or similar. It will feel right and you'll immediately be comfortable with it. As you grow with the job, you'll accept your chosen career path without hesitation. You won't even question how you originally got into the industry or why you do so well in it, you'll merely acknowledge it. Plus, you'll really enjoy what it is you're doing.

On the other hand, if the job you started doesn't feel right and every day makes you feel miserable, then maybe it's the wrong career choice you've made. Rather let it go and find your real niche. This doesn't mean you can sit back and relax and wait for it to happen. You will still be faced with choices plus you'll still need to get out into the market place and compete for the occupation in your field because life is competitive. There are no gifts. Best man always wins, but when you do choose the right path, you will instinctively know it's right. Sometimes you may even do several different professions before you finally slot into the right one. This happens for a reason. It could be a short-term project designed to teach you a lesson in life or it could be a trade you need to learn in order to acquire the necessary skills before you start the big one. Worst case scenario is taking the easy way out to walk the wild side. This road is lonely and dark and seldom ends well.

When we commit to a particular career, we naturally put a lot of energy into it. This is positive energy. As you get more involved with the company, the more energy you'll generate. Occasionally things don't go right and you lose some of that positive energy, even allowing yourself to absorb some negative energy, which influences you against work. By being aware of this two-way energy flow you can avoid these stressful situations. Understand, everybody has their good days as well as their bad days. It's all part of life. The energy you put into your work can be huge. You need to control it. Don't let it control you.

There are people in the marketplace who over time put their heart and soul into their work. Their energy imprint's so significant; when they leave their job, the respective company suffers and even deteriorates. The person's energy imprint was so profuse it couldn't be replaced. This also has a huge personal effect on the person who left because they were so used to giving everything they had to the job. They now suddenly feel empty, at a loss. They still have all the energy but they can't use it. It takes a little time before people like this are able to settle into a new position or project and get going again. Sometimes you just have to give time...time.

Getting Fired...

This is always a stressful experience no matter what the particular situation is. Earlier on, we covered *'Life'* situations and compared them to the game of Golf. Well, this situation definitely applies here, *'Pick up and move on'*. The longer you spend commiserating about why and who, could have, should have, would have, blaming everybody, stressing out, allowing loads of negativity to flood your self-esteem, the longer you are going to take before you finally accept it and successfully move on.

When you get fired there are obviously financial implications as well as the dent in your self-esteem, which takes a huge knock but you have to understand, a serious situation like this will have been a part of your life plan so try to accept it, no matter how difficult it is. It's a life lesson you evidently needed to learn. You have to get through it in order to move on. The world is not against you. Your only enemy is yourself. Stand tall, pick up and move on, knowing full well, when doors close it's for a reason. Bigger doors will open with new opportunities and yes, new challenges will arise. Whatever you learnt in your previous job has now equipped you to handle these new challenges. Everything happens for a reason. Anyway, getting fired means you had the wrong job in the first place…!

Be aware, when a door closes and another one opens, you don't spend so much time commiserating over the closed door, you miss the new one that's just opened…!

Making Mistakes…

A man was sitting on the edge of the bed, observing his wife, looking at herself in the mirror. Since her birthday was not far off, he asked what she'd like to have for her birthday. "I'd like to be twelve again", she replied, still looking in the mirror. On the morning of her birthday, he arose early, made her a nice breakfast, then took her to

Alton Towers Theme Park. He put her on every ride in the park; the Death Slide, the Corkscrew, the Wall of Fear, the Screaming Monster Roller Coaster, the works. Five hours later they staggered out of the Theme Park. Her head was reeling and her stomach felt upside down. He took her to a Take Out and ordered her a *'Happy Meal'* with extra fries and a chocolate shake. Then it was off to the cinema with popcorn, a huge Cola and her favourite sweets. She felt exhilarated but very tired. Finally, she wobbled home with her husband and collapsed into bed exhausted. The husband leaned over his wife with a big smile and lovingly asked, "Well Dear, what was it like being twelve again...?" Her eyes slowly opened and her expression suddenly changed. "I meant my dress size, numb-nuts...!"

The moral of the story: Even when a man is listening, he still gets it wrong. We all unfortunately make mistakes in life, especially when it comes to enamouring women, men seldom get it right...!

We've all done things in the past, we're not essentially proud of. Get over it. Pick up and move on. Sometimes it takes a little longer to get back on track. The longer it takes, the harder it becomes. We get offered so many tasty alternatives in life and the tasty path always seems so much easier.

You'll know when things aren't right because your intuition will subliminally alert you that whatever it is, you're currently doing, isn't spiritually motivated or harms people, animals, the environment, abuses your health and so on. Sometimes it takes a friend or a member of the family to advise you and confirm it. When it happens and it doesn't really matter how it happens, this is when you need to make a conscious effort to refocus. The good news is, due to the balance in life, you'll always be drawn back towards your original life path.

Getting back on your path is a decision you alone have to make. You may even need to change your circle of friends or your current job. You get to decide how and when. Once you've made the decision, it'll feel right, you'll know it. Every time we fail, we get to learn from these important experiences in life. However good or bad a situation is, it will change. It always does. Time heals almost everything. Frame every so-called disaster with these words, 'In a few years' time, will this really matter...?'

'In life there are no mistakes, only lessons'
Vic Johnson

The following is a fun story about how *'time'* and *'decisions'* affect us every day. Imagine you'd won an incredible prize from your bank: Each morning your bank deposits $86,400.00 in your private account for your personal use. This prize is however accompanied by a few standard rules...

The first set of rules:

1.) Everything you fail to spend during each day is taken away from you

2.) You may not transfer the money into another account
3.) You have to spend it all every day

Each morning upon awakening, the bank opens your account with another $86,400.00 for that day.

The second set of rules:

1.) The bank can end the game without warning. At any time, the bank can say, "It's over, the game is over…!"
2.) The bank can close the account and you won't receive another deposit

What would you do…? You'd buy anything and everything you wanted. Not only for yourself, but for everyone you love. Even for people you don't know because you couldn't possibly spend it all on yourself. You'd certainly endeavour to spend every cent and use it all…right…?

Actually, this game is reality. Each of us is in possession of such a magical bank. We just don't care to see it because the magical bank is in fact 'time'. Each awakening morning, we receive 86,400 seconds (24 hours) as our God given gift of life. When we go to sleep at night, any remaining time left isn't available for credit to us. What we haven't 'lived up' for the day is forever lost. Yesterday is history and the bank (God) can dissolve our account at any time without warning…!

Question is - what would you do with your 86,400 seconds every day...? Aren't the life seconds worth so much more than the same amount in dollars...?

Enjoy every second of your life. Get the most out of every day because time races by very quickly. Ensure you share your time like you would have shared the $86,400.00 in dollars.

Friends...

You can select friends who make you happy or you can select friends who make you feel dark and unhappy. You also have friends you trust and friends you don't fully trust so don't share personal information with them. Remember, time spent with the wrong friends means less time spent with the right ones...!

When you start meditating regularly, you naturally increase your awareness of life and mindfully evolve your thought patterns and the way you view life. With time you may find you mentally have less and less in common with your existing friends. Don't be alarmed by this. Most of all, don't proselytize, let them be. It's time for you to move on. Accept it. Observe it as part of your growth.

There will be many new friends and acquaintances you'll meet in the future, who are on a similar 'Life' path to you. Due to the balance in life, you'll always be drawn to like-minded people. However, don't suddenly ignore old friends or burn bridges with them, just gracefully move on. Still recognise all your friends and harmonise but don't be afraid to make new friends and broaden your friendship base.

They say, light travels faster than sound. This is why some people appear bright until you hear them speak...! Okay, it's a joke but it can also apply to how you choose your friends. Try not to evaluate people on face value alone. People are generally categorised into the following:

- The Chinese talk about the *'doers'* and the *'talkers'* and the *'in-betweens'*. There are those who think of an idea, get off their butt and do it and there are those who think of an idea, talk about it but seldom get it done. The *'in-betweens'* talk a lot and do little

- In the West there are the *'creators'* and the *'destructors'* and the *'others'*. There are those who create and there are those who destroy and then there are the *'others'* who choose to sit on the fence

- In the South, they talk about *'white'*, *'black'* and *'grey'* people, which has nothing to do with race. They define *'white'* as those who are spiritually inclined and try to live in God's white light. The *'black'* are those who live in the dark zone, meaning they don't accept God and then there are the *'grey'* who run with the hares and hunt with the foxes. They believe in God but will gladly run with either side

- New Age people talk about the *'takers'* and the *'givers'* and the *'fence-sitters'*. The *'takers'* are those who constantly take from society, each other, earth and so on and never give back. The *'givers'* are those who create, give back to society, share, are spiritually advanced and walk in God's light. The *'fence sitters'* don't even need further clarity.

It all seems to come down to three distinctive categories in any language. Unfortunately, in our mixed-up world the destructors/takers types make up the largest slice of every nation. They have little care with regards to life, be it spiritually or physically, so they'll destroy in order to survive. And then there are the extremists or wealthy who are often quite happy to destroy in order to make yet more money.

You've heard the axiom: *'God must love stupid people. He made so damn many...!'*

Whereas Oscar Wilde said, *'It's like some people cause happiness wherever they go. Other people only cause happiness whenever they go!'*

Subtle difference but you get the point. You need to choose your friends carefully. Try and avoid the obvious *'destructors'* and *'takers'* of this world who will only consume your good energy and leave you with loads of bad energy.

Selecting friends is also about magnetic energy. If the flow is strong, you will connect. How do you think lovers meet and instantly bond...? It's because their vibration frequency resonates, it's perfectly matched. It may not stay like that forever and it may also strengthen further over time. Whomever you've attracted into your life, friend or foe, is where your consciousness currently is. You've attracted these people into your life because this is where you're at, right now.

An eminent man once walked a wonderful spiritual path for years. He was wise at an early age, travelled extensively and gave freely of his knowledge and time wherever necessary. He was always a humble, quiet man, totally at peace with the world, with a lot of love in his heart.

Years later he got involved with friends who were on a very different and difficult path. He thought he could maybe influence them to his way of thinking but their energy was too strong for him and he was sadly led astray. He soon became a taker and a belligerent and selfish person, very unpleasant to be around. It took a divorce, when his wife and kids left him, before he realised what had happened. For him, it was a major wake-up call and a hurtful one. Today, he is his wonderful old self, definitely wiser than before, having learnt from his struggle. This can happen to anybody.

The Sages say, friendship isn't about whom you have known the longest, it's about those who never left your side when you needed them the most. Preferably, select friends who share similar interests or sports or have a similar outlook in life to you. These will be people you'll instantly bond with.

This is exactly how tribes originated. Small groups of similar minded people broke away from the main body because they couldn't accept the direction or way of life of the main body and started out on their own. This also happens in religion. In fact, it happens every day in companies, sports clubs, political parties and so on. Tribes have always been infectious because you have a core group of similar thinking, similar spirited people, who because of their collective positivity, develop far more easily and advance a lot faster, often leaving the original main body behind.

Sleep...

As one falls asleep, the senses withdraw in a specific order: Smell, Taste, Sight, Touch and lastly, Sound/Hearing. As the sense of hearing is the only link to the outside world, this is the time when the Conscious mind takes a backseat and the Subconscious and Unconscious minds become active.

On an average, mammals (humans included) spend at least a third of their lives in a sleep state, alternating from a deep sleep to a light sleep. When in a light sleep mode (REM – Rapid Eye Movement) we are dreaming. The fun thing is, because this mind state is open to suggestion, we are able to program the Subconscious with sleep inspired desires. If you desire to travel while you sleep, you can go on any mental journey you wish, merely by instructing your Subconscious mind whilst you are in your drowsy state. Ever watched a horror movie before going to sleep and then had nightmares about the movie...? Same principle applies. The movie made an obvious imprint on the Subconscious and mentally replayed until you woke up screaming or similar.

Getting to sleep and remaining asleep for some people though is a problem. One of the biggest causes of restless sleep is diet. If you consume a high protein diet (animal flesh) in the evening, then the chances of you getting a good night's sleep are going to be difficult because your digestive system will be working throughout the night trying to digest your complicated, heavy dinner.

Whereas having a light dinner will assist you considerably in getting a good night's sleep. Another factor is fresh air. Make sure you have at least one window open when you go to sleep at night. Fresh air circulating throughout your bedroom is a huge aid to ensuring a good night's sleep. Air-conditioners, heaters and stale air can impair your breathing.

You can also spend a couple of minutes prior to bedtime, massaging pressure points on the inside and outside of your heels. These specific pressure points are connected via the nervous system to sleep functions in the brain (the hypothalamus) which help you to relax. Alternatively, if you suffer from insomnia or regular sleep disorders that aren't diet related then meditation offers a wonderful way to relax.

Insomnia is normally caused by patients having an overly active supply of Beta brainwaves. The Beta waves are so intense, even when the patient feels sleepy at night and retires to bed, he/she cannot get those busy brainwaves to shut down. To overcome these sleep disorders, you can use the tip of the nose breathing technique (see the chapter on Meditation), which is about relaxed breathing. Focus on the tip of the nose as you inhale and again focus on the tip of the nose as you exhale. This is pretty much guaranteed to slow your Conscious mind down and bring your mind into the present. As your relaxation deepens, you'll fall into a deep sleep.

You can also use a repetitive affirmation to imprint your Subconscious. Prior to going to sleep, instruct your Subconscious mind to fall asleep immediately and to sleep right through the night. If you repeat it continuously, you'll fall asleep. Your Subconscious responds to pictures or images so to encourage sleep with this aloof mind state you can also mentally go on a visual fantasy journey. If your fantasy journey is one of peace and harmony, you'll become increasingly drowsy until you drift off into a wonderful peaceful sleep.

Memory...

Our active Beta brainwaves are so controlling in our daily Conscious mind, we try to hoard every thought and emotion. This often sends the senses into overdrive, which results in confusion. Sadly, the Conscious mind cannot cope with so much incoming information. The memory banks don't get a chance to capture everything. We get agitated when we forget things, especially simple things.

If you want to learn something, you can learn it parrot fashion by repeating it out loud several times. This may be sufficient to imprint the Subconscious for some people but it may not be for others. If you write the information down as well as repeat it, your chances of remembering it suddenly double. However, to really remember information, in addition to the above techniques, you need to create a visual of the information or generate a rhyme about the information. A rhyme works well because it creates harmony, which the Subconscious can hold onto.

When Mick Jagger was once asked how he remembers the words to all his songs, he replied, *"Cause I wrote 'em...!"* Writing the lyrics and then singing them to a beat imprints the Subconscious. They're with you forever, especially if you're constantly repeating them.

If someone listed ten items, showed the list to you briefly and then asked you to recall them, you'd probably remember the last two items or anything that stood out as being unusual on the list. However, if the person showed you a list of items and next to each one was a picture of the item or alternatively, provided a rhyme that linked all the words together, you'd remember around 80 - 90% of the words.

This is because you're now talking in a language (pictures, music, arts, feelings) that your Subconscious responds to, which is why using visualisation techniques in meditation are so effective. The same reasoning applies when you use affirmations. Make up rhymes or batches for your affirmations.

Consider the letters of the alphabet. Guaranteed, if you repeat the letters out loud right now, you'll say them in batches. For example:

a,b,c,d,
e,f,g,
h,i,j,k,
l,m,n,o,p
and so on.

This is due to what brain researchers refer to as 'chunking'. You only recall small chunks of information at a time, which coincidently also coincides with your breathing pattern. As your memory increases you get to remember larger chunks of information. To accelerate this trend, include a rhyme and rhythm to your chunk, you'll definitely imprint your Subconscious and remember it for a long time.

The main reason spiritual eastern mantras work and are easy to remember is because they consist of a specific chunk of words in rhyme and are usually practiced in a nice catchy rhythm, which are also breath friendly. A similar reasoning applies to the Psalms in the Bible. How about our youth, they can effortlessly remember the words to a pop song but will struggle recalling history dates and mathematical formulas...? The one is fun. The other is boring. We are naturally drawn towards the fun things in life. If all learning could be done in a fun way there would be relatively few failures in schools.

Why does the *'fun way'* work...? It's because we invoke our senses when we do this. Plus, we are relaxed, happy and intrigued. We get to visualise the scenario and easily imprint our Subconscious.

This is why when we meditate, we use melodic background meditation music, have soft lighting and sometimes burn incense. It all heightens our senses, sharpens the mind and helps us to focus, stilling the busy Conscious mind whilst opening up the wonders of the Subconscious mind.

Sportsmen...

There are professional sportsmen who use breathing techniques and claim they couldn't succeed without it. Take the game of golf for example, which is a game of extreme concentration. When golfers get into position to strike the ball, they stand over the ball and waggle their butts but the real magic is about what's happening with their breath. It may not look like it to the casual observer but there is intense focus happening here. When they are ready to swing the club back, they breathe in for a count of three (or whatever is comfortable to them), then they momentarily stop the club on the top of the back swing (that 'space' thing again) before swinging down and through the ball, while exhaling.

The motivation here is to bring the mind into the present moment, still the active Conscious mind and visualise the shot. Why do sportsmen do this...? Simply because a keen or even a professional sportsman cannot afford to let his Conscious mind interrupt his focus. Random thoughts cannot be allowed to enter and cloud the situation. This is why a lot of sportsmen rely on affirmations for motivation.

By visualising the shot, a golfer for example, is using language the Subconscious mind understands. By avoiding the Conscious mind, the sportsman connects directly with the Subconscious, allowing him to play instinctively, in 'autopilot' mode. When you watch professional sportsmen, they have those stern unsmiling faces. Now you know why. These guys are in focus, concentrating on what they are doing. They are not robots. They are professionals and to remain at the top of their game, they need to be in control.

Respect...

Simon and Walter are old friends. They often debate on subjects. Simon is a dedicated and highly respected songwriter and musician. Walter is a respected biochemist, resident at Groote Schuur Hospital in Cape Town. They've known each other since junior school and kept in touch over the years. Today, they are having a quiet drink in the Lord Nelson lounge, a prominent hotel in Cape Town.

"So, tell me Simon, who in your opinion, are the top five songwriters in the world…?" Walter asks.

"Aah, that would be Paul McCartney, followed by the late John Lennon and then probably Bob Dylan followed by Brian Wilson and Neil Young. Yup, that would do it." Simon replies, scratching his head thoughtfully.

"You know I love music Simon but I must agree, you're on the button there. That would probably be my choice as well." Says Walter, nodding his head in approval.

"Your chance Walter. Tell me something nerdy." Simon challenges, smiling. "Yah, right," Walter replies quickly, "nerdy, umm, okay, let me see, how about the only part of the body that has no blood supply is the cornea of the eye. It receives oxygen directly from the air; or a new born child can breathe and swallow at the same time for up to seven months; or your skull is made up of 29 different bones; or the human heart pumps 182 million litres of blood during an average lifetime."

"Whoa, okay, okay, I got it…!" Simon cuts in laughing, "You win…!"

Two close friends existing in almost different worlds and yet they can joust each other as friends without any offence taken. This is because each respects the other for what he does. Respect is a revered award that is earned.

You cannot buy it. Some people have it, some alas, will never have it.

How do we earn respect...? The major key is to stop focusing on you. Rather think about the people you really respect and what they do differently, i.e. - they keep their promises; they stop apologising for everything; they don't waste people's time; they don't get involved in gossip and sarcasm or try to be too nice or condescending; they have a moral code, are open minded and listen when people talk to them; they don't talk about themselves; they are usually inspiring and are never afraid to stand up and say no; they thread their own path in life with innovative ideas, have an original view on issues and prefer being in the background in crowds as opposed to the spotlight; they're not afraid to speak their mind if they believe in something and will usually side with the underdog; they genuinely care about people, animals, the environment and always seem to have their emotions under control; they readily take responsibility and will do things without waiting for someone to ask; they're always happy to lend a hand or an ear. Know anybody like this...?

Jokes aside, there are many who fit into some of the above character traits and that's why we respect them. Respect can also be earned in sport, music, careers, the creative arena and so on because it's about what they do or create, rather than what they say. People who have earned respect are normally strong-willed people who don't need the latest fashion, the super cool friends or the latest gadgets. They rather prefer their own company. They are comfortable with themselves, in their own space.

We can learn respect. It starts at school, we respect a certain teacher, older kids, an older brother or sister, anyone who makes an impact on you will gain your respect. Your parents (if they're loving parents...!) are obviously your biggest motivators when it comes to respect, even if your mother has just said, "You did WHAT...? OMG, you are so grounded until you are at least 30...!" You'll still naturally respect her; it is your mother after all. Most of all, learn to respect yourself...!

Learn to Give...

Giving and sharing is something we all need to actively pursue. Maybe it's the competitive arena we live in or the way we are raised but sharing doesn't come easily for most of us. We have to work at it.

We all know the adage, 'War doesn't necessarily determine who is right. It merely determines who is left...!' So true, war is such a waste of life. Unfortunately, it's the politicians who determine these issues and make the decisions but when it comes to us, we alone make our own everyday decisions. Decisions that shape our lives, decisions that determine right from wrong and decisions that will ultimately determine how and when we share.

The following is a wonderful story about the folly of not sharing. It concerns two Scotsmen, Fraser and McTavish: Fraser lives in a quiet, orderly suburb in a well kept house with the usual white wooden picket fence around his garden. His neighbour moves out one day and McTavish moves in as the new neighbour. Fraser is the first to welcome McTavish to the neighbourhood and shakes McTavish's hand over the fence but then notices he has chickens running around his garden. Fraser's a bit perturbed about this because he feels it will reduce the standard of the neighbourhood and devalue the surrounding properties. He holds his tongue however until one day a chicken flies over the fence and lays an egg on his front lawn. Fraser smiles and eagerly runs over to pick up the newly laid egg. As he is about to retrieve the egg, McTavish leans over the fence and says, "That egg will be mine, thank you." Fraser stands up abruptly, glares indignantly at McTavish and replies curtly, "The egg is mine, it was laid on my lawn."

"Where I come from," says McTavish, "if my chicken laid the egg, it is mine." Fraser ponders on this for a moment and then replies, "Okay, we'll settle this the old way."

'Fine by me, what do you propose...?" Challenges McTavish, now leaning arrogantly over the fence.

'I propose a testicle kicking competition. We each have a good kick. The one left standing is the winner." Fraser offers. McTavish raises his hands in the air, sighs and agrees.

"Okay, because it's my lawn, I'm going first." Says Fraser and quickly disappears inside his house. He returns wearing his big spiky hiking boots.

"Climb over the fence McTavish, drop your pants, bend over with your legs spread wide and lean against the fence with both your hands on the fence." McTavish grudgingly obliges. Fraser takes a run at McTavish and releases a mighty kick into McTavish's dangling crutch. McTavish crashes through the fence, landing in an upheaval on top of the broken fence, screaming in agony. As he struggles up into a sitting position, Fraser notices with glee, McTavish's testicles have shot up his spine into his neck. His neck now has two swollen lumps the size of golf balls on either side, just under his ears, plus his face has turned blue. Fraser howls with laughter while McTavish doubles over, writhing in agony. McTavish's wife fortunately arrives and gently massages the swollen twins back down his neck and spine to their rightful positions. McTavish is finally able to stagger to his feet. His eyes are still squinting from pain, tears cascading down his cheeks. He glares at Fraser and says, "Now it's my turn…!" Fraser swiftly bends down, scoops the egg off the lawn and hands it to McTavish. "Nah," Fraser says "it's okay, you're the winner, you keep the egg…!"

If only they'd shared…! The moral of the story is, learn to hold your tongue. The majority of issues are just not worth it. All giving is good but we're talking about giving in the greater sense. Like giving of your best in your marriage; your family; your job; projects; hobbies; sport; your friends and so on. It's about giving the best of what you are capable of giving in whatever it is you do.

The emphasis is not about what you can get from others, as opposed to what you can or want to do for others. It's about giving as opposed to taking because ultimately due to life's balance, with giving comes receiving anyway. This can be difficult because we've been conditioned from our youth; the future is all about us. We live in a Capitalist world. Suddenly, now we get told to help all those we've been trying to beat. They say life isn't about how to survive the storm, but how to dance in the rain. The reality is, it's merely a different mindset. Giving your all makes you feel special. You experience complete joy when you give.

Please note: Giving doesn't necessarily mean giving money to the nearest street beggar. You may well be promoting their drinking or drug problem. When it comes to beggars, give them food. That way it hopefully won't be abused or go to waste. Real blessings arrive when you do good deeds to those who cannot repay you, which means giving silently.

When we talk about giving, you can also give your time and your energy to welfare causes, or animal shelters, to old age homes, hospitals, to the older members within your immediate family and so on because the Universal guarantee is; every blessing you give in this way, provided you give it of your own free will, with all good intentions, will be repaid to you in abundance.

And here's the best part - when you're giving your all it's infectious, it rubs off on everyone around you. This is the power of positive energy. Like a virus, it spreads and grows, attracting everyone, pulling them all in the same direction. Immerse yourself in giving of your best and you will attract similar people with equal enthusiasm. It works.

This is a different *'giving'* story. It's about a father who needed his son to help him plant the annual potato crop on his small holding but the son was in prison so he wrote to his son and told him how he really needed his help, as he was now too old to do this big job on his own. The son read the letter and thought about it. He felt bad he wasn't there to give his father the help he needed so he penned the following letter:

'Dear father, sorry I can't be there to help you. You know my situation. However, please do not dig up the big field as that's where I buried all the money I stole.' At 6:00am the following morning, a large Police force arrived and promptly dug up the entire field. They didn't find any money so they apologised to the father and left. The next day the father received another letter from his son. It read, 'Dear father, under the circumstances, that was the best I could do. Hope you have a fantastic potato crop this year...!'

Just goes to show, all giving is good...! It's really all about how you give, not how much you give. When you're giving of your best, the chase is the excitement, the passion and the foreplay.

The ride is everything...!

Having spent many years in an Advertising Agency, the most incredible times were when we pitched for a new account. The amount of passion and excitement, the cohesive working, the ultimate planning and formulated strategies, the creativity produced by the art department, the shared commitment, all culminated in a brilliant strategic and creative pitch to the client. Everyone in the Agency was collectively dedicated to giving of their best. If we won the account it was always an incredible high but even if we lost, it wasn't totally defeatist because as a team, we'd all pulled together and individually done the best we could. The positive energy generated was electric. Anybody walking into the Agency from the outside immediately felt the synergy, the excitement, the positive vibrations, knew something awesome was happening within. Once we won the account the passion wore off until the next pitch came along and so it started all over again. This is why it's all about the journey, not the destination, always give of your best. No-one has ever become poor by giving from the heart.

Dominion...

Biblically, God gave man dominion over all living things (*Book of Genesis*) but dominion actually means: 'To ensure the survival and well-being of all living things.' In other words - Caretaker. No matter your religion, it still applies.

Therefore, one of our responsibilities as Dominion Keeper or Caretaker is to ensure the co-existence between earth and nature is always maintained. This is one of the reasons why we shouldn't interfere or leave damaging footprints. We need to co-exist, not destroy. Fishing out the oceans, killing all the animals, cutting down the trees, poisoning the environment and so on, isn't what we're here for.

What does this mean…? Simply put, if any of the major components of nature are deleted, the system collapses. For example: The North Pacific Gyre in the Pacific Ocean is thought to be more than twice the size of the USA, known as the *'Great Garbage Patch'* to Marine specialists and sailors. This vast patch of once pristine ocean is where the world's plastic waste accumulates and is still accumulating.

The plastic slowly breaks down into tiny pellets, which are then ingested by marine life who mistake the pellets for plankton. This releases deadly toxic pollutants into the worldwide food chain from commercial fishing. This is our shocking human footprint.

Once we've removed all the trees, we'll have no oxygen. Remove all the animals and insects and we'll have no plants, flowers or trees. Increase the size of the hole in the ozone and we'll lose our atmosphere.

We have been given a perfect earth and a perfect nature to caretake. We therefore need to collectively ensure the survival of this symbiotic nature/earth or we'll no longer have anything. We were the last to enter as *'Life'* forms on earth. If we don't look after it, we'll be the first to exit.

Earth can survive without us but cannot survive without nature. We learnt in an earlier chapter how earth and nature survived successfully for millions of years prior to mankind's arrival. It can do so again.

All nature's entities co-operate with each other, creating a balance. Mankind therefore equally needs to co-operate in order to 'Caretake' effectively. We need to fit into earth and nature's way of doing things, not the opposite. It's all about synergy. Once we've learnt to tune into the energy around us, we'll understand this. Whatever we cut down, hunt, kill or destroy has consequences, not only for us but for earth and nature. We have already learnt so much about nature. The time has now arrived to connect with nature and tune into nature's wonderful energy.

There is an intelligence in nature that brings balance and harmony to the mind, heart and soul. Nature expresses a consciousness that is peaceful and balanced in a serene way, a joy that is omnipresent, touching everything. Nature's cycle of life, death and rebirth is effortless, without fear or intimidation, just a natural flow and order of everything there is. We still have so much to learn from nature. Spending time in nature can be a spiritual rejuvenation. Commit to this, it's worth it.

Part of the problem is the ever-expanding population of earth. Nature has balance. Humans don't. We are literally killing the world with our massive human footprint. There are insufficient resources on earth to feed and support almost eight billion people. Human population is out of control. Restrictions need to be imposed on birth numbers worldwide immediately if we want to genuinely save our planet. Over population is generally worse in third world, poorer countries because mothers earn government allowances or subsidies for every child they have. There is no way we can win this race to save our planet if governments continue with this practice (usually to win votes) because in poor countries a subsidy means an income, where often there is no other source of income. The domino effect is catastrophic.

One of the resultant problems facing mothers is starvation when they eventually, can no longer feed all their children. We are damaging the environment faster than nature can repair it, potentially leading to an ecological and societal collapse. Worldwide education on birth control is vital for our future survival.

3-𝒟...

Architects and designers talk about 3-D designs and projections of objects. The 3-D formulae consist of:

- A 'Plan' (overhead view)
- A 'Side Elevation' (side view)
- And a 'Front Elevation' (front view)

Artists create paintings in 3-D on canvas. You can wear 3-D glasses and experience an entire movie with the full 3-D effect. The 3-D phenomenon basically means, you get to see everything in its entirety, in all its glory, warts and all. It's no different in life. The more we look within and discover the meaning of life, the more we get to understand how the Game of Life works. We begin to see the full 3-D affect. It's like the gate has been opened and we suddenly have this realisation; there's so much more to life than merely plodding on day by day, just getting through from the time we wake up to the time we go to sleep at night. When we look at this bigger picture and take it all in, it is initially overwhelming but then we get to accept it and our hunger and thirst for more knowledge becomes insatiable.

It's like the story about if you were a point, all you'd see is just the point. Then when you become a line, you get to see the point and the line and that's all you see. When you advance to 3-D, you get to see all the lines, all the points, all the angles. However, just because you can't yet see a fourth dimension it doesn't mean it's not there. The moral of the story is, *'We never stop learning...!'*

How then do we get to feed this hunger and grow our knowledge...? There are several ways. Reading the right books will certainly enlighten and inspire you. Meditation will teach you to look within. Talking to people who are already on a *'Life'* discovery path will also help but probably the biggest contributor is simply to travel.

When you travel, the mind sees, hears and learns things you've never previously experienced, which add to the memory banks and considerably expands the mind.

Travel introduces you to life and teaches you so much because you get to experience life first hand. It's all up close and personal. The people you'll meet, countries you'll see and the cultural experiences you'll have can never be learnt in a classroom.

Joy...

Bob Dylan once said, "There's no black and white anymore, only up and down and down is close to the ground. I want to go up. That's where the joy is...!"

We all get to enjoy moments of pure joy in life even if it's only for a brief moment. It's that incredible moment of *wonder'* we occasionally experience. We call it euphoria, ecstasy, exhilaration, elation, rapture and so on. When something really good happens to us, the adrenalin pumps, Gamma brainwaves accelerate, dopamine flows, we experience that giddy *'feel good fuzzy'* feeling that completely consumes us. It's a brief moment of absolute joy. The pleasure zone in the brain (the nucleus accumbens) is stimulated, dopamine is released and we get to feel the energy and the euphoric love of the Universe.

On stage experiences for most performers, generally consist of a period of initial fear followed by a heady surge of adrenaline plus a cocktail of highly enjoyable endorphins. Music is a sublimely creative process, coming from deep within. Kind of like a sonic vibration, an explosion of inner feelings, leaving you wanting only more of the same. If the performance is a success, a powerful sense of validation sets in, the ego literally sparkles with overwhelming joy, making even simple speech a difficulty.

This can last a while, dissipating as the adrenaline slowly drains, leaving one empty and void. Like all balances in life, the extreme highs are followed by dismal lows. The following morning is an uncomfortable physiological experience filled with some wonder but often torturous regrets re the many imperfections still recalled of the gig, known by performers as the 'morning-after-blues'.

We unfortunately lose it the moment we slip back into our Conscious mind. Beta brainwaves become active, the ego takes over and we confront reality again. Facing conflict, we start demanding, competing, vocalising - it's called being human...! It's no wonder performers take to drugs and alcohol abuse to continue their joyous profession.

Pamela Stephenson, in her autobiography book on her husband, Billy Connolly, says although Billy was basically just speaking his mind when he performed, he found himself in an accelerated state of magnified consciousness that wasn't really him. This ethereal awareness occurs with most performers when in the zone. Joy has this Subconscious effect.

Aldous Huxley once claimed, ingesting a few psychedelics provided an insight to complete joy and also represented a good way to open up the *'doors of perception into the Subconscious'* which coincidently is where the alternative rock band, *'The Doors'* (Jim Morrison) got their name.

Long distance runners enjoy getting in the zone. The loneliness of running and the constant rhythm stills the Conscious mind. The mind then begins to drift, heightened by the consistent breathing pattern, easing them into their Subconscious where they experience a wonderful feeling of well-being and joy.

Sportsmen achieve it in their respective sport. As a surfer, being in the zone is when you're surfing a wave and you get to ride in the tube of the wave. It's all about flying down the line on the steep face of an overhead wave when all of a sudden it curls over and covers you. There's no real way to describe the feeling. You can hear the hiss of the spray, feel the smooth wall of the wave around you, pulsing with energy, you taste the salt in your mouth, see the tunnel ahead, smell the vibrant ocean, as all your senses lock in. It's a mind blast. Dopamine readily flows. Complete joy.

Soccer players experience joy when they score a goal. Athletes break a record and get a high. Artists go into the zone when they paint or draw and express their creativity.

So, what happens when we experience these joyous moments of glory...? With this sudden adrenaline rush, the *'Real You'* is briefly revealed, completely naked, totally in the present. It's an orgasmic feeling you have no control over, leaving you wanting only more.

The reality is, experiencing joy in life is all about how we live our lives, which means ensuring we take part in activities that regularly bring us complete joy without the help of stimulants like drugs and alcohol.

Unconditional Love...

One of our objectives on our *'Life'* discovery path is learning to love unconditionally, which is a whole new level of commitment. At this level you no longer have a dark side, i.e. no hatred, no anger, no lust, no resentments, no fears, no greed, a controlled ego and no limitations.

Essentially, this means becoming *'light'* and continually seeking to become even lighter. Becoming light takes a lot of sacrifices in life because it means letting go of the tasty side of life completely. Your life then ultimately revolves around one word – love, or unconditional love. You are filled with the Universal love of God and everything that represents God and if God ultimately represents everything then love becomes your realm.

The holy men from the east surrender all material possessions and vices in their quest to love unconditionally. They experience a feeling of euphoria from the love they receive in return. Recognising one's enlightenment in this instance becomes a return journey from consciousness to the heart, from audible words to silence, from the Conscious to the Subconscious, from being somebody to being nobody but realising, you are a part of everybody. It's also about finally controlling the mind to exist fully and only in the present moment and allowing the rhythm of Mother Nature to flow through you in a never-ending pure energy cycle as an expression of God's unconditional love. More on this deep subject in the following chapter.

Knowledge & Intelligence...

The guru's say, 'knowledge can be learnt, but intelligence has to be earned' and wisdom is even more difficult to attain because you can learn knowledge but you can only become wise.

When it comes to knowledge and intelligence, we need to accumulate a sufficient base of information on a specific subject in order to acquire knowledge on the subject. It is only by *'doing'* that one accumulates the knowledge and is then considered to be qualified. It's almost like one initially needs to bank sufficient knowledge on a particular subject before intelligence can be gained.

Understanding a situation doesn't necessarily mean you now have knowledge on the subject either. Understanding is actually just the beginning of mentally accepting your initial desire to continue learning more about the respective subject.

At birth, the mind is formless. As we progress in life, the mind accumulates knowledge, which we then convert into intelligence and so the mind develops. Making subtle changes in our daily lives has a profound effect on how we think as well as helping us to advance. Unfortunately, we are still captivated by material issues and possessions, which describes how much we are still chained to this world. It's not easy to break free. We are after all human.

With time we learn to focus and concentrate within. Once we do this, we're able to achieve a relative state of peace of mind. This helps us to be mindful re the need for anchors and burdens in life, which can now be released. Having released our desires, allows us to simplify our lives. By leading a simple life, we are able to access deeper meditation, which ultimately leads us onto a wise path.

This is a heart-warming story about wisdom. A wise woman who was travelling in the mountains found a precious stone in a stream. The next day she met another traveller who was hungry so she opened her bag to share her food with him. The hungry traveller saw the precious stone and asked the woman if he could have it. She gave it to him without hesitation. The traveller left, rejoicing in his good fortune. He knew the stone was worth enough to give him security for a lifetime. Later, he returned to the wise woman. "I've been thinking," he said, "I know how valuable this stone is but I'm giving it back to you in the hope you can give me something even more precious."

"And what may that be...?" She asked.

"Give me what you have within you, within your soul, which enabled you to so readily give me something this precious."

Aaaahhh - the noble gift of giving...! The next level or

challenge in life will require a different you, a wiser more prudent you. The sages say knowledge is knowing what to say while wisdom is knowing when to say it...! Alas, you cannot buy wisdom, wisdom will only find you when you are ready.

'Life is like an echo. Whatever you send out – you get back When you give – you receive'

And so...

We are born completely clean, innocent. As we grow, we learn, we gain knowledge. Talents emerge, which are talents we've brought with us from previous life experiences. As we walk our path, a bunch of challenges and opportunities are thrown at us. How we deal with these challenges/opportunities determines how we progress. We'll meet people along the way who may be part of our challenge/opportunity or they may be part of our life plan to assist us on our journey. We'll experience tragedy and we'll experience love and joy. It rains one day; the sun shines the next. There is fame and fortune if we choose and there is spiritual awareness or we can walk the dark side and go our own way. Life is about choices. Change is the only constant in life.

This is life. This is who we are...! The principles we use to get us through life are readily available. We don't have to be an old soul to realise and enjoy this wonderful gift of life. Live your life to the best of your ability and trust in your ordained life plan. Love God like no other and treat your neighbour with respect. Always choose good over evil and seek quality knowledge and wisdom about life. Constantly pursue the truth and give readily when you can. Try and spend time alone, preferably in a garden park or forest, even if it's only occasionally. Observe a vow of complete silence for at least ten minutes a day. This not only creates inner happiness; it'll boost your self-esteem. Collecting your thoughts and coming to terms with yourself is self-medicating. Focus on the abundant energy around you and adopt a loving and optimistic outlook, knowing positively, whatever it is you are trying to achieve, will ultimately happen.

Be aware of spending too much time alone as it can lead to mild depression, whereas mixing with people (the right people) energises you into a happy state of mind. It's a balance. You need to spend time alone to collect your thoughts, to wash your 'mind linen' but you also need to let people into your life, to socialise, laugh, share stories and feel liberated. This is joy. This is life. Attract only waves of positive energy. Do things that bring you joy, peace and harmony without harming anything or anybody. You know the saying: 'If it ain't fun, don't do it...!'

A real 'life' objective is to reinforce inner happiness. Once you have achieved inner joy your outer perception will radiate joy and you will attract joy, people, opportunities, events and circumstances in abundance into your life. Doors will suddenly open where there were once only brick walls facing you at every juncture. This is essentially how the balance in life works. Why not use it to your advantage...!

Walking Your New Path...

To walk your new path and enjoy what you're doing, think about the following actions. They'll go a long way towards giving you peace of mind and direction in life...

Slow down, think about things before rushing into them; spend more quality time with the ones you love like your family and friends; travel as much as you can afford to; broaden your horizons; write that book you've been thinking about; visit that friend you haven't seen for so long; become a human and not a robot; lose all your obsessions; talk to God; listen to people when they talk to you; try and listen to nature; spend time gazing up at the stars; take a week off from television and the newspapers; read a book; visit an art gallery or a museum; once a month try and do something you've never done before; it's okay to cry now and again; learn to give; learn to forgive; don't judge anyone; learn to love and be loved; be especially kind to all animals; protect God's environment – Mother Earth; surrender your vices, you don't need anchors; take up yoga; exercise regularly; eat less; drink more water; fast for a day at least once a month; make Sundays a fruit and liquid only day; meditate regularly; do only what is morally right; live a healthy lifestyle; learn to overcome greed, your ego and your fears; cultivate and maintain a positive state of mind; avoid negative thoughts, negative people and negative situations; never fear failure, for it is just the beginning of an adventure; create causes for happiness and positive energy; become aware of who you are, what you are here for and where you want to go; ensure your living space is spiritually friendly; have a more profound loving and caring attitude for those close to you and around you; and finally, accept God as your Creator and love God (the Universal Consciousness) with all the passion you have. Realising true love within and without, will fulfil your 'Life.'

This may seem like a huge mountain to climb but with persistence and a positive mind, it's a wonderful journey. All we really seek in life is – Peace, Love & Happiness…!

Are you ready to play this awesome Game called Life…?

'Most people consider life a battle, but it's not a battle, it's a game'
Florence Scovel Shinn

Part Three

FROM ABOVE

Prayer is when you talk to God;
Meditation is when you listen to God'
-Buddha-

There are three religious' truths: Jews don't recognise Jesus as the Messiah. Protestants don't recognise the Pope as the leader of the Christian faith. Baptists don't recognise each other in the liquor store or at Hooters...!

It's a joke...relax...! When it comes to numbers, the number *'three'* has always been significant in spiritual terms because three refers to the Trinity. In Christendom - In the name of the Father, the Son and the Holy Spirit. In Hindi - Brahman the Creator, Shiva the Destroyer and Vishnu the Preserver. In Buddhism - The Three Universal Truths; The Four Noble Truths; and The Noble Eightfold Path. With Yogi's, it's Mind; Body and Spirit.

The number *'three'* actually features continually throughout the Bible, like Jesus telling Peter how he'll deny him three times…

Before a rooster crows, you will deny Me three times.'
And he went out and wept bitterly' - Matthew 26:75

The number *'three'* also represents a *'perfect triangle of balance'*. If we superimpose a triangle over a human body, the top of the triangle is the third eye position located in the centre of the temple, just above the eyebrows. The bottom left and right points are the left and right nipple positions extending across the chest or breastbone, creating an *'energy'* triangle of balance. Similarly, when we sit in a lotus position for meditation with our legs crossed, we once again have a triangle from the left and right knee up to the third eye position.

The Truth…

Religion as a principle, is an abstract concept upon which ideals of humans are reflected. Originally, direct contact with God by a chosen few, sufficed to transfer the word of God or the *'truth'* to the masses.

In order to accept or believe this, there had to be a leap of faith though, because none of the words written or spoken from any of the great books can actually be proven, on an empirical level. No test can prove or disprove these theories either. It happened too long ago. This seems to imply, Faith and Religion cannot exist, one without the other – unified balance…!

Religion should always be about seeking the truth. Henry David Thoreau said: "It takes two to speak the truth. One to speak and another to listen!" As much as the Bible represents the truth to Christians, conversely so do the Vedas represent the truth to Hindus, the Koran to Islam, the Torah to Jews and so on. In this way, all religions seek to find and establish the truth. However, you'll be denying yourself the opportunity of ever getting to know the teachings of the great spiritual leaders, like: Jesus, Buddha, Mohammed, Krishna, Gandhi and so on if you dogmatically disregard all other religions.

When it comes to seeking the truth, it was Christ who said: *'The truth will set you free'* - *John 8:31*

Truth can be subjective though so we need to tread warily because *'truth'* by definition has to be absolute, no question, without a doubt, without repose. If it fails to stand up to any of these criteria, how can it qualify as the truth…? We are such masters of delusion (especially self-delusion) and rationalisation. We tend to bend and mould the truth to protect ourselves, which can also be an ego influence but logically it's probably more about self-preservation, which is possibly genetically inherent.

We so easily tell blatant lies, some of us do it without guilt or remorse. It comes naturally. We tell lies to cover our mistakes, to guard our pride and self-esteem. We exaggerate in staggering quantities. What begins as a small story soon advances into a huge story. We add excitement, vigour, danger, colour and whatever else we can conjure to make our story even more believable and make us appear even more invincible. Our whole life soon becomes a complete lie.

When it comes to religion, we're then quite content to accept whatever the minister/pastor tells us because we're drowning in lies anyway. However, if we start questioning everything, with time, we start living a life without lies. Obtaining the truth suddenly becomes real, it matters, it's important. We turn a huge corner - Hallelujah...!

'There are no priests dressed up in puppet style to be admired by men; for every son of man is a priest of love. When man has purified his heart by faith, he needs no middleman to intercede' - Chapter 80 15:15 The Aquarian Gospel

At the best of times, humans are strange creatures. We are the only species who kill and destroy out of greed and who willingly express a blatant disregard for our fragile earth. Unlike Mother Nature, where the warp and weft of life is played out in a manner of the natural order of things.

In reality, most of us are quite happy to hurtle down a turbulent and rocky 'life' road without a map. We have talking GPS in our cars but no GPS to guide us through life. Religion was supposed to serve this purpose but has it...? The teachings are certainly there but they've been largely ignored, sometimes even twisted to suit individual needs for personal gain and power.

Take Christianity for example. Unfortunately, although the Christian faith is the world's largest belief, it's also, the most divided.

Different religions within Christianity have disagreed with each other for centuries. Kings have even manipulated the Gospels to suit their own political agendas. It has also been about power and money and probably always will be for eons to come. Can you imagine what a huge spiritual power base of energy could be generated if all religions accepted each other as one, even for just a day...? What an incredible blessing that would be...!

Ultimately, via prayer, we learn to let our spirit override our ego and self-preservation, requesting God for: *'not my will but thy will'* and hope when the time comes for the hard answers, we can rise to the occasion, regardless of the religion we have chosen.

For many, religion is a way of life, which is great. Adopting a religion doesn't mean you have to change your way of life though. You can still be who you are and enjoy life. For example: If you were born in California and you've always lived the California lifestyle and you were recently introduced to Buddhism, it doesn't mean you have to shave off all your hair and walk around in sheets and beg from everyone with a rice bowl. You can still live your accustomed life. All you're adopting are the principles. If you're an Indian or Asian then live like an Indian/Asian. Likewise, if you're an African, live like an

African and if you're from the Western world then live the way you do because it will make you happy and comfortable with what you're doing.

The Dali Lama had this to say about religion: *'My true religion, my simple faith is in love and compassion. There is no need for complicated philosophy, doctrine, or dogma. Our own heart, our own mind, is the temple. The doctrine is compassion. Have love for others and respect for their rights and dignity, no matter who or what they are.'* The great mystics like the Dali Lama are always able to simplify just about anything and wrap up a complex subject in only a sentence or two.

This is an old *'tongue in cheek'* story that touches on the time it takes to understand religion - Once an old King went to see a hermit who lived in a tree. He asked him, "What is the most important Buddhist teaching...?" To which the hermit answered, "Do no evil, do only good and purify your heart." The King had expected to hear a very long explanation so he protested, "But even a five-year old child can understand that!" The old hermit sighed deeply and replied, "Yes, but even an eighty-year old man cannot do it."

If this little story has any merit then understanding religion is simple. Unfortunately, some of us only practice religion for an hour or so on Sundays, then ignore the principles until the following Sunday. If you commit to a way of life and you really want to get the best out of it, you need to at least try and abide by the values. This is not about becoming obsessed. Obsession is yet another vice no one needs. Rather commit yourself in a way that makes you feel proud to freely discuss your beliefs, without any hang-ups or guilt, anger or embarrassment. Know what you are talking about and where you want to go in life.

Either you desire a Godly presence or you don't. There isn't a halfway mark where one day you accept, you are part of the Universal Consciousness and the next day you don't. By lacking confidence in yourself you are creating obstacles to block your spiritual flow. When you are confident, calm and collected, you are in balance.

Nonattachment and Renunciation...

Two characteristics of spiritual practice are nonattachment and renunciation. You can renounce bananas all you like but if you continue to live in your banana home on banana street, work at the banana warehouse and hang with your banana gobbling friends, you're going to be eating bananas forevermore. It's time to pick up and move on.

Renunciation means an abandonment of your pursuit of material comforts, in the interests of achieving spiritual enlightenment but it's probably the most difficult step to take. Letting go usually means changing one's lifestyle, including one's friends.

In the Western world, we are steeped in Judeo/Christian beliefs, re sin and guilt from an early age. We live this ashamed life of sin and guilt, carrying this ridiculous burden on our weary shoulders for life, usually forced upon us by Pastors and Priests who are really no better or more pious than any of us because we're all human. We all possess similar human desires of want, greed, lust, etc., some more than others but we all have our failings and weaknesses.

The problem is, our opinions, our identities, our way of life today, is dependent on how we are judged by others, our social circle and society at large. We live in a society that refuses to grow up. Eternal youth is everything. We become perpetual validation seekers controlled by our massive egos, which constantly require massive stroking to keep the dopamine flowing upstairs. It's an empty life without reason, which is why folks turn to religion for direction.

Part of our 'life' journey therefore is to eliminate blocks to our progress and cultivate positive energy for spiritual growth and we do this by letting go. It's a gradual acceptance that grows with time and some personal effort.

We seem to know more about our friends than they know about themselves. We know so little about our real selves. Think of someone you know who is always smiling, calm and loving and seems to always be taking right action to everything. We watch in envy as obstacles fall away before this person and wonder why. The reality is, it's because this person lives by right action every day, every moment, not just for an hour on Sundays. Taking a continual right spiritual attitude/action in life infuses you with positive, flowing energy and the inherent ability to therefore take the next right action, and the next, and the next, ad infinitum, because this is what makes you happy, makes you content with the life you're living, inspiring you with wonderful enthusiasm to wake up tomorrow to yet another incredible day.

This is a story about a shoal of salmon who, mistaking themselves for beaver, vigorously set about damming up a river. They however, find this task extremely difficult, even daunting, considering they don't have beaver teeth or paws but they plough on relentlessly for a lifetime, day after day to complete their mission. One day an enlightened salmon arrives and explains to the shoal, there is no need to dam the river because by following the river's flow, it'll lead the entire shoal out to the open sea and total freedom, a place of unimaginable abundance. All it requires is for the shoal to stop blocking the flow of the river with their misguided efforts and archaic beliefs.

The message – Go with the flow...! It's not necessary to accumulate possessions if you don't need them. In addition, finding endless fault with everything, being constantly negative, looking for flaws that aren't even there and so on, causes blockages to your natural flow in life. Get over it, pick up and move on to that open sea...!

Discover within yourself the absolute peace of your true nature and accept it with love. Love is an action, an emotion to share. We carry love with us as part of our natural being.

The Guru's tell us, information is always available but we are not always available to the information because most of the time, we are so caught up in ourselves, we are blind to everything else around us.

When you stop conforming to other people's models and learn to be yourself and allow the natural channels of love to open and flow from within, you get to live from the inside out, which strengthens your ability to continue. Try to smile with the complete joy of a dog and embrace life, knowing you never have to *'earn'* God for God is already within you.

The story of, *'Once I get there, everything will be okay'* is not okay, because there is no *'there'*, there is only *'now'* and you are the solution. Love is your natural inheritance. Only you have the ability to sense who you are and who you are not. You can make more friends by becoming interested in other people than you can by trying to make other people interested in you. The reality is – if you come from a place of love, the world around you will equally respond with love because love represents balance in all its formats. What you give out, you will receive…

Having a dog as your companion is an incredibly rewarding spiritual experience. Dogs have unconditional love which they share with you constantly. Their exuberance and love of life is intoxicating when you get to understand it. Dogs embrace the world and equally, the world embraces them in return. There are no hang ups, they merrily go with the flow from one day to the next.

All they ask for is your love in return plus food and water and a roof over their heads. They want to be as close as they possibly can to you constantly, which many humans find irritating but when you mindfully realise the extent of their love, you appreciate and hopefully learn from it.

Part of your spiritual growth, is to leave your familiar pond and try new waters now and again. Be aware though, when you leave your safe pond, you are ready to go. This is because we always think the grass is greener on the other side. Well, the grass sometimes is greener but that's because its covered in sugary manure. Yup, it's full of everyone else's manure and you will soon be full of it as well when you step into it because it sticks like crazy. You will absorb all that 'tasty' manure and it's very difficult to get rid of it.

The caution here is, it's necessary to try new waters but do it with caution, don't leapfrog into it and think you'll own it once you're in. You never own it. It owns you. The judging, the gossip, the me, me, me, the lights are on me because I am 'Mr. Cool', I wear the right clothes with the right labels, say and do all the hip things, hang with the right people, play follow the hedonistic leader – it's all there, mountains of it. It's called society and the majority of it is false and terribly ego controlled. Tread very lightly with dignity and honesty and you will survive.

We are our fears, our desires, our thoughts and we

should all be aware of our limitations. In the present moment, we are exactly who we are. The more we let go and stop resisting the natural ebb and flow of life, the quicker we get to understand our spiritual purpose in life. Going against the flow is like a dog chasing its tail, we go nowhere, completely losing sight of everything that matters to us.

Religion means different things to people and can be extremely controversial. However, when we share our religious beliefs and experiences, it makes us that much stronger because we get to learn from each other. It really all depends on what you value the most. Right now, only you know if your spiritual path is on line or not. We're all in this together so there's nothing to hide. Make peace with your higher self and share your feelings. This is not about if you're a good or a bad person, this is about how you see your spiritual path. We all do things that aren't spiritually correct. We've all committed misdeeds we'd like to forget. If we didn't, we'd all be enlightened spiritual Gurus.

Sometimes a God 'need' only happens when tragedy strikes or we are faced with what appears to be insurmountable challenges in life. This is when we suddenly want to talk to God. It's a lot easier however, if you talk to God regularly. This way, you build trust. Once you trust in God, your faith grows and once you have faith in God, you have everything. Soon, you won't do anything without consulting God and then you'll come to appreciate, God is indeed within you. Slowly but surely, you'll convert your thought patterns into spiritual thought patterns. Everything you do will then ultimately be for the spiritual good of your life.

You can pray anywhere and feel comfortable, it doesn't have to be in a church (your sanctuary at home is fine), because God is omnipresent. Find your haven of worship wherever you can. Sounds effortless enough but it isn't because life, as mentioned before, is so tasty it's very easy to get side tracked. We are complex beings with vastly different characters, attitudes, personalities, cultures, habits and customs and on top of it all we face many life challenges along our destiny path, which often makes us do extreme things.

The following story is about having faith, which is very appropriate here. It's about a Pastor who had been on a long flight between church conferences. He was just sitting back in his chair and relaxing when the sign on the above console flashed: 'Fasten Your Seat Belts.' After a while, a calm voice said: "We won't be serving beverages at this time as we're expecting a little turbulence. Please be sure your seat belt is fastened." As the Pastor looked around the aircraft, it became obvious, many of the passengers were becoming apprehensive. Later, the voice on the intercom cut in, "We unfortunately still cannot serve the meal because the turbulence is now directly ahead of us." And then the storm broke. The menacing cracks of deafening thunder echoed above the powerful roar of the engines. Lightning lit up the darkening skies, within moments the huge plane was tossed around like an infinitesimal cork on a vibrant ocean. One moment the airplane rose on forceful currents of air; the next, it dropped as if it were about to crash. The Pastor confessed, he shared the discomfort and fear of those around him. He remarked later, "As I looked around the plane, I could see nearly all the passengers were upset and alarmed. Some were praying. The future seemed ominous and many were wondering if they would make it through the storm." The Pastor stopped and took a breath before continuing, "Then I suddenly saw a little girl. Apparently, the storm meant nothing to her. She'd tucked her feet beneath her as she sat on her seat, calmly reading a book. Everything within her small world was serene and orderly. Sometimes she closed her eyes, then she would read again; then she'd straighten her legs, but worry and fear were not in her world. The plane was being buffeted by the terrible storm, lurching all over the place as it rose and fell with frightening severity. All the adults were scared half to death but that incredible child was completely composed and unafraid." The minister could hardly believe his eyes. It was not surprising therefore, when the plane finally reached its destination and all the passengers were hurrying to disembark, the Pastor lingered behind to speak to the little girl whom he had watched for such a long time. Having commented about the storm and the behaviour of the plane, he asked her why she hadn't been afraid. The child replied, "Because my daddy's the pilot and he's taking me home."

'Experiencing turbulence during flying must be one of the best laxatives known to man' - Billy Connolly

Nice story. Have faith. God will take you safely home, no matter your religion. You may well be happy with Christianity and later switch to something else. We're all ultimately one with everything anyway so it doesn't really matter which spiritual direction you choose. Sadly, it's normally our religious beliefs that separate us when they should ideally be uniting us. Rather ignore the age-old direction of religious separation. Choose a path that presents itself to you, offering direction, an understanding of the truth and a belief that intuitively feels comfortable to you without fear or intimidation, which many religions use rather liberally. When your time is ready, you'll be instinctively led anyway.

This is what the truth is all about. It's about being true to yourself, discovering what path you should take, knowing within, it's the right choice and not allowing yourself to be led astray by others who tell you their religion is the only one because the truth is: *'All religions have some truth but none have all the truth…!'*

Jesus...

This is a lovely story about Christianity and how Jesus gave his life to save his people. There was once a man named John Thomas, from a small New England town. One Easter Sunday morning he came to Church carrying a rusty, bent, old bird cage and set it by the pulpit. The congregation stared; eyebrows raised. As if in response, John began to speak. "I was walking through town yesterday when I saw a young boy coming toward me swinging this bird cage. In the bottom of the cage were three little wild birds, shivering with cold and fright. I stopped the lad and asked, "What do you have there, son...?"

"Just some old birds," came the reply.

"What are you going to do with them...?" I asked.

"Take 'em home and have some fun with 'em," he answered. "I'm gonna tease 'em and pull out their feathers to make 'em fight. I'm gonna have a real good time."

"But you'll get tired of those birds sooner or later. What will you do then...?"

"Oh, I got some cats," said the little boy, "they like birds. I'll give 'em to them."

John was silent for a moment. "How much do you want for those birds, son...?"

"Huh...? Why...? You don't want them birds, mister. They're just plain old field birds. They don't sing, they ain't even pretty."

"How much...?" John asked again.

The boy looked at John as if he were crazy, "$10.00...!"

John reached in his pocket and took out a ten-dollar bill. He placed it in the boy's hand. In a flash, the boy was gone. John picked up the cage and gently carried it to the end of the alley where there was a tree and a grassy spot. Setting the cage down, he opened the door. By softly tapping the bars, he set the birds free.

"Well, that explains this empty bird cage." John said to the stunned congregation, "but I'm not finished yet. One day Evil and Jesus were having a conversation. Evil had just come from the Garden of Eden. He was gloating and boasting. Jesus looked concerned but Evil eagerly rubbed his hands together and said, 'I just caught a bunch of people. Set me a trap, used bait I knew they couldn't resist. Got 'em all...!'

'What you going to do with them?' Jesus asked.

Evil replied, 'Oh, I'm gonna have fun...! I'm gonna teach em how to marry and divorce each other, how to hate and abuse one another, how to drink and smoke and curse, be cruel to innocent animals, feast on their blood and how to destroy the natural environment. Then I'm gonna teach these people how to invent guns and bombs so they can kill each other. I'm really gonna have fun...!'

'And what will you do when you are done with them...?' Jesus asked.

'Oh, I'll kill all those left over.' Evil answered proudly.

'How much do you want for them...?' Jesus enquired.

'Oh, you don't want these people. They ain't no good. If you take them, they'll just hate you. They'll spit on you, curse and rob you. If you give them work and wages to earn, they'll go on strike and burn your business down and then they'll blame you for everything. You definitely don't want these people...!'

'How much...?' Jesus asked again.

Evil sneered, 'Your life and when you die you must be crucified and die in pain and agony.' Jesus agreed and paid the price."

John picked up the cage and slowly walked through the rows of silent people, out the door of the church.

For anyone who accepts Jesus, he was indeed a holy, perfect, divine and spiritually correct soul. The absolute power and conviction of Jesus' teachings has crossed all paths at one time or another. His word, has morally spread throughout the world with unequivocal conviction, passion and belief. We have to ask the question: Why was he so successful considering the incredible mountains he had to climb...? The answer is simply because he told the truth and the beautiful thing is, he accomplished this purely by leading by example. The miracles obviously helped but Jesus' purity, his conviction and sincerity, is what won the day.

We need to honour and remember Jesus, not as a man trussed up on a cross in pain and agony (like Christian churches do) but rather as a gentle soul who came to show us the way, to teach us right from wrong, enlighten us about God and prove to us, God truly is a God of love and not a God filled with human qualities and emotions, like anger, jealousy, etc.

The portrayal of Jesus has always been one of

perfection so if you chose Jesus as your role model and the Bible as your belief then so be it but don't look down on others who decide not to choose this path. Whether you accept Jesus was the son of man, born a normal birth and then ordained to be a Prophet or whether you believe Jesus was the son of God, manifested as God on earth, doesn't really matter because the simple fact of the matter is: *'Jesus Was Here'*. This is the single most important fact that all religions seem to overlook. What Jesus said or didn't say, suddenly loses its significance and should never have segregated religions the way it has. Jesus was here on earth and there is factual written and archaeological proof to substantiate it.

No religion actually disputes Jesus was real. They rather prefer to get caught up in the semantics of Jesus, instead of accepting the simplicity that he was here. Jesus walked and preached on planet earth. He preached the word of God and ultimately gave his life to forgive everyone for his/her sins:

'Christ, our Passover, was sacrificed for us' - 1 Corinthians 5:7

Jesus's mission was to re-unite the twelve tribes of Jerusalem, bring some balance to their religious path, stamp out the paganism and hopefully reduce the power of the corrupt Pharisees and Sanhedrin's. Sadly, this perfect, beautiful soul of spiritual peace, was crucified by his own people, the very people he set out to educate and unite.

The betrayal was about power, fear, finance, hierarchy, ego's, jealousy, greed and other wicked stuff – human stuff. Unfortunately, these issues are still very prevalent today amongst humans. So, nothing has really changed.

The Jewish nation were all aware a Messiah would one day arrive and walk amongst them because it was written in the scrolls. When they saw Jesus, it wasn't quite what they wanted. They were expecting a King of wealth and status to free them of their Roman tyranny, line their pockets and lead them to the *'Promised Land'*, similar to what Moses had achieved in Egypt. Instead here was Jesus, a mortal human, made of flesh and blood, a hands-on carpenter by trade, teaching them how to live a more spiritual life, a life free of the shackles of the then ruling Judaic religion, plus Jesus preached of a God of love and forgiveness instead of a fiery pit of hell.

Jesus' teachings showed the Christians and the Jewish people, if they lived good, wholesome lives, he'd lead them to a spiritual Promised Land on the *'Other Side'* as opposed to a material Promised Land on earth. This of course went against the grain of the Pharisee's teachings. Nor could Jesus tell them he'd spent a large part of his youth studying with the holy men in the East and what he'd learnt. Divulging information like this would have been unacceptable. The local people were incredibly naïve, even ignorant. They were basically uneducated and illiterate. These were extremely difficult and untrusting times. Jesus therefore picked his words ever so carefully, choosing rather to speak in parables. He was constantly challenged by the leaders of the Judaic faith, the intolerably harsh and brutally arrogant Romans and even the Jewish and Christian people.

Jesus personified perfection in every possible manner. We have so much to thank and learn from this remarkable 'Saintly Soul' - his dynamic and unwavering faith, his divine leadership, his unadulterated love and compassion for fellow man, his purity, his wisdom, his inspirational teachings, his celestial passion for God and for how he converted an entire nation, against all odds, to follow a strong spiritual path, with good and purity prevailing over evil.

Much like today there was a distinct line drawn between Christianity and the Judaic faith. The split came about after the crucifixion of Jesus, when Jesus' brother James, was the leader of the Church of Jerusalem. Jesus appeared to his disciples after his crucifixion (proving resurrection and life after death exist) and later appeared to the apostle, Paul. He tasked Paul to spread the gospel to Christians. This caused conflict between James and Paul, which resulted in divisions between the Christian and Jewish faiths. Paul was so successful, he even convinced Emperor Constantine, then Emperor of the Roman Empire, to abandon the pagan Greek Gods they had adopted and accept Christianity. Constantine believed Christianity would bring the nation of Rome together.

This was the beginning of the Roman Catholic faith,

the wealthiest Christian denomination in the world today. Based in the Vatican and led by the Pope, it's the largest of all the branches of Christianity, with about 1.3 billion followers worldwide. Roughly one in two Christians are Roman Catholics and one out of every seven people worldwide. In the United States, about 22 percent of the population identifies Catholicism as their chosen religion.

Sadly, a lot of the popular religions today are focused more on money than faith and even the Pastors, Priests and leaders, who are seen as *'The Shepherds'* of their respective flocks, succumb to the *'money magnet'*. They are human after all, no different really to other humans.

And Jesus said, 'These scribes and Pharisees are not the scions of the tree of life, they are not plants of God; they are the plants of men. Let all these men alone; they are blind guides; they lead a multitude of people who are blind' – Chapter 126 29:30 The Aquarian Gospel

With regards to Christianity, the synoptic Gospels – Mark; Mathew; Luke & John were the only gospels canonized, by general consensus in the church. Having four gospels does give credibility to the story of Jesus because all four gospels do tell a fairly similar story. However, they were written over a long period of time. Plus, there were numerous additional gospels written, all delivering their various versions on Jesus's journey, which obviously caused worldwide contention by the many who seek the truth.

One can only surmise, from all this internal politicking,

the Jewish Hebrew Bible probably represented the original written word because the Church of Jerusalem and Jewish history, particularly back then, represented the core of Judaism. The other writings, i.e. the Gospels in the New Testament, all came later.

Israel...

The Land of Israel, also known as the Holy Land, is the birthplace of the Jewish people, the place where the final form of the Hebrew Bible is thought to have been compiled and therefore the probable birthplace of Judaism and Christianity. It contains sites sacred to Judaism, Samaritanism, Christianity, Islam, Druze and the Bahá'í faith. The region came under the sway of various empires over time and as a result, hosted a wide variety of ethnicities.

However, the land was predominantly Jewish (who are themselves an outgrowth of the earlier Canaanites) from roughly 1,000 years before the Common Era until the 3rd century of the Common Era. The adoption of Christianity by the Roman Empire in the 4th century led to a Greco-Roman Christian majority, which lasted until the 7th century when the area was conquered by the Arab Muslim Empires. It gradually became predominantly Muslim after the end of the Crusader period (1099-1291), during which it was the focal point of conflict between Christianity and Islam. After 1516 it became part of the Ottoman Empire until the British conquest in 1917/18.

A Jewish national movement, Zionism, emerged in the late 19th century. During WWI, the British government publicly committed to create a Jewish National Home. The Jews were therefore granted a mandate to rule Palestine by the League of Nations for this purpose. Rival Arab nationalism also claimed rights over the former Ottoman territories with the intention to prevent Jewish migration into Palestine, leading to further growing Arab/Jewish tensions. Israeli independence in 1948 was accompanied by an exodus of Arabs and a subsequent Jewish exodus from Arab and Muslim countries to Israel. Over 40% of the world's Jews live in Israel today, the largest Jewish community in the world.

History shows these nations are all therefore historically connected in one way or another so, why are they still fighting each other...? Why is religion still the divider amongst all these people who are all so true to their respective faiths...? How can it be possible for religion to divide nations, create wars, destroy families and control masses with fear and so on...?

You are an individual, free to make your own choice in life. Free to choose whatever religion works for you on your life path of discovery. Do not be blinded by all this hate and division. We're all on a path to eventual enlightenment, whatever avenue you choose, is your God given right.

Unfortunately, through the ages, children have been taught by churches to mix only with those who share similar religious beliefs. Throughout life we are expected to accept only like-minded people when we should be accepting everybody, no matter their religion, because ultimately, we were all originated by the same divine thought, which is Universal Consciousness, who we accept as God.

Do you for one minute really believe you have a better chance on the *'Other Side'* with your chosen religion as opposed to anyone else...? Surely not. No one can be that naïve. The fact most people practice a religion is awesome because it proves they are at least searching for their spiritual path but don't let this blind you into thinking only you are right and all other religions are wrong or pagan. Religion should never control you. Your life should only be controlled by yourself and you were given the right to choose. Use it wisely...!

The Room...

This is a superb story that empowers the maxim of *'forgive and forget'*. It's about a teenager who only had a short time to write and prepare something for a class assignment, so he wrote an essay. The subject title was, *'Forgiveness'*. The boy's teacher was so impressed with his essay, he submitted it to the Regional Schools writing competition. It won first prize. The young boy was ecstatic as were his parents. Unfortunately, it was also the last essay the boy ever wrote. He died a month later. He was a passenger in a car driving home with a friend when their car went off the road and struck an electrical power pylon. He emerged from the wreck unharmed but stepped on an exposed power line and was electrocuted. His family framed a copy of his essay and hung it among the family portraits in the living room. "I think God used him to make a point. I think we were meant to find his essay and make something of it." His mother later remarked. They decided to share their son's vision. This is his essay, which he aptly called, *'The Room'*.

In that place between wakefulness and dreams, I found myself in the room. There were no distinguishing features except for the one wall, covered with small index card files. They were like the ones in libraries, listing titles by author in alphabetical order, but these files, which stretched from floor to ceiling, were seemingly endless in either direction with very targeted headings. As I drew near the wall of files, the first heading to catch my attention was one that read 'Girls I have liked.' I opened it and began flipping through the cards. I quickly shut it, shocked, I recognised the names written on each card. And then without being told, I knew exactly where I was. This lifeless room with its endless files was a detailed catalogue system of my life. Here were written the actions of my every moment, big and small, in detail, which I knew my memory could never hope to match. A sense of wonder and curiosity, coupled with horror, stirred within me as I began randomly opening files and exploring their content. Some brought joy and sweet memories; others a sense of shame and regret so intense, I often glanced over my shoulder, shrouded in guilt, to see if anyone was watching.

A file named 'Friends' was next to one marked, 'Friends I have betrayed.' The titles ranged from the mundane to the outrightly weird, 'Books I have read; Lies I have told; Comfort I have given; Jokes I have laughed at'. Some were almost hilarious in their exactness: 'Things I've yelled at my brothers.' Others I couldn't laugh at: 'Things I have done in anger'; 'Things I have muttered under my breath at my parents.' I never ceased to be surprised by the contents. Often there were many more cards than I expected. Sometimes fewer than I hoped. The sheer volume of the life I'd lived overwhelmed me. Could it be possible I'd had the time in my years to have completed each one of these cards...? But each card confirmed this truth. Each was written in my own handwriting. Each signed with my signature.

When I pulled out the file marked: 'TV shows I have watched', the cards were packed tightly and went on forever. I shut it, ashamed, not so much by the quality of the shows but more by the vast amount of time I knew each file represented. When I came to a file marked 'Lustful Thoughts,' I felt a chill run through my body. I pulled the file out only an inch, not willing to test its size and drew out a card. I shuddered at its detailed content. I felt sick to think such a moment had been recorded. An almost animal rage fired within me. One thought dominated my mind: 'No one must ever see these cards...! No one must ever see this room...! I have to destroy these cards...!'

In an insane frenzy I yanked a file out. Its size didn't matter now. I had to empty it and burn the cards but as I got hold of the one end and began pounding it on the floor, I could not dislodge a single card. I became desperate and pulled out another card, only to find it as strong as steel when I tried to tear it. Defeated and utterly helpless, I returned the file to its slot. Leaning my forehead against the wall, I let out a long, self-pitying sigh. The next file caught my eye immediately. The title was etched, 'People I have shared my Gospel with.' The handle was brighter than those around it, newer, almost unused. I pulled on its handle and a small box not more than a few fingers long fell into my hands. I could count the cards it contained on one hand. And so, the tears came. I began to weep, sobs so deep they hurt. They started in my stomach and reverberated right through me. I fell on my knees and wept. I was embarrassed from the overwhelming shame of it all. The rows of shelves swirled in my tear-filled eyes. I cried out, 'No one must ever, ever know of this room. I must lock it and hide the key...!'

As I pushed away the tears with my sleeve, I saw him. 'No, please not him. Not here.' I desperately pleaded, 'Anyone but Jesus...please hide me, hide my shame...don't let him see me, see what I have done with my wasted life...!' I watched helplessly as he approached and methodically began opening the files and reading the cards. I couldn't bear to watch his response. In the moments I could bring myself to look at his face, I saw a sorrow deeper than my own. He seemed to intuitively go to the worst boxes. Why did he have to read every one…?

He turned and looked at me from across the room, a look of pure love in his eyes. I dropped my head, covered my face with my hands and sobbed unashamedly. He walked over and put his arm around me. He could have said so many things but he didn't say a word. He just cried with me. Then he got up and walked back to the wall of files. Starting at one end of the room, he took out a file and one by one, began signing his name over mine on each card. 'No…!' I screamed, rushing to him. All I could find to say was 'No…! No…! No…!' as I tried to pull away a card he was holding. He gently took the card back. His name shouldn't be on these cards but there it was, written in red, with his blood, so rich, so dark, so alive. His name, 'Jesus' covered mine. He smiled a radiant smile and completed signing the remainder of the cards.

I don't think I'll ever understand how he did it so quickly but the next instant I heard him close the last file and walk back to my side. He placed his hand on my shoulder and said, 'It's done, now we go forward together.' I stood up slowly, still dazed. He led me out the room. There was no lock on the door. I had no desire to ever go back there and I knew I never would. From here on, my journey would be different. I'd been given new eyes and this was indeed a new and enlightened day…!

This is a beautiful story with strong morals. We all know life doesn't exactly come tied with a pretty bow but it's still good, especially if you can accept your mistakes and move on, more importantly, if you can learn to forgive and forget.

I'm dreaming of a white Christmas but if the white runs out, I'll drink red…!

Christmas…

We all love Christmas time, the vibe, the coming together of family and loved ones and the exchanging of gifts on Christmas day, originated by the *'Three Wise Men'* who arrived bearing gifts for baby Jesus. What a beautiful concept Christmas is. Sadly, there is also a dark side to this wonderful occasion only practiced by Christians. Many pose the obvious question - does this concept really acknowledge the birth of the Christ or is it just a massive cash boost for the economies of the world and a virtual bloodbath for innocent animals…?

And how does a chubby little guy with a big white beard, dressed in a red suit, feature…? Is he the merry man who hands out gifts to all the children, especially the needy (we sincerely hope so), or does he merely represent the icing on the cake to boost further profits…? Apparently, he used to be dressed in a green suit until the popular American soda company, Coca Cola got hold of him and changed his green suit into a red suit, which was more in line with their brand colour…!

Is anyone even the least bit mindful, this is a time to celebrate the birth of Jesus or is it lost in the holidays, the financial profits and the Christmas dinner, where billions of innocent turkeys, fowls and animals are murdered and consumed, creating immense animal hardship and additional wealth for sadistic profiteers...?

The needless slaughter of animals and birds actually originated in the Jewish temple's way back in biblical times when animals and birds were slaughtered as a sacrifice, offered by the people to *'cleanse'* themselves of their sins. The spilling of innocent blood in itself is surely a satanical practice...?

'And Jesus called the priests and said, Behold, for paltry gain you have sold out the temple of the Lord. This house ordained for prayer is now a den of thieves. Can good and evil dwell together in the courts of God...? I tell you, no. And then he made a scourge of cords and drove the merchants out; he overturned their boards and threw their money on the floor. He opened up the cages of the captive birds and cut the cords that bound the lambs and set them all free' - *Chapter 72:7-10 The Aquarian Gospel*

This *'Cleansing of the Temple'* narrative tells of Jesus expelling the merchants and the moneychangers from the Temple. It occurs in all four canonical gospels of the New Testament. According to the gospels, Jesus was horrified to learn animal sacrifices were still being made in the name of God, plus these innocent animals and doves were being sold by the moneychangers to the pilgrims because their animals had to be pure, with no flaws, otherwise they were deemed unacceptable, resulting in additional profits being made by the moneychangers who were charging excessive prices for their 'pure' animals and profiteering unashamedly. Even the high priests during the first century seemed to have given up their love of God for the love of money. Apparently, due to 'tithing', the Temple high priests were wealthy beyond imagination. Similar to some worldly Pastors today...!

Of particular interest, Jesus carried out what is euphemistically called the 'Cleansing of the Temple' several hundred years after prophets like Isaiah, Jeremiah, Amos and Hosea had long since denounced the sacrificial slaughter of animals for any ceremonial or religious event. Christian scholars and religious leaders continued to ignore biblical denunciations of this bloody worship. They also tried to obscure the reason for Christ's assault on the system. They did this by focusing on the moneychangers, although they were only minor players in the drama that took place.

It was rather the cult of sacrifice that Jesus tried to dismantle than the system of monetary exchange and the blatant deception of the ignorant pilgrims. In all the gospel accounts of the event, those who provided animals for sacrifice for the Passover, are mentioned first. They were the primary focus of Christ's outrage. It is deeply disturbing to see Christian leaders joining hands across the centuries with their ancient counterparts to this day, in order to validate a system of worship in which the house of God becomes a giant slaughterhouse, awash in the blood of its innocent victims.

Animal sacrifices are a human way of transferring our own guilt and sins onto an innocent animal, which is then offered to God in the form of a pagan sacrifice. Not cool, considering God lovingly created every animal just as God lovingly created every human. We cannot scapegoat an animal to be a substitute for our own sins, for they are our sins and not anyone else's. The balance in life has direct consequences. Hail Mary's are not a substitute either.

"If only you had known the meaning of 'I desire mercy, not sacrifice,' you would not have condemned innocent animals" - Mathew 12:7

This is not about whether we should or should not celebrate Christmas and the sharing of gifts, it's about the needless sacrifice of innocent animals and birds at a time when we should be full of joy, celebrating the birth of gentle Jesus. For Christians, it is their given right to celebrate Christmas or any other religious festival for that matter; share gifts, spend quality family time together and praise the Lord but do so without harming anything or anybody, especially innocent animals.

'The more I get to know humans,
the more I prefer the company of animals'

A Visible God...

How do we accept a loving and gracious God exists when we cannot see God...? Well, we can look around and see what God created in our perfect world because it obviously couldn't have all happened by accident. It's too perfect and too precise for that. In addition, Jesus and the other prophets are surely tangible and living proof God exists. Plus, we can read about God in the Christian Bible or the Islam Koran or the Hindu Bhagavad-Gita and the Upanishads or the Jewish Torah plus all the other various religious text books and history books but so many of us still desire to see God in order to accept and believe.

The problem with this is, God is ultimately divine and we are mere humans, simple mortals living on earth, here for a brief stay to learn and develop. God cannot parade around on earth like a human for all to witness because God is not human. Plus, having God living next door to us would remove all the mystery of the Universe.

Due to this, one of our greatest 'life' lessons is to create trust and have pure faith in God, knowing within, God does exist (God Within), for this is what 'putting your trust in God' is all about. God consists of formless divine energy but assumes any form because God is in everything. When you realise this you'll understand, whatever you look at, you're seeing God. From the highest mountain to the smallest flower, it's all God. Meditation, prayer, living right and constantly developing your spiritual path will certainly help point you in the right direction.

When you first notice religion, it's like looking through a small telescope, you're gobsmacked at what you see. As you progress in life you look through bigger telescopes and soon realise, what you first saw was only the tip of the iceberg. Life's spiritual depth is infinite. Walking a spiritual journey can take a lifetime (in fact, many lifetimes) but it's a wondrous journey. Since Universal Consciousness (God) has infinite intelligence, as your spiritual awareness develops, the closer you'll come to defining your own spiritual intelligence.

'If you truly believe in yourself, anything is possible'

This is a story about a young woman who experienced the wonderful love of God. She came to Calcutta in India with a group of college students from the USA. They were on a mission trip and wanted to help make a difference to the lives of poor people. The young woman's name is Helen, she thought she was mentally prepared for what she was about to experience but nothing could have prepared her for what she encountered.

Part of Helen's tour took her to visit Mother Theresa's *'Home for the Dying Destitute'*. The setting is an elegant old building, adjacent to the Kali Temple. This is one of India's most sacred sites. Inside the building, the scene was however far from elegant. The Home for the Dying Destitute is a home for dying people who have nowhere left to go.

Helen was initially appalled by the sights around her.

Wherever they went as a group they discovered terrible poverty, overwhelming filth, pop-eyed, skin-and-bone children plus human waste lying sometimes knee high. They were surrounded by hordes of marauding flies and a foreboding smell, which she described as a mixture of death, faeces and rotten food. Helen was devastated.

One of the workers approached her and suggested she feed one of the patients. Helen was shown to a lady in a cot. She weighed about fifty pounds, had three teeth and paper-thin skin. The diaper she wore needed changing and she babbled constantly in her foreign tongue. Helen looked away in disgust. This wasn't in her plans but she tentatively moved towards the cot anyway. "I didn't want to go anywhere near her." She said, "I could barely even look at her but then as I began to feed her small bits of rice, she looked up at me and slowly started to inch her frail body closer and closer towards me. She ate very little and I quickly established she wanted something else. She wanted to touch me. And then it happened. After a few seconds, as I held a cup of water to her lips, she pointed at her heart and then pointed at me. In that one moment God opened my eyes. I experienced a whole new kind of love. My initial disgust gave way to pure love. I knew then I would do anything for this poor woman. I blurted out unashamedly, 'I love you,' and as I did so she looked at me, looked deep into me. Tears involuntarily an down my face for I knew instinctively, right at that instant, I had just seen the face of God."

What happened to Helen is her desire for *'self'* diminished as her desire for *'service'* increased, which then converted into unconditional love. Even at this elevated state though, the Mother Theresa's of this world still desire to challenge the Universe in order to evolve yet further, searching for even higher sources of love, reaching deep within their inner selves, constantly probing whilst still trying to reconcile being human and facing a daily barrage of human challenges.

If this is what it takes, then so be it. To feel that one instant moment of heavenly love, that divine warmth that completely envelopes you, however momentarily, has to affect you, no matter who you are or how hard core you think you are. It should be sufficient to inspire anyone to continue on their spiritual path. And here's the good news, as you grow and let your brilliance shine, it rubs off on those around you and helps them to grow. Ask Mother Theresa...!

Judgement Day...

Just as the weeds are collected and burned up with fire, so will it be at the end of the age. The Son of Man will send his angels and they will collect out of his kingdom all causes of sin and all evildoers and they will throw them into the furnace of fire, where there will be weeping and gnashing of teeth. Then the righteous will shine like the sun in the kingdom of their Father. Let anyone with ears listen!'
Matthew 13:40-43

Christian churches still challenge their members with talk

about Satan, the Devil, eternal suffering in hell and how everyone's soul will one day be judged when Jesus finally returns and you will either go to heaven or hell, which is disturbing, in fact intimidating. This one passage is probably the most feared story within the Bible, used bountifully by religious leaders to put the fear of hell, into their followers. Surely, no-one is naïve enough to believe, they will be banished to either heaven or hell, for all eternity, based purely on their one Christian life on earth, even babies who live for only ten minutes.

The biblical story of Jesus returning one day on a golden chariot, flying through the sky, to land and judge each and every soul since time began, is just as puerile. It may have entranced Christian followers many years ago but in this advanced age, does anyone really still accept these hypothetical stories…?

The bible is a wonderful account of the history of the Jewish nation in the old testament and describes captivating stories of Jesus in the new testament. However, like all religions, ardent followers tend to go a little overboard in their understanding and belief of their respective religions. No matter what your faith is, you need to keep an open mind because if you adopt a totalitarian dogmatic view, like many followers do, it's going to hold you back spiritually.

No one is against churches. Like-minded people get together for an hour on a Sunday, share fellowship and praise God. The combined energy created is incredible.

It's very focused and directed at God. The return energy can therefore only be good and uplifting for all. Plus, a full gospel choir singing their hearts out with passion and vigour is awe inspiring, mesmeric and entrancing, creating lighter and higher vibrations for everyone.

The problem we have with the youth of today, who represent our future leaders, is they are far more educated and wiser than before. They aren't concerned with fear and damnation. If they can't get what they want, they'll look elsewhere. The old adage of, *'if you read it in the Bible then it must be true'* no longer holds merit. People of the new world demand proof for anything and everything.

The reality is, God is all about love, definitely not evil, or threatening with fear and damnation. God is a divine spirit, above all human desires, needs and wants. The Old Testament depicts our Creator as a God of wrath and even jealousy. It's not possible. God is not human and therefore doesn't have human flaws.

God represents absolute perfection. Gaze around you or as previously mentioned, above you and you'll see it. Look at a simple flower for example and be mindful of its incredible perfection, just like every other flower. This is God's creation, in absolute perfection.

If we believe and accept God is divine, then God only has heaven. God cannot have a hell. God is about love and creating. The Judgement reference in the Bible is rather a parable indicating to mankind the need for all nations to live harmoniously or we'll destroy each other and the world through conflict (fire), creating untold sorrow (weeping and gnashing of teeth) in the process. Alternatively, logic dictates the Judgement Day prophecy as: 'When one has attained enlightenment on earth and never has to return for another incarnation. He/she is finally Karma free.

We're talking about our Creator who created the Universe. Don't get God's status mixed up and compared with humans. There is no comparison. If a preacher talks to you and awards God with human qualities, leave. Mankind only created this human image of God based on their own imperfections. We cannot walk our life path with blinkers on and hope to advance spiritually, oblivious to everything happening around us. It's only when we open our eyes, are we able to see. Our intuitive and spiritual senses will always guide us anyway. Break free and search for the truth. It will set you free (Jesus said so...!). If there is any issue in your current religion that doesn't sound right to you, question it. You have the right to choose.

At the end of the day we were all created by the same God. The path you choose to reach God doesn't matter. Think of it like a tree. God sits at the top of the tree. On this tree are many branches. If you climb the tree, you may well choose a different route up the tree to reach God compared to someone else standing right next to you. What religion you choose to get there isn't important. How you handle the journey, is what counts.

It was Kiko Michel who said: *'We are actually all the same life force, created from the same magnetic energy, which cannot be destroyed so I need to discover how I can stay conscious enough and focused as a spirit in a very tasty material world, in order to remember, I am just a drop of water in the same river with an infinite amount of other spirits, all with bodies, all headed for the same ocean in order to join back together as the 'One' which is represented by the many...!'*

We spend time walking through our lives, room by room, drawing up a list of work to be done, cracks to be patched, things to be replaced, when we actually shouldn't be looking for flaws at all. We should only be focusing on opportunities, on ways to improve our life, ways of developing spiritually and ways of increasing our levels of consciousness to at least make that journey down the river an enjoyable one. Judging a person doesn't define who they are, it defines who you are…!

'Remember to enjoy the little things in life'

Reincarnation…

'Men are not motes to float about within the air of one short life and then be lost in nothingness. They are undying parts of the eternal whole that come and go. A cause may be a part of one brief life; results may not be noted until another life' – Ch:114 29:30 The Aquarian Gospel

This is a rather contentious and sensitive subject but the reality is very real. Reincarnation is a fact. Back in the day, reincarnation was voted out by one vote (299 years AD), at a gathering of the Christian Ministry. The decision was that close amongst the clergy, a long time ago.

The big questions against reincarnation are hypothetically - how is it possible for there to be three billion people on earth and a few hundred years later we have five billion people and so it compounds continually...? Where do all the additional lives come from considering only so many died and were then reincarnated and just how much of a human footprint can our earth actually handle before it collapses...?

For the first question - we experience many *'Earth'* lives. However, it may not be a life spent solely on our planet earth, it's rather a mix of lives spent on any one of billions of similar earth planets like ours, spread throughout the Universe. We are not the only souls existing in this Universe nor is our earth the only earth, so the amount of souls crossing our current earth's path is in fact timeless, it's of no consequence.

For the second question - the one billion people mark on earth was passed in the early 1800s; the two billion mark in the 1920s. As it stands now, the world's population is heading for eight billion. According to United Nations predictions, it could reach 9.7 billion people by 2050 and over 11 billion by 2100. However, if certain factors become less plentiful, the carrying capacity will drop, i.e. if resources are used faster than they are replenished, then we'll have exceeded earth's carrying capacity and for this there will obviously be consequences. Populations will decrease accordingly. Over populated countries like China are already in a negative birth growth. This trend will no doubt continue.

As discussed previously, over population on earth is a major concern for world leaders and needs to be addressed with the same urgency as Climate Change or the natural order of balance will apply, which could be catastrophic. The human footprint on earth and earth's resources are already top heavy, a *'trimming of the human herd'* is bound to happen and it won't be fun.

To justify reincarnation on our earth, there are now thousands of documented case studies, focusing on children who claim a previous life. The individual cases have been dissected and evaluated in depth.

Leading psychiatrists, including luminaries like Jim B. Tucker, an associate psychiatry professor at the UVA Medical Centre's Division of Perceptual Studies, failed to find fault in these cases. Rather, they were captivated by the results. For many years, Tucker investigated claims made by children, usually between the ages of 2 and 6 years old, all claiming to have had previous lives. The children are able to provide such finite detail about their previous lives, for their stories to be traced back to the actual person the respective children claim to have been in their previous life, via history records. And the detail is remarkable. The children even tell their parents, how they select their parents before entering their new life. A similar scenario occurs with patients who have been under deep hypnosis and discussed their previous lives.

'When men see no further than one little span of life it is no wonder, they say, there is no God' – Ch:114:42 The Aquarian Gospel

The subject of reincarnation was historically brushed off by many as *'New Age'* nonsense but with all these documented case studies now coming to the fore, a lot of scholastic and even theologian opinions are changing and accepting reincarnation as reality.

Take for example celebrities. Personally, knowing legends or heroes is what makes us feel better about ourselves. It gives us a target to strive for, an image to aspire too. They're heroes because that's how *'Joe Public'* sees them. These are people who were born into this world the same as the rest of us and yet achieve incredible feats we can only dream of. How do they do this…? What makes them so special…? Why can't everybody excel at a specific career, profession, sport or the arts…?

The reason is because these highly gifted people are souls reborn with talents they learnt in previous lives. This would substantiate why some people are born with extraordinary gifts and go on to greatness so effortlessly, at so young an age. We're focusing essentially on exceptional people here like great sportsmen who earn their titles or maestro musicians who bring so much joy to the world, artists who create masterpieces on canvas, surgeons who perfected heart transplants and so on, individuals who are able to absorb energy off others so naturally.

If we studied and played music for example in one lifetime, in our next lifetime we carry that gift over and easily achieve greater heights in music in our new life. We'll in fact be magnetically drawn to music in our new life so we can continue where we left off before we passed over.

'In heaven there is no death' - Revelation 21:4

Lennon and McCartney are probably one of the greatest song-writing duos who significantly changed and influenced music throughout the world. Have no doubt, these two iconic souls crossed paths in previous lives and wrote incredible music together. When they came into this current life, they merely picked up where they left off in their previous lives and continued. Their paths were destined to cross so they could continue spreading joy throughout the world with their music.

John was sadly murdered and left our world early but was probably re-called for another music expedition on the *'Other Side'* or another *'earth'* planet somewhere in the Universe. Lennon and McCartney were born with their wondrous talent. They didn't merely by chance learn it after a few years at art school. You can't learn a talent like that. It comes from within, takes a huge commitment and many life incarnations with loads of practice and perseverance before one gets anywhere near acquiring that level of musical genius.

The late, great Jimi Hendrix was a legendary guitarist. He played left-handed. When guitar companies like Fender, didn't have a left-handed guitar for Jimi, he simply played it upside down, transferred all the chords, everything. You have to understand, playing a guitar at the kind of level Jimi played, is one thing but playing a guitar upside down at that level is unthinkable.

Jimi also wrote incredibly beautiful music and he wasn't technically schooled. He played by ear with the ability to intuitively feel and sense his notes. Jimi used his acute senses to navigate his way up and down a Pentatonic or a Chromatic scale with dignity, playing intricate blues runs that flowed seamlessly between unorthodox chord structures, which to him sounded right and somehow, they always were. This totally astounded the music gurus. Jimi also saw music in colours. He mentally witnessed waves of colour for different sounds (Synaesthesia) and therefore played his music in an esoteric explosion of colours.

By now you're beginning to see just how deep this incredibly gifted man was and how intuitively in touch he was with his senses and he was born with this talent, he didn't go to Berkley Music College to learn it. Jimi obviously spent a lot of time in his Subconscious mind. This alone, immediately set him apart from the rest. He obviously perfected his talent over a period of many 'life' journeys. Jimi was a troubled soul though because he didn't accept fame very well, sadly turning to recreational drugs for dependence.

The Sages always talk about the emptiness of personal victory because normally with victory comes some form of sacrifice. It's all part of life's balance. Sometimes the greater the victory, the heavier the sacrifice. When one climbs to the top of the pile, it's a long way down and usually once one has made it to the top of his/her profession/art/sport, a huge void is left in one's life because there is little else to achieve. This is why some of these over achievers turn to recreational drugs, alcohol and often suffer depression. It's to fill the void and of course it never does. Jimi may have surrendered to this void but he did however leave a legacy of music that inspired more guitarists than any other musician has to-date.

David Crosby, of Crosby, Stills & Nash fame, claims in his life documentary on 'You Tube', from an early age he already knew how to sail a boat without anyone teaching him. It was a similar situation with music. Says he was magnetically drawn to it. He didn't need to learn scales and music; it was already in him. He's convinced in his previous life he sailed and played music. In this life, he merely picked up where he left off in his previous life.

If we're looking at great musicians, what about Beethoven and all the other classical maestros, who all created incredibly complicated symphonies (which are still relevant today) without all the add-ons, music schools, You Tube and so on we currently have at our disposal...? Surely these maestros serve as prime examples of unbelievable talent, which they couldn't have possibly evolved in only one life span...?

If you take time out to read up on Beethoven's life story: He started writing and playing the piano at around six years old, played his first public performance at the age of eight, wrote his first symphony at the age of eleven...! It's a long stretch to accept, an average little kid back then could have achieved a level of brilliance at so young an age. He obviously spent many lives honing his art as a musician. Beethoven succumbed to deafness at the age of twenty-six from lead poisoning and only at forty-four years old did he stop performing live. This means he continued playing complex classical pieces live while he was stone deaf...!

Alas, he died eleven years later. One can only imagine what life Beethoven chose to be re-born into on his next visit to any one of the billions of earth planets existing in our Universe...!

The problem is, it may be part of your destiny to bring joy to the world by writing beautiful music but ultimately, you're still going to have to advance spiritually. Being born with an inherent talent doesn't necessarily make you spiritually better than anyone else; it merely provides you with opportunities to increase your talent, while you're on earth.

There are many elevated spiritual souls amongst us

who are already spiritually advanced. They've experienced numerous lives on earth, overcome challenges and played the *'Game of Life'*. Their future focus is essentially on furthering their levels of consciousness and deepening their spiritual awareness. Old souls exist in every society, every culture and every country.

On the *'Other Side'*, an older soul is not any more or any less important than a younger soul because everyone has the same connection to source, the same ability to be part of a journey. *'No one hoards the jelly beans'* as hypnotherapist Jimmy Quast (Easton hypnosis) quantifies it.

If you happen to connect with an older soul here on earth, you'll find it's the older souls who seem to select the more difficult lifetimes because they can handle them. It may be someone who has had many lifetimes and returned to have a contemplative experience, living in isolation or in some place of calm and repose or it may be someone who has chosen the most difficult of journeys because they know it's only temporary. This is why we cannot only have one life and our indestructible spirit then disappears for all eternity. It's not possible. Heaven is absolute.

You also have Subconscious memory of your past lives, which is why you enjoy particular hobbies and interests, or are drawn to certain people, have a need to travel to certain places and so on. There are filters in place that deny you access to this information. If you knew your life plan, it would be a scripted play and not an adventure. Plus, your entire life isn't planned moment by moment. Only main events and characters are planned. Many accidents often occur, which may alter your life plan. Earth is a dangerous planet with wars, epidemics, natural disasters, crime, illnesses, etc., which can totally derail your soul plan. It's a learning experience – the adventure of a lifetime…!

Stop for a minute and ponder on how magnificent life is, how precious this God given miracle called Life, actually is. Every human is unique, there is only *'One of Each of Us'*. Out of the millions of sperm cells in an ejaculation, you are the one that was fertilised in an egg, so you definitely are not a *'one-off'* mistake.

Think about that. Make sure you treasure your life and use your time on this earth prudently. Live every minute, every second to its fullest. This incredible life is yours, a God given gift. You also have the gift of *'Freedom of Choice'*. Use it or abuse it….

The Other Side...

'Find the cost of freedom, Buried in the ground
Mother Earth will swallow you, Lay your body down'
- Crosby Stills Nash & Young –

We're on planet earth for such a short time. Our seventy to ninety odd years on this planet are merely a blink in spirit time. We all however accept and understand, one day we'll cross that Rainbow Bridge to the *'Other Side'*.

So, what is the 'Other Side…?' The wise men from the east have their theories as do the Spiritualists who are in contact with the *'Other Side'*. Christians believe in Heaven and Hell. Every religion has their belief. We can analyse each religion and pick out what suits us as individuals and make up our own minds or we can take one day at a time and see where it leads us. Go in blind, so to speak.

Thankfully some of us need more than this. It can be a scary topic for some because we all want to accept, the *'Other Side'* indeed exists. We all want confirmation of sorts; the life we are currently living isn't merely a one-off, there is an afterlife.

'The veil that separates the worlds is but an ether veil. For those who purify their hearts by faith, the veil is rolled aside, they can see and know death is an elusive thing' - Ch:129 19 The Aquarian Gospel

On the *'Other Side'*, the spirit energy frequency levels are a lot higher, which is why we can't see Celestial Beings. However, the clairvoyant amidst us can see them and they verify this. Hypothetically, think of it as if there are two worlds, i.e. a second world co-existing with planet earth. The difference is the second world resonates at a higher frequency with many levels of consciousness in existence.

In passing over, life begins with a breath and ends when we can no longer breathe. Our breath is therefore the catalyst to life. Our breath is our umbilical cord to the *'Other Side'*. When we are born into this world, God gives each of us the *'Breath of Life'*.

So, in essence: Breath is life and life is the breath. It's a perfect balance. Anything else can and will happen in life but remove the breath and you will die. When you die, all you strive to do is hold onto your breath. At that moment you cannot buy another breath no matter how wealthy you are. When you fight with every aching muscle to live, you are really fighting just to breathe. There is nothing more important than breathing and this is something so inane, we daily take it for granted, without ever sparing it a thought.

In dying, it eventually comes down to that last breath. There is no more pain as the mind effortlessly slips into an unconscious state. When the last breath goes, so the *'life light'* disappears, the body's Auric light shines no more. Our indestructible spirit peacefully transfers over to the *'Other Side'* and continues, celestially existing, resonating on a higher frequency, a different vibration, in another dimension, another realm, surrounded by God's unconditional love, in what we call heaven. In passing over, our dominant ego is left behind. Only the *'Real You'*, your soul, transcends in the form of divine energy.

The joy is, everybody goes to heaven. There is no hell. It doesn't matter if you're a Saint or a murderer, everyone goes. And this is the lightbulb moment - there are many frequency levels of consciousness existing on the *'Other Side'*, for all sentient beings. Those on the lower levels, i.e. the murderer, are unaware of the higher consciousness levels above (the Saint), nor do they have access to the higher levels of consciousness because those levels resonate on a higher frequency. The higher the level, the higher the frequency, ad infinitum.

Meaning: In my father's house there are numerous levels. Consciousness in the afterlife therefore exists on many levels, many dimensions, many realms. It's complicated but its reality.

How do we know this – we know from those who have experienced Near Death Experiences, those who have crossed over and returned, plus there are also the clairvoyant amongst us who confirm this.

In our simple world, we have a tendency to look up when seeking heaven or God in prayer. This is not because we think heaven or God exists in the sky or somewhere in scary space, it's because heaven resonates on a higher frequency, unseen by us mere mortals. We therefore naturally look up because it's in our Genes to do so.

Why do we come back to earth...? In a nutshell - we come back to learn and overcome previous mistakes we made, face new challenges and advance spiritually so we can acquire lighter vibrations and transcend to higher planes or levels of consciousness on the *'Other Side'*. We may also return to help others in need or deal with specific missions.

There are many reasons for reincarnating. Life is ultimately like a school. We are merely here to learn. Problems are simply part of the curriculum, similar to being in an algebra class but the lessons we learn, last forever. Lao Tzu says - a journey of a thousand miles begins with a single step…!

'For God so loved the world, whosoever believeth in him should not perish, but have eternal life' - John 3:16

Spirit Guides...

For some of us, Spirit Guides are spiritual helpers, assigned to us at birth. To others, Spirit Guides represent a Celestial Being, symbolically assisting us to find wholeness. And still, to others, Spirit Guides are parts of our Higher Self, revealing themselves whenever we need them.

No matter what you think of Spirit Guides and no matter how *'New-Age'* or pragmatic your understanding is, we all need guidance, direction and support in life, beyond our own capabilities. Spirit Guides teach, warn, support, comfort, remind and reveal things we need to learn about ourselves in order to advance along our life path.

When we're re-born, we get to pick our Spirit Guides or Guardian Angels, whatever you want to call them. Sometimes your Guide even volunteers for the job. They are there for us from birth until the day we die and pass over. They enjoy raised vibrational levels to the point where they glow a golden colour, if you're ever able to see them. They are Celestial Beings, dedicated to personally guiding us through life. And yes, they witness everything we do, but without judgement.

You have one main Guide, who is typically from your soul group, meaning you are fragments of the same soul. Then you have Guides that come and go as you need them, depending on whatever activity it is you're currently active with.

You can talk to your Guides as they are always there for you. The best time to receive answers is in a light meditative state (Alpha brainwaves present). It may sound as if you're talking to yourself, but when you receive an answer, you'll know it and then you'll appreciate how real they are. The message arrives via the Pineal Gland, situated within the brain. You usually call on Guides for guidance and often do so without realising it. It's your Spirit Guide who stimulates your intuition. When you've established a direct contact link, you'll talk to them about everything. It takes time but doesn't everything...!

Should you for any reason no longer require your Guide, merely instruct your Guide and they will disappear. They may then only get involved to save your life in dangerous situations. Remember, they are your Guardians, so their job is to heal, guide and watch over you. If you want to commit suicide, they will try to save you, even though your conscious desire will be the opposite. They will also work with you to help others.

Bear in mind, they are not directly responsible for you. Nobody is going to punish your Guide if you decide you now prefer to walk the dark side of life. They can also work with your Higher Self (a part of your own energy existing in higher densities, not incarnated in the body) to make changes in your Soul Plan if circumstances change and the original Soul Plan becomes impossible to complete.

They help you stay on your path by sending you dreams, putting thoughts into your head, creating opportunities and synchronicities, arranging meetings with necessary people, or sometimes forcing you to avoid danger by implementing last minute changes. Spirit Guides have been known to cognitively alert you to switch on the radio or television because there's something they want you to hear or see. They also try and connect you with people they want you to learn from. They can even make you sick to avoid a possible offensive situation. Guides can also heal you and will talk to you directly in meditation or hypnosis sessions.

To get a mental picture of Spirit Guides at work, think of a plane flying through the sky with a pilot at the controls. On the ground is a group of experts (traffic control) guiding the pilot to his destination. In life, you are the pilot. The ground crew are your Spirit Guides guiding you safely to your destination. Isn't it comforting to know you have loving help to guide you on your 'life' path.

Always try to be guided by Spirit, not driven by ego…!'

Clairvoyants/Mediums…

Clairvoyants or Mediums are those amongst us who have psychic *'gifts'* allowing them to see or visit the *'Other Side'*. These earthly souls enjoy many different levels of powers. Some can see Spirits and converse with them, others can only hear them, some are guided by writing and still there are others who do transformations where the Spirit takes possession of the psychic's body.

A lot of people are in awe of these gifted people who are able to guide and inform us re the *'Other Side'*. Be aware, there are also a lot of fakers out there who will scam you for money and completely misdirect you. If you feel the need to consult with a clairvoyant/medium, ensure you check their credentials carefully. The safest way is to attend a service at a Spiritualist Church. You have a better chance of meeting the right people and receiving genuine guidance there.

When we talk about Spirits, let's first deal with the difference between Ghosts and Spirits. There is a difference between the two. Spirits are those who have died and made the transition to the *'Other Side'*. Ghosts are those who have died but haven't made the transition, for whatever reason. Normally because they have unfinished business on the earth plane or they still have strong emotional anchors, which have prevented them from letting go, from releasing their emotional bonds.

They will eventually make the transition but it can take time for them to accept they are actually lifeless and need to move on. Making the transition is not an issue; it's a matter of personal acceptance.

This is some advice from an anonymous clairvoyant re having the gift to *'see'* the Spirit world when asked if she enjoys her gift: "I'm going to tell you something you may not want to hear. You don't want to see them. I know, because I can see them, hear them and feel them. Increasing your sensitivity to these things is, in my opinion, not in your best interest. I realise you may disagree and that's your right. I'm going to advocate for you not to attempt to increase your sensitivity. Once you see these things, they know you can see them. This highlights you to them. That's great if they're *'nice'* but there are also spiritual entities who can be very persistent, demanding you immediately contact their loved ones on the earth plane and give them an urgent message. It can be very annoying when you're on their radar. It's definitely not fun. The effort you must expend to keep yourself grounded and sane, is immense when you have that level of sensitivity. It's a full-time job. And to be honest, mental illness and addiction are real threats to us. Our *'gift'* comes at a cost and it's a cost I would dearly surrender, if only I could. Imagine, if you will, this scene from my own life - I'm walking down a street. I see a man walking toward me. I know immediately from his energetic attachments; he is molesting children. I see flashes of the faces of his victims and there's nothing I can do. It's not like I can go to the police and say, 'Excuse me, but I'm psychic and this dude is molesting kids.' Sometimes I am in a book store, I see a woman, she is consumed by gluttony, it sickens me. She purchases expensive items on credit and hides them from her husband. I see from her Aura; she also has a gambling addiction. The woman looks at me and she's immediately angry at me. She doesn't know why she's experiencing such negative vibes. She stalks away, confused and enraged. Do you know what it's like to see human suffering all around you...? It's tiring. Do you know what turns off the sensitivity...? Drugs and alcohol. Oh, you might say, you're not prone to doing that. Give it a few years. A glass of wine can easily turn into a bottle for us sensitives. Before I leave home, I have to *'armour up'*. I have to ground centre, do certain things to protect myself. It's exhausting. I'm being very honest with you. Many of us end up with severe mental health problems due to this *'gift'*. I struggle every day with keeping myself sane and grounded. It's definitely not for the faint of heart."

This is a captivating insight into the world of the ultra-psychic sensitives out there. We are however, grateful for their presence because they offer vital guidance to us all.

Demons...
Ghosts and Demons, can both attach themselves to a live

human or animal host but there is a radical difference between the two. We'll start with Ghosts. As mentioned above, Ghosts are merely the Spirit of a dead person who hasn't crossed over. These entities will sometimes search for a living individual to attach to. When this happens, usually the Ghost fails to realise they are in fact dead. So, in defiance, they will jump into the body of any bystander who was nearby at the time of their death. They often choose a nurse in a hospital or a hospice volunteer, or somebody who was a witness to a car crash. People who work in hospitals often have small children attached to them. As the little ones die, they are confused and are therefore drawn to kind women with loving energy.

Alternatively, if the Ghost accepts it died, it can refuse to go into the light for many reasons, i.e. - addictions, unfinished business, fear-based religious beliefs, fear of Hell, judgment, meeting the spirits of its victims, etc. So, it will remain as a Ghost, but might eventually start looking for a living body to attach to. Typically, they are looking for people with similar addictions or similar emotional states. They will attach to drunks in a bar, a 'foodie' in a restaurant, a sex addict at an orgy, a drug user, etc. Normally, addicts have a lot of Ghosts attached to them, which makes recovery more difficult as they are demanding their fix. Sometimes they attach to somebody depressed or in fear because the Ghost felt the same emotions when they died and are therefore drawn to negativity. Horses for courses…!

Getting rid of these attachments requires spiritual intervention from a medium or clairvoyant who will discuss the situation with the Ghosts and convince them to transcend to the other side by removing their fears.

Ghosts are essentially lost souls. They require guidance, some more than others. Thankfully the *'gifted'* among us, like the Spiritualist's, are able to deal with this sensitive and often scary situation.

Demons, on the other hand, are another story altogether. According to the Bible, demons are fallen angels who joined Satan in his rebellion against God. They were defeated and cast out of heaven along with Satan *(Revelation 12:7-9)*. In the Gospel of Mark, Jesus meets a man on the far side of the Sea of Galilee who is possessed, he asks the demon to identify itself. It replies: "My name is Legion, for we are many."

If you accept the writings of the Bible then you probably accept, demons exist. Demons are regarded as spiritual, noncorporeal beings, but have been depicted in religious iconography as hybrid creatures with horrifying characteristics or as caricatures of opposing religions. Today, only in rare cases is the ancient rite of exorcism performed to cast out a demon from someone who has been diagnosed as possessed.

Darwin's notes on the subject included, *'A being infinitely more sagacious than man, one with penetration sufficient to perceive differences in the outer and innermost organization quite imperceptible to man, and with forethought extending over future centuries to watch with unerring care and select for any object the offspring of an organism produced under the foregoing circumstances.'*

This sort of slippage still happens today, as when an inventor such as Elon Musk warns, 'We are summoning the demon' with Artificial Intelligence. Such invocations are not necessarily theological, although a devout scientist may well make such appeals. However, they are not scientific, they are simply metaphorical.

There are theologians who claim, demon spirits inhabit another dimension here on earth, which they say explains some cases of *'alien'* sightings, where weird visions appear before our eyes and then disappear.

So, do demons actually exist or are they mere antiquity fables...? Part of my research for this book included a fascinating and completely illuminating, frank discussion with a very sensitive Medium who had a lot to say on the subject. I also interviewed people, who disclosed their vivid experiences with demons. They related very similar accounts while under deep hypnosis. Our Medium wants to remain anonymous for obvious reasons so we'll call her Mary, for her explanation.

According to Mary, demons definitely exist. She says they are not of our world. Their appearance is like that of a wisp of smoke energy, which twirls indefinitely like a small funnel, storm cloud. Existing in various sizes, from quite small to fairly large, adult human size. They range in colour from a light greyish blue to extreme black and can briefly take on any animal or even part human form, if they so desire. These evil spirits often pout freakish animal faces to scare Mary because they know she can see them. They exist within many vibrational frequencies, which is why we can't see them but the more powerful ones are able to transform into complete human form and possess the human body.

Mary says, demons transport from Solar System to Solar System throughout the Universe, in search of earth like planets, teeming with life. They seldom stay on a planet for long periods, preferring to move on until they find a comfort zone suiting their type of evil, which comes in many different flavours – murder, theft, sex molestation, obesity, gluttony, you name it, they got it covered.

They enjoy humans and animals with weak personalities; character traits they can easily bend and sway; absorb their energy and inspire them to commit evil before leaving the host and moving on to find a new host and new energy to absorb. Drug addicts, drunks, negative souls, depressed souls, basically those who are at an all-time cognitive low with no spiritual direction or belief, present easy pickings for the demons to devour one's energy, for this is how they continue to exist. They don't appear to be interested in the elderly or children because their energy levels are too weak.

The more powerful demons will target rock stars, politicians, people in power, etc., for their energy because then they have access to a huge audience of followers to bend and twist as they desire.

Demons cling or attach to a human or animal, often on the back, hip or leg. Once they've attached themselves, the host will immediately feel out of sync. Sudden aches and pains develop around the attached body area with no medical explanation. From here on, the host is coerced to walk a terrible dark path, committing all acts of bestiality. Humans often end up committing suicide to escape the horrors they've committed. Hitler and his henchmen, Serial Killers, humans committing acts of cruelty to animals, etc., all serve as prime examples of hosts possessed with powerful demons.

Not all demons have the same levels of power. The weaker ones will attach to a host and cause the host to be constantly in a foul mood or state of depression or have an eating disorder. There are many negative levels demons operate in.

Although we can't see them, with our intuition, we can sense them. It's that weird existential sensation you sometimes feel when walking into a room or down the road or whatever. Your whole body briefly shivers, leaving you wondering what has just happened. A demon has just cruised past you, testing your energy. This is what they do. Sometimes you can smell them. Mary says they all carry an acrid, foul smell, some worse than others. She says they know she can see them so they purposefully descend on her relentlessly, hissing their evil all over her.

Next time you smell a disgusting smell and you can't

immediately trace its source, it's probably a demon near you. According to Mary, the evil of demons represents the 'balance', compared to the good of God. Wherever we have the one (Good), we'll always have the other (Bad). We fortunately have Spirit Guides who are our protectors, our angels, that guide us through life but sometimes the demon is too strong even for them and will attach to you, upset your balance and absorb your energy, especially if your spiritual path is weak. How do you prevent this…?

By walking a strong spiritual path to begin with, will obviate demons targeting you. Remaining fit and healthy is another good protector because then your Aura and energy are too strong for them. Being aware of these weird entities and the relevant signs of their presence will keep you on your path, ensuring you remain positive, blocking their presence.

You're always going to be seeking to maintain your balance in life anyway, which is difficult in a world filled with hatred and conflicting wars, often fuelled by contradictory religion but whether demons are real or not, we cannot actually quantify because there is no empirical proof or relevant science to prove their existence. However, we are aware, evil only exists because it's part of the balance and will always tempt us for a walk down the tasty side of life. Be conscious of it. Knowledge is everything…

'Sometimes Life is a long lesson in humility'

Prayer...

'When the dark side of the moon slips into the thunder of the night, sounding clear across the sky, asking man to stop his wars and open his doors to love and light'

When you pray, you spiritually connect to the God Within, not to a God existing somewhere in the clouds like so many still believe. Prayer is your personal lifeline to God, the Universal Consciousness. Once you accept this, you'll achieve a wonderous peace of mind and comfort. Prayer is a direct way of communicating with God. This is where you simply leave all your problems in life up to God. The more you believe in prayer and have faith, the more you'll enjoy total peace of mind by having handed over your concerns/problems to God. Prayer has this incredible fixing effect in life. Everything is now okay, because you've given it to God and God will never let you down.

Throughout time, we've become conditioned in this belief. We have total faith; God will sort everything out and take care of it. The incredible thing is, it normally pans out right and it's all because we have *'faith'* it will happen.

Our belief is so strong we imprint our Subconscious with such conviction, the result is practically guaranteed. The thing is, you cannot buy faith. It is a virtue you have to accept within, unconditionally. It comes with time and dedication to all who persevere in prayer, without prejudice. Once you have it, your life will definitely change for the better.

Of course, you also need to be aware of what you pray for and how you do it. Sometimes, if you pray for peace, God will send you a hurricane...! This is because with suffering comes learning, which means you may have to initially learn a lesson in life and overcome a challenge or two before you are awarded with your desire. Sometimes we don't get what we want because the majority of us don't even know what it is, we want in life...!

When Buddha was once asked how he'd preserve and prevent a drop of water from evaporating, he answered candidly: *'Throw it into the ocean...!'* Sometimes the obvious is right under our nose and we still can't see it.

The following is a beautiful story about a young woman and an ant that portrays the power of sincere prayer. This young woman was an avid mountain climber. One day she was almost halfway up the top of a steep cliff. She stopped for a bit on a ledge to take in the view and catch her breath. As she rested, the safety rope snapped and just clipped her eye, knocking out her one contact lens. "Great", she thought, "here I am on the edge of a rocky ledge, hundreds of feet from the bottom and hundreds of feet still to go to the top of this cliff and now my sight is all blurry." She quickly dropped to the ground and desperately searched the rough, rocky surface of the ledge, hoping somehow it had landed somewhere but she couldn't find it. She felt the panic rising in her, so she began praying. She prayed for calm and she prayed she would find her contact lens. When she got to the top, a friend examined her eye and her clothing for the lens, but it was nowhere to be found. Although she was calm now that she was at the top, she was saddened because she couldn't take in the magnificent view. She wasn't able to clearly see across the range of mountains. Everything was a complete blur. So, she thought of the Bible verse: *'The eyes of the Lord run to and fro throughout the whole earth'* - *2Chronicles16:9*

She prayed again. 'Lord, you are omnipresent. You know all these mountains. You know every stone and every leaf and you also know exactly where my contact lens is. Please help me…!'

Later, when they had hiked down the trail to the bottom of the cliff, they met another party of climbers starting up the face of the cliff. One of them shouted, "Hey, you guys, anybody lose a contact lens…?" Well, that would be startling enough, but the reason why the climber saw the contact lens is because an ant was moving slowly across a twig on the face of the rock directly in front of them and theant was carrying the contact lens...!

The story doesn't end here. The young woman's father is a cartoonist. When she told him the incredible story of the ant, the prayer and the contact lens, he drew a cartoon of an ant lugging the contact lens with the caption: *'Lord, I don't know why you want me to carry this thing. I can't eat it and it's awfully heavy but if this is what you want me to do, I'll carry it for you...!'*

Lovely story to illustrate the wonderful power of prayer. Sadly, the reality is most of us do carry unseen loads; some are just bigger than others and the majority of them, we make ourselves. We do have the ability though to unlock these loads and get rid of them. The problem is, the longer we leave them, the larger the load inevitably becomes.

God's Reward System...

Everything you do has a consequence. It's like whatever you put into a project, your job, a relationship, even life, is what you're going to get out. If you put nothing in; you'll get nothing in return. Simply put, this means *'no work, no pay'*. This is how God's reward system works.

We are more interested here though in the spiritual direction of reward. If we take the above *'no work, no pay'* example then it goes without saying, the more spiritual you become, the more you'll love God, the more you'll love your neighbour, the more you'll give of yourself, the more you'll look after your health and ultimately, the more spiritual rewards you'll receive in return.

This reward formula is repeated indefinitely throughout the Biblical books about how mankind will earn for whatever he/she does:

- In biblical terms it is: As ye sow, so shall re reap

- Scientists refer to it as: Cause & Effect

- Buddhist's refer to it as: Karma

The subject of Karma or Cause & Effect was covered lightly in an earlier chapter so we'll look at it a bit more in depth here. According to Science; causes will always happen before effect and never the other way around or else the entire Universe would collapse into chaos. However, every cause creates an effect.

And Jesus said, 'Afflictions are all partial payments on a life debt. There is a law of recompense that never fails and it is summarized in the true rule of life. Tooth for a tooth; life for a life.' – Ch:138 4:7 The Aquarian Gospel

Karma is often explained as *'the ripple effect'* meaning if you were to drop a pebble into a pond, as it lands in the water it sends out ripples. In a similar manner, so do our words/feelings/vibrations, create ripples. The difference is our words/feelings/vibrations create consequences, which due to the balance effect in life, are then returned, sometimes not quite as we would prefer to have them returned either…!

Basically, it's all about: *'Do good, receive good. Do bad, receive bad'*. It's that simple. Life is all about *'Balance'* and we've covered this so many times already but once again, the evidence is all there – if you give out *'Good'* you will receive *'Good'* in return. Give out *'Bad'* and you will receive *'Bad'* in return – which would you rather have…? No-one escapes this balance effect. It is Universal. Whatever you do to create joy for yourself is how you should ideally treat others with the same line of respect.

In an earlier chapter we learnt how atoms consist of molecules containing protons and electrons in perfect balance and everything consists of atoms. Therefore 'Balance' exists throughout the Universe including all life on earth. We all receive or conversely pay, no matter how long it takes. It can even take several lifetimes. The problem is, every day we continue to incur more Karma. The debt can therefore, become infinite.

Christians have a wonderful outlook on Karma. They believe by handing over their sins to Jesus, who died for them on the cross, they no longer have any outstanding or future Karma as Jesus will shoulder all their Karma for them. All they have to do is give their lives in sincerity over to Jesus and then live their lives according to Biblical Christian law. Hmmm....

Baptists believe all original sin is inherited from their parents, which remains with them until their heart is fully cleansed through baptism with the Holy Spirit. Whereas their personal sin is only when they voluntary commit a violation of a known law of God.

Not to punch holes in any religion but when did God appear as a human and write a list of laws...? Okay, these are obviously human laws, written by humans. The idiom – 'If you live in a glass house, don't throw stones' comes to mind. If you're comfortable abiding by a bunch of spiritual laws created by humans a couple thousand years ago, who in reality are no better or worse than you, then so be it, go with it. Bear in mind, Karma isn't defined as a law – it's about balance…Universal Balance…!

Most religions accept this based around a similar concept. It does however go deeper than this because it's a magnetic balance, which affects everybody personally, no matter who you are or whatever your circumstances. The reverse also applies for the good you do. How you treat others is your Karma. How others treat you is their Karma. The bottom line is: There are no free lunches. We all want good Karma.

If you truly desire success and total joy in life, try to do the best you can in life without hurting or destroying other life forms or nature or our wonderful world. When it's purely for personal gain and others suffer because of your success, you will pay. It's a guarantee. For example: Farmers, who farm innocent animals for profit, will pay dearly. No-one escapes. Even the spoken word can hurt, so tread softly.

Forgive and Forget...

You have to forgive and forget in order to move on in life. It's the only way to get rid of the negative vibes clinging to you. It's a cleansing process and difficult to do, especially when you're the one who has been hurt but once you release the bondage and finally let go, you'll enjoy the wonderful relief it brings. When you sincerely forgive, it depolarises a situation. Problem is, when you throw stones, you get boulders thrown back at you. No-one wins, everyone gets hurt. Learn to forgive and try and forget it ever happened.

We all know life doesn't exactly come tied with a pretty bow but it's still good, especially if you can accept your mistakes and move on, more importantly, if you can learn to forgive and forget your neighbour's mistakes.

Forgiveness is the one overwhelming key to reducing one's Karma. Learn to genuinely forgive your enemies, your family, your loved ones, anyone who has wronged you in the past because this will reduce your Karma. It must come from your heart with love, intensity and sincerity. We are essentially living this current life to learn the many lessons of love and especially forgiveness. By forgiving someone, you free the negativity you've been holding for so long. You can finally move on, free of all burdens. Learn to quieten your mind, stop listening to the news and learn to love again once you have completely forgiven whoever wronged you.

This is a heart-warming story reinforcing the human 'success' attitude for personal gain: There was once a blind girl who hated herself because she was blind. She hated everyone, except her loving boyfriend. He was always there for her so one day she said to him, "If I could only see the world, I would marry you." A week later, someone donated a pair of eyes to her. When the bandages came off, she was able to see everything, including her boyfriend. He asked her, "Now that you can see the world, will you marry me...?" The girl looked at her boyfriend and saw he was blind. The sight of his empty eye sockets shocked her. She hadn't expected it. The thought of looking at his daunting eyes for the rest of her life led her to decide against the marriage. When she told her boyfriend, he didn't reply, just forlornly walked away. Days later he wrote her a note: 'Take good care of your eyes, my love, for before they were yours, those eyes were mine.'

This is how our human personalities work when our status changes for the better...! Very few of us are capable of remembering or looking back to what our life was like before and who was always there by our side in the most painful situations.

As previously mentioned, it's always good to better your situation but not at another's cost. Let life lead you in a manner that makes you feel proud to have achieved what you've accomplished without damage to anything or anyone. Preferably, your success should encompass and equally benefit all those who helped you achieve your success. Together, you'll always be stronger.

The Journey...

If you want to know what you were in your previous life, look at your current life, your current situation. It won't be a lot different. You'll have faced similar challenges. Your next life journey, depends entirely on how you manage the challenges you're facing in this life, right now.

Why...? Because everything you do in this life automatically impacts on your next life. It's like a rollercoaster. You actually get to choose your destiny for your future life, as of today. If you decide to regress, then your future life will be filled with even more demanding challenges. However, if you choose to lead a good and harmonious life now, then your future life will be a lot easier to manage because you'll have less Karmic baggage. It also depends on what you and your Guides choose for your next life but if you can reduce your Karmic baggage, it's always going to work out better for you.

It has been said before: 'We are not humans having a spiritual experience; we are spiritual beings having a human experience on this earth plane'. You need to remind yourself occasionally, your life is a journey. The only limits on your life are those you yourself set. If you are however, prepared to push beyond those limits, you can unlock mental and physical reserves you never knew you had. There is nothing noble about being superior to another person. True nobility lies in being superior to your former self. With every mistake in life comes lessons because from struggle comes strength and knowledge.

There's an old Buddhist story about the butterfly who was initially denied a chance to struggle. A pupa was having difficulty releasing from its stubborn cocoon. A kind hearted human walking past noticed the struggle and decided to intervene and help by carefully tearing the bottom end of the cocoon, thereby releasing the new butterfly, which emerged safely but instantly fell to the ground as it didn't have the strength to fly. The reason was because the butterfly needed to struggle out of the cocoon on her own in order to develop sufficient strength to help her fly.

And so, it is with life. We are often faced with immense struggles to prepare us for our next challenge. Accept this because now you know the reason why. We all have to start somewhere. Success on the outside means nothing unless you start making an effort to grow spiritually within.

When your current life reaches the twilight years you should ideally, already be preparing for your next life. All it takes is a little conditioning every day. Your general attitude towards life is a major contributor to your spiritual progress.

Oneness...

Oneness is a state in which a person gets to experience consciousness in its true form, utterly devoid of subject material. Self is inextricably interrelated to the rest of the world, meaning we are all a part of the same whole in this Universe.

Imagine you're the whole universe; you live in total joy and bliss. Imagine there is no past or future, only now. Imagine there is no space or time, only an unbounded eternity. Imagine endless peace, harmony and unconditional love. Imagine no fear and equality in everything. This is Oneness or John Lennon's version of Oneness...!

An easy example is to imagine a river of moving water. It is strong and invincible until it reaches a waterfall. When this happens, the water disintegrates into singular little streams and droplets. The closer you get to the waterfall; you'll see the tiny droplets of the falling water. If the waterfall is high, the droplets take a long time to reach the bottom. However, once they reach the bottom of the waterfall the singular streams and droplets unite once again into a complete river of flowing water. In other words, – they have reached Oneness. Now they are complete, they are once again strong and indestructible, whereas when they were singular droplets, they were powerless and vulnerable.

And then we get the other side of the balance: There's a rose bush growing on the side of a road surrounded by weeds. A dog walks by and sees vegetation, gives the rose a sniff, sneezes and walks on. Whereas a human walks by, sees a rose bush and weeds. For the human, it's a good plant surrounded by bad plants, a pretty rose bush with value, which is so much better than useless weeds. Reality check – we need to learn to see the rose flower and equally, the weeds, because they are all God's creation.

When you have learnt to see both, you have Oneness because each entity has life. Each one is a creation. Each one has a right to survive and they're all intrinsically connected. One is not necessarily better than the other, maybe more attractive to look at but they both exist. It is what it is, no more, no less.

A human will not simply see what is, a human will judge what is, will evaluate its value, will compare it to something else and decide, which is better and which is worse, which is desirable and which isn't, which is good and which is bad. Balance at it's extreme...humans...?

All this evaluation, judging, estimating, assigning of value and importance is what the human mind does. It's how the human mind interacts with reality, how the human mind perceives life. It's our normal mental process. The mind evaluates, compares and judges everything it encounters. And we do it without thinking about it. We do it in autopilot mode (Subconscious mind).

If you hear of someone having a different experience then we don't simply see two different experiences, we see a better experience or a worse experience, a valuable and useless experience or a superior versus inferior experience. We relate to the experience by comparing, evaluating and judging endlessly. This is because the mind only knows separatism, me, me, me. It cannot grasp Oneness, or the concept of Oneness.

For humans, more will always be better than less. More is superior to less because no one wants to be inferior. And this happens in every facet of life, sadly, including religion. Humans have no guilt or remorse re standing on another human to better themselves. This could be seen as a fault in the human dynasty but obviously our Creator created us this way in order to make it a challenge for us to overcome.

Some will say, it all falls back on the parable of Adam and Eve, succumbing to the forbidden fruit in the Garden of Eden and creating evil thereafter, where in reality, they received consciousness, (or so the 'other' story goes) activating a dominant ego, which allowed them to think for themselves, compete and compare everything, find fault in everything, express emotions, discover ways to better themselves, release themselves from Oneness and spiritual joy and join the vibrant tasty world, incurring truckloads of Karma for evermore. Relax...it's only a parable...!

Anyway, you have only really begun to awaken when you can comfortably re-experience Oneness with everything and everyone, friend, foe, animal, tree, plant, planet Earth, the Universe - no exceptions.

Judging, estimating and evaluating is a 'greed' emotion but also a competitive 'ego' emotion because we don't only want more of everything we also want to be 'seen' as the best at everything we do and this is what separates us. This is not to discourage humans from being competitive because it's in our genes to constantly better ourselves, which is probably why the human race has evolutionary advanced so radically over all other species.

And yet, there are many amongst us who have recognised this separatism ego challenge and learnt to overcome it. They now assist others to create a balance between separatism and Oneness, whilst still retaining a relatively competitive edge for the ego. Isn't balance a bitch...!

To achieve a state of Oneness, we need to go beyond the mind, intellect and our dominant ego. Tough call...! Oneness is the coming together of all opposites, meaning complete balance. It's always with us as the basis and underlying essence of everything. It's nothing in itself, but holds potential for everything. We need to go beyond the senses, beyond duality, to find Oneness. It's unique and difficult to maintain.

We've all had random, unexpected glimpses of existential Oneness. Perhaps you were watching a beautiful sunset and had that moment when you felt like you merged with the whole of creation; or saw your new born child for the first time and fell in love with the whole world. We even have expressions for these glimpses. We say, *'It took my breath away'* or *'Time simply stood still.'* This is Oneness. We became one with the totality of the experience. When we return from the moment of Oneness, we find it impossible to properly express it. Simply put - It is what it is. There are no words to describe the feeling or joy of Oneness.

We can also achieve a direct experience of Oneness via meditation. When we settle our awareness to quieter levels of thinking and finally transcend thought completely, we can slip into the spaces between our thoughts and enter into a state of sublime Oneness. Not easy but certainly possible.

We are all connected via Earth's Geomagnetic field so,

attaining Oneness should be relatively easy but it isn't because of our constant desire for separatism. Like everything, it takes patience and perseverance...

Spiritual Awakening...

The majority of the contents of this book, have been a preparation for this section, hence, the title of the book. We will endeavour to unpack a fairly simple *'Awakening Experience'* procedure for you to follow, based on what we have covered to-date.

This is it in a nutshell, so to speak, the entire enchilada. You've managed to get this far, you now have the tools, so grab a cup of your favourite beverage, digest and enjoy...!

The Spiritual Awakening process differs from person to person but there are some common themes. It invariably begins when you finally separate your busy ego from your quiet Higher Self, realising that the constant flow of superfluous incidents your ego relates to you every day are not only negative and false but incredibly self-boosting as well. Slowly but surely, selling your soul to the highest bidder to be seen as *'Mr Cool'*, loses its attraction. You begin to see the light and desire to move on. However, even when walking a spiritual path, your ego still wants you to believe you're progressing spiritually and you are now more virtuous, compared to others. It takes some deep direction from the Higher Self to realise, this is merely your *'ego'* at it again.

From here on, ensure your spiritual connection is only

with your Higher Self, bypassing your ego thoughts, realising we are all a part of the Universal Consciousness and therefore no one is better than anyone else. The good thing is, by understanding your ego has been misleading you, means you are already progressing on your journey. You have opened the door...!

Stages...

There are several stages to a Spiritual Awakening. When you first see the light, it's a light bulb moment; your quest to learn and see more, can be overwhelming. At first, it appears to be light-hearted and fun but at some point, life will start proposing you practice spiritual life changes aimed at shedding away any and all previous beliefs, identities, systems, constructs and anything else you previously associated yourself with, both internally and externally. It's one thing enthusiastically following a new spiritual path but now you need to actually walk the path with all honesty and passion. There's a huge difference. Walk the walk, talk the talk – got it...!

The removal of these things is not a nice experience. You invested a lot of time and effort in creating them, mainly to boost your ego. You believed in them. They were important to you. Shedding these things will be painful...

Eventually, you settle down into an acceptance mode and walk a focused spiritual path of light and love with no encumbrances or regrets. Once you really accept this, you become elated, confident, filled with joy and flowing positive energy, which feels like it will never subside. You are at peace, serene and content. It's a good thing to feel these moments of complete joy. Allow them to happen but be aware, attachment of emotions can also prevent further growth.

Due to the balance in life, the good feelings of joy will be followed by feelings of depression as you begin to relive your past, some of it joyous but a lot of it will leave you disappointed and even depressed with whatever happened in your past. These fears are being sent to you for the purpose of purging them out of your system. Once each situation is accepted, made peace with, negotiated from a place of positivity rather than negativity, they simply fade away. You can use positive affirmations to cleanse your past (see page 193) and always maintain a solid spiritual practice to keep you balanced and grounded. Meditation, prayer and exercise (yoga) will also help you purge your previous regrets in life.

Once you've covered this stage, which is always the most difficult, you'll gradually move on from your old self into your new self with complete acceptance and contentment. This is also a period of rest and contemplation as you work on releasing your dominant ego, letting all 'ego' thoughts slip by without hindrance. You no longer worry about what others think of you. You are yourself, complete in every way. You have achieved a semi state of Oneness.

The following stage is about getting completely grounded on your new path. Accepting that life, is what it is, with all the good and the bad opportunities and challenges, crossing your path in everyday life. You have to face them all in order to grow.

The Guru's say, life is like a tree, the deeper you plant your roots, the higher you will climb and therefore the more spiritual you'll become. Good advice. You will need good roots to stay grounded.

At this stage, you have accepted your new spiritual direction with conviction. Remember, you need to completely surrender in order to progress spiritually. Affirmations like, *'I surrender my control to my soul'* and *'My ego is now under direct control'*, plus many other similar affirmations, will become your mantra's for evermore in order to constantly keep your busy ego under control.

Give it your all and always listen to your heart, your love centre. You can do this by putting your hands over your heart and mindfully bringing your awareness to your heart. You can also softly tap your heart with your forefinger to awaken and stimulate your heart chakra. With practice, you will feel an abundance of love surrounding you. This is an incredible spiritual feeling of God's divine love, which will impact on you eternally.

The final stage is about putting into practice what you've learned and constantly striving to continue learning. It is infinite, you will never learn it all. Sharing what you've learnt, being focused and strong on your path with complete devotion, will keep you on your path. Quieten your mind every day, even if it's for only a few minutes. Detach yourself from your thoughts completely and merely observe your thoughts. The more you do this, the easier it becomes.

The only way to speed up your journey is to completely let go of everything. Currently, it's your attachment to your personal ego that is holding you back. Try to refrain from telling yourself, *'your Awakening isn't happening because your spiritual gifts haven't awakened as yet or they're taking too long to surface'*, because this is the very *'you'*, which you need to let go of in order for the process to complete. You can't be attached. You need to let go of everything. Go with the flow, it will happen naturally…

Above all, enjoy your journey because you will not progress if you can't experience genuine passion and joy for what you are doing.

And so...

This scenario is a rather brief unpacking of a standard Spiritual Awakening procedure. The more you develop your spiritual practice, the further you will grow into an Awakening because once you're in, it's like no other human experience. You'll soon appreciate the change in your inner world is the key to long-lasting joy.

As humans, we tend to spend most of our time reliving traumas and past successes over and over or we systematically project ourselves into the future, convincing ourselves that if only this or if only that happens, then everything will be perfect thereafter. Many of us think getting the optimal career or the ultimate soulmate, guarantees happiness. Yes, these things are good and will support you but long-lasting peace and true happiness can only really be accessed spiritually from within for this is where you'll find inner peace. When the present moment starts to become your main focal point; you are definitely on a path to a Spiritual Awakening.

The truth is – we cannot guarantee the future. However, we can create the future in the present, right now, with patience and dedication. Getting your health together is probably the biggest motivator to begin getting you to notice positive change within. The more you go within and start healing the most tender parts of yourself, (maybe an offensive past incident that really offended you) the more you'll experience longer periods of peace.

One thing more difficult than Spiritual Awakening, is to trudge through life unaware, stumbling through pain, grief, difficulty, etc., and not knowing how to handle them. Merely accepting everything, is what it is. Unaware there's a different way, a different path to walk every day, a new way of life to live, filled with love and light and joy.

A Spiritual Awakening is difficult. It's not for the faint hearted. It's not for the one who asks *'what are the benefits of an Awakening…?'*. It's not like going to the supermarket to buy something. It's for the one who knows life isn't good enough without it. For the one who knows there's something more, something better, something real out there, just waiting for you. Bear in mind, this adventure is for the long haul. There are no shortcuts. It's forevermore and all depends on how much you are prepared to commit to your spiritual path...100% is always good...!

Gently remind yourself – 'All You Have, Is Right Now'. This simple truth is extremely liberating. If you allow yourself to mindfully explore it further, the realisation of 'existing in the moment' becomes reality. Live it...Love it...!

Enlightenment...

Is this the ultimate, elusive state of Nirvana we're all searching for and if so, how do we achieve this and how long does it take to get there...?

So many questions...! Back in the day it was defined as: 'A movement of the 18th century that stressed the belief that science and logic give people more knowledge and understanding than tradition and religion.' A later example: 'When you become educated about a particular course of study or a particular religion.'

It's also a popular spiritual term, commonly used in Buddhism. There are many books available re – 'The Path to Enlightenment.' They mostly follow a similar pattern with the final resting place resulting in when you've reached a state of enlightenment. They describe many progressive stages of spiritual evolution to get there.

The Buddhism version is probably the most illuminating:

'Enlightenment is a state of perfect knowledge or wisdom, combined with infinite compassion. Knowledge in this case does not mean merely the accumulation of data or a description of the world of phenomena down to finite details. Enlightenment is an understanding of both the relative mode of existence (the way in which things appear to us) and the ultimate mode of existence (the true nature of these same appearances). This includes our own minds as well as the external world. Such knowledge is the basic antidote to end ignorance and suffering.

In a similar scenario, how do Sages become Sages and who decides when they become Sages. The same scenario applies to Guru's. In the Christian religion, it's Pastors and Priests, etc.

Ad infinitum for all religions who have Spiritual leaders they admire. They are respected because they have studied, done the hard yards and now have abundant spiritual wisdom to share, teach and educate. In this manner, they assist to overcome ignorance and suffering for all humanity. Is this a state of enlightenment...to become a spiritual teacher...?

Suzuki Roshi, a Zen Buddhism Master, says Buddha wasn't really interested in the elements comprising human beings, nor in metaphysical theories of existence. He was more concerned about how he could exist totally, completely, in the moment.

This is more like it...it's an elevated state of being. With knowledge, eventually comes wisdom and a mental state of celestially existing in the moment, residing completely in the Subconscious with raised frequencies, heightened senses, perfect balance, peace, harmony and unconditional love. Sounds like a magic mushroom trip...love it...!

This is one of Buddha's metaphors for understanding enlightenment: - Bread is made from flour. How flour becomes bread, once admitted to the oven, is the essence of enlightenment because simple flour dough becomes perfect bread, over and over again. Every time the dough is admitted to the oven, the result is always the same – perfect, tasty, edible bread.

It's all in the continued *'practice'* of making the bread, resulting in absolute, timeless, perfection. So, the process of what happens to the bread, to transform it from rudimentary flour dough, to perfect bread is metaphorically, the road to enlightenment. Therefore, once you understand the example of how dough becomes perfect bread, you will begin to understand the process (the practice) of enlightenment. Ultimately, repeat the process indefinitely until you eventually gain sufficient wisdom to *'become'* the bread, for this is when you have arrived...enlightenment.

What Buddha is saying is, spiritual advancement has no ceiling. You will spend many lives understanding the process, committing to the practice of existing in the moment and walking a profound spiritual path (what happens in the oven), before you can actually become the bread (enlightened).

Suzuki Roshi uses a pair of glasses as a metaphor to explain enlightenment. Making a pair of glasses is the practice. Eventually, putting the glasses on to see properly, is enlightenment. There are many forms or scenarios of enlightenment that we can entertain without upsetting the Gurus amongst us. Here are a few simple examples…

1.) Consider an insect on a windowpane. The insect can see the free world on the other side of the windowpane but cannot get there. Day after day he struggles relentlessly to get through the windowpane but cannot do so. One day a human comes along and opens the window just a little. The insect still struggles to get through the windowpane because he cannot see the window has been opened. Eventually, the insect finds the small opening and escapes to enlightenment.

2.) A baby elephant is captured in the wild by poachers and is sold to a circus or a zoo. For over fifty years the elephant is locked in a cage, let out only with heavy leg chains to perform or entertain humans. One day, a real human purchases the elephant and releases him back in to the wild where he was originally captured. He is united with his brothers and sisters he hasn't seen for fifty years. He is so overwhelmed with joy; he has Oneness once again and remains in a state of enlightenment for the remainder of his life.

Be a lot easier to merely take a bunch of hallucinogenic drugs or ingest some Magic Mushrooms, kick back, idly talk to the Godly on the Other Side for a few days and discuss religion and the afterlife over a jug of Rooibos tea…!

Problem is, when you come back to reality, you'll still be carrying your Monkey Mind around with you and you'll still be walking in the dark. Truth be told, enlightenment is a state of being, a wondrous state of being. In order to achieve it though, you need to undergo a practice of learning, a gaining of spiritual knowledge and intellect, sometimes suffering and overcoming challenges in life, before you can achieve any state of enlightenment, which brings us back to the original three roads example. If you've only walked the middle road towards enlightenment, you'll never get there until you've walked both the high and the low road because only then will you have knowledge of all three roads.

The big question, is what comes next. What happens once you've reached a state of enlightenment…? The answer is nothing. Why…? Because you can never really reach a state of complete enlightenment. In other words, there are many stages of a heightened awareness or enlightenment, whatever you want to call it.

Reaching the first stage is really about having reached your initial Awakening stage. You have arrived, you have spiritual knowledge, you've done the practice (sufficient cushion time in meditation) to live in the moment, you have forgiven those who wronged you in life and you have renounced your superfluous material possessions, you have found balance in life and your life is now complete, or so you thought it was.

Reality is, you've only just begun because now you need to seek wisdom and that is infinite, there is no ceiling, there is no end. In the true sense, you will always be practising, you will always be seeking the light and you'll ultimately get lighter until as Buddha says, *'you become the light'* and even then, you will still continue seeking...

It's really about how much you personally want to commit to walking your spiritual path. Small bites to begin. As your faith, your balance in life, your compassion, knowledge and your confidence cultivate and matures, you will find your own path to existing completely in the moment, attaining a level of wisdom and a relative state of enlightenment.

In Conclusion...

Life and religion have been in competition forever. The tasty side of life is very tempting and religion is one of those subjects few can agree on. The objective of this succinct spiritual overview is to encourage the reader to think about his/her current religion, where it's taking them and realise, there are alternative spiritual paths you can walk, free of intimidation and fiery pits of hell. You don't have to be blinded by dogmatic pastors/ministers.

You, as an individual, have the right to make your own choices in life.

Try and avoid conflict when talking religion and personal beliefs. Everyone is entitled to their own belief so refrain from forcing your beliefs on others because they may not be on the same vibration as you, they haven't as yet 'seen' what you've seen and vice versa but you do have the right to question anything that concerns you in your current religion. If you really want to make a point you can always lead by example.

Too many religions today are still steeped in history and beliefs that originated eons ago. Science has since leapfrogged into the future providing truth to so many questions. We all love Jesus, Buddha, Krishna, the Saints and all the other deities and we'll always honour them for their beautiful and heartfelt spiritual messages and guidance, which have stood the test of time and helped many of us through difficult times but you don't have to live your life according to their age-old traditions. We are blessed to live in this day and age of advanced electronics, which has made the world a smaller place. Via the internet we can contact loved ones and have a live discussion on camera. Who would have thought this was possible twenty years ago let alone a few thousand years ago...?

The point is, the world has advanced at an incredible rate whereas religion hasn't, it's actually stagnated, become tired, boring and even nonsensical to most.

Currently, there is a huge move away from Christianity and other clerical religions to a more spiritual based, personal path. There is surely enough proof to substantiate a Godly presence consisting of divine intelligence exists, controlling and creating throughout our Universe and this Godly presence is omnipresent. Most humans accept this in one way or another, even if they feel a little awkward to verbalise it, they know internally, a Universal Consciousness has to exist. Our Universe and especially planet earth, couldn't function without a superior presence in the driver's seat.

We all want to leave this world one day, having made it better than when we arrived. We do this by walking a divine spiritual path, creating an everyday *'Heaven on Earth'* lifestyle, knowing we can remove the *'I'* from everything we say and therefore maintain some control over our dominant ego and enjoy life, guided by our Creator's Universal love and light because the truth is - if you follow the light, you'll never be in darkness…!

Denying yourself of your God given right to a good life, is defeatist. Let it go. Lighten up, laugh with this wonderful world, find your balance in life and begin your Spiritual Awakening…it's worth it…!

'My true self is free - it cannot be contained'

Meditation

"Quiet the mind and the soul will speak."
Ma Jaya Sati Bhagavati

Visualise a world filled only with love. Love all around us, love in the air, love everywhere. No hatred, no egos, no dark side and no hunger, no poverty and no police force, no need to worry and no need to care. Envisage a world as one. One government. One world currency. One law enforcement. One language. No passport, no border control, no customs and no fences. Living together in perfect harmony...

Don't think the world is ready for all this yet but nice idea. The problem is, we're all so different. In our world, we have way too many cultures and religions and outlooks on how to live this life. With only one government we'd end up imposing one view of life on everybody. No can do...! One day though, maybe we could encourage a large number of the world's population to meditate. Now there's a possibility...

It almost happened at Woodstock. This was the music festival that ran from the 15th-18th August 1969, drew half a million people, was recorded as one of the largest peaceful gatherings ever. A lot of people were introduced to meditation at this event but it unfortunately wasn't the entire half a million.

Meditation is an ageless practice. It goes right back to even before Buddha's time, some five thousand years ago when the effects of the practice were discovered by ancient men who spent their time staring into the flames of flickering fires, evoking visions and putting them in touch with their esoteric senses. It's considered to be one of the oldest forms of mental, spiritual, health and wellness practices in existence today.

Since then, several meditation techniques have developed, spreading across the continent of Asia. Meditation was controversial for its time because it eliminated the need for religious dominations to a large extent. In short, it cut out the middle man. However, meditation only took off and was globally accepted when the holy men from the east introduced the practice to the western world.

Today, there are people in every country who practice meditation in one form or another. A lot of people use meditation to enhance their ability to relax because being able to fully relax is about letting go of the ego, frustrations, greed, anger and so on. In meditation we learn to cultivate, transmit and receive subtle nuances that emanate from deep within. Sometimes we release the creative artist within us and use our minds as a canvas. Whatever we create on the canvas, if we mindfully meditate on that scene and hold it joyfully within our thoughts and then merely observe it without becoming attached, we begin to generate powerful feelings of contentment. Meditation is a time for reflection within, you're able to completely relax and let go, focusing only on your breath as your anchor. Your mind soon comes to the present as you let go of all the busy Conscious mind chatter, allowing your dreamy, calm Subconscious to take over.

If you visualise specific desires and don't become attached to them, you begin to attract energies and circumstances to make your desires happen. Meditation also helps increase spiritual awareness. In essence, it is a self-awakening. We get to remove the blocks, barriers and obstacles that accumulate through life. With consistent meditation, via this new awareness, an inner healing slowly takes place.

One of the first obstacles we encounter when we begin meditating is doubt. We seek every excuse to stop and surrender and it happens to all of us. With continued practice, you will learn to push through this barrier and move on. It is our human nature to endure hardship for a higher vision. The results you are seeking are not material, they are spiritual, emotional. Slowly, we learn to understand how everything comes together and that to better ourselves, we have to stop thinking only of ourselves, remembering that this new entity is actually a very old timeless entity, a path that so many before us have already walked, a path we failed to recognise but now do and accept, without doubt, without remorse or contemplation, we just do it.

Sitting quietly for a while, trying to meditate is difficult at first because the busy Conscious mind explodes with thoughts that bounce in every direction. With time and perseverance this gets better as you learn how to focus and relax. When we talk about focusing in meditation, we mean focusing on issues pertaining to meditation like breathing, chanting mantras, exploring our senses and so on. When you are in focus mode, nothing else matters. Time stops. All other thoughts, both positive and negative, are meaningless. Normally this happens automatically when you are focused on a real-life situation, but it's also a useful skill that can be developed.

What breathing means to life so does your breath, equally impact when you're meditating. If you're able to use your breath to slow down your mind, you'll soon come to experience new rhythm patterns to help you relax and calm your nervous system.

Mindfulness...

Mindfulness is a Buddhist term. Defined as the quality or state of being Conscious or aware of something. A mental state achieved by focusing one's awareness on the present moment, while calmly acknowledging and accepting one's feelings, thoughts and bodily sensations. Sometimes used as a therapeutic technique.

Being aware of your mind wandering when meditating is important as this is essentially your first step in self-awareness – you are aware your mind is wandering. Now you can gently bring your focus back to your anchor, which is your breath. This proves once again; the Real You is not your mind (thoughts - ego).

By valuing stillness and silence, we get to seek deep within and explore our soul, uncover the mystique and embrace our true selves and we do this by simply becoming mindfully aware of the internal spirit residing in all of us.

'Mindfulness is having awareness of something
Meditation is having awareness of nothing'

Ideally, Mindfulness is when we focus in on something meaningful, maybe an issue that has being troubling but we don't get attached, we merely observe as the story or thought patterns unfold.

Mindfulness is therefore a powerful tool within meditation. Mindfulness also releases *'happy'* chemicals in the brain; lowers blood pressure, improves digestion and relaxes tension around pain. It's simple to practice and wonderful in effect.

Not a bad deal when all that's needed is to slow it all down, pay attention and focus within, which sounds like something we should all be doing but mostly don't. When we do pay attention, change becomes possible.

"I could never still my mind. And then, as I was approaching my seventieth birthday, I thought the time has come. Part of aging is that as the externals begin to fray so you are beckoned inward. As my mind became quieter in meditation, I discovered this place that seemed to be suspended behind my forehead, like a chandelier hanging from the top of my skull. It was a place of complete stillness." The Unexpected Power of Mindfulness & Meditation - Jane Fonda

Mindfulness is also about being mindfully aware of redirecting the Conscious mind to be still, enabling us to enjoy intentional actions, willpower and decisions. We become mindfully aware of how the brain functions, how the Subconscious and the Conscious minds work. How the mind so easily wanders and how we are able to prevent this from happening by focusing on our breath. The more we activate these complex mind states, we stimulate neuroplasticity, activating our grey matter, which instantly sprouts new, active and demanding neurons. All this vibrant new mental activity is what makes it so difficult to still the mind and stay focused.

Take the game of golf for example. It is a *'mindful'* game. Try staying focused, pulling a golf bag on wheels around 18 holes and still be mindful about each shot and each putt. It takes extreme concentration. Who says thinking, isn't hard work...!

If you mindfully think of an idea and try to remember it, you're going to immediately raise your stress levels. However, if you write the idea down, your mind instantly releases the idea and your stress levels return to normal. With mindfulness, we become aware of this cognitive ebb and flow. With meditation, we learn to control it.

Meditation isn't about becoming a different person, a new person, or even a better person. It's about training in mindfulness and getting a healthy sense of perspective. You're not trying to turn off your thoughts or feelings. You're learning to observe them without judgment. Eventually, you may start to better understand them. Mindfulness is the ability to be present, to rest in the here and now, fully engaged in whatever you're doing in the moment.

Don't worry about achieving perfect meditation. Sometimes your focus will wander or you'll forget to follow your breath. That's okay, it's part of the experience. What's more important is to meditate consistently so you can get into a pattern. It's definitely one of those things where the journey is more important than the destination.

It's estimated, 95% of all behaviour is Subconsciously driven. This is when we are in our *'autopilot'* mode, meaning we are unaware of our actions. Our behaviour patterns are expressed Subconsciously because neural networks underlie all our habits, reducing our millions of sensory inputs per second into manageable shortcuts so we can function without too much thought in this weird world. These default brain signals are very resourceful, making it easy for the brain to cognitively function in the most efficient way possible.

When meditating, we often get little narratives running through our minds, which we didn't choose, i.e. 'I've got to pay accounts tomorrow' or 'I don't have time to sit still, I've got so much work to do'. By practicing mindfulness, we learn how to recognise when our minds are doing these wacko activities. By merely observing this, we're able to become more aware of ourselves and take control.

In the realm of meditation or even in applying creative work, a strange switch is thrown in the brain. You no longer ponder or cogitate about what happens next. You are completely immersed, absorbed, you almost feel possessed by the abstract, creative internal force within you. It's almost as if you've been wonderfully liberated or temporally cut off from the everyday busy world.

Contemporary researchers are exploring whether a consistent meditation practice yields long-term benefits, noting positive effects on brain and immune functions among meditators.

However, the purpose of meditation is not to achieve benefits, rather the goal of meditation is *'no goal'*. It's simply to be present. In Buddhist philosophy, the ultimate benefit of meditation is liberation of the mind from attachment to things it cannot control, such as external circumstances or strong internal emotions. The liberated or enlightened practitioner no longer needlessly follows desires or clings to experiences, instead he/she maintains a calm mind and sense of inner harmony.

The reality of course is, we consciously need to accept the transient nature of everything in life, warts and all without trying to sidestep or avoid the transience, which is simply temporal life, nor can we celebrate the impermanence with which we address our daily struggle or attempt to denude our life path of discovery.

Meditation Techniques...

Buddha said it takes great effort to become '*effortless*'. With our busy minds this is true. For this reason, there are many varied preferences of meditation. Some meditations promise enhanced concentration or deep relaxation while others promise a path to enlightenment. There are religions that require meditation as a sole form of spiritual practice whereas others see meditation as part of a requirement necessary to awaken the spirit.

Buddhists prefer the '*observer*' method. The objective is to try and become a witness or observer to the movie or scenario playing out in the active mind. The desire here is to casually sit on the side line, never getting involved or partaking in the endless mental debates. You merely observe what's happening but you do it from the outside, kind of like from a distance but you still remain constantly aware so you can return to your anchor (breath) should you drift off or get involved in the mental activity you're observing.

With breath and body scan-based meditations, the focus is on self-awareness, health, memory status, deep relaxation (without sleeping) and achieving a state of calm and serenity.

Hindus prefer using a series of repetitive vocalised chants or hum effects, called Mantras, to promote tranquillity. They are easy to do as there are many well practiced Mantras, handed down from various eastern religions that are timeless. They suit people on a religious or devotional expansion of growth. People sometimes become dependent on Mantras preferring to use them in everyday situations, which can become an irritation.

New Age people prefer to use a visualisation. They visualise a peaceful nature scene or a beautiful setting. This is a very relaxing practice, which very quickly gets Alpha and even Theta brainwaves active.

Sense only meditation can be used for enhancing one's senses. These meditations have the depth to also enhance ones' intuition and spiritual senses as well.

Third Eye meditation is when you focus only on your abstract third eye (centre of the forehead, above the eyebrows). The longer you can stay focused, the more chance you'll have to 'see'. Normally it begins with colours. With practice you'll see images. This is when it becomes interesting. Meditation is the key to turning on our third eye. It's important to avoid distractions like a runaway imagination. Simply relax and gently observe your breath. When you're completely relaxed, slowly bring awareness to your third eye position. Whatever comes to your mind, remain calm and maintain a non-reaction attitude. With time, you'll realise you're observing yourself from within the third person. No matter how intense the scenario impacts on you, remain calm and merely observe. In meditation, you close your eyes but via your third eye you're still able to enjoy prodigious visions. This is your third eye-opening. Enjoy it, it's free and it has no encumbrances...!

For some people, their preference is to just kick back and get in tune with nature. Aids like serene music or a calming visual series on a screen or even a simple lit candle to focus on or a nice log fire to gaze endlessly into are often used to help relax the mind and explore within. It's all meditation. There are many techniques. They vary from country to country and within various cultures.

The above represent some of the more typical examples. The main criteria for all types of meditation are to: Relax, sit still, focus on an object or activity and rid the mind of all else, thereby creating a 'still mind', a mind that essentially exists in the present. It's a type of 'mind cleansing' if you wish.

The Monkey Mind...

On a daily basis we are mentally overrun with regular activities and situations, all requiring thought. These constant battles with inner conflicting personalities try to emerge; often based on people we met earlier in the day. As the day builds, all these thoughts, worries and concerns culminate into the *'dreaded stress'* syndrome, if we let them. Clearly, we have to let go of these mental plays if we ever want to really relax and as we all know, with an extremely active Conscious mind, letting go can be difficult. Buddhist's refer to this build- up of activity as the *'Monkey Mind'*. They say, *'Even in dreaming you are only observing...!'*

One way to cease being bothered by your continual rising thoughts is to realise and accept, they are nothing more than insignificant ripples in your consciousness and don't originate from the *'Real You'*. Once you apperceive the reality, they are not you, but simply phenomena rising and falling in self-awareness, your concern will diminish. You will then take control of your thoughts.

Meditation can be a form of concentration. The word *'con'* means *'consciousness of'* and the word *'centre'* means centre. Put together it's about becoming aware of the centre of who you really are.

One way to describe this is to see your busy thought chatter as clouds rising in a clear blue sky. The thoughts that arise are the clouds, which you then observe (prefix *'ob'* means towards while *'serve'* means service). You acknowledge the clouds as being present but then gracefully return to the clear blue sky (your anchor). You accept them but you don't get involved. You don't avoid the clouds (thoughts/pain), you move towards them and accept them, which forces the thoughts to lose their intensity (once the mind accepts, it moves on). You are then able to return to your clear blue sky and continue in your observer mode.

Another nice metaphor is to imagine the surface of the ocean in a turbulent and agitated state. The stormy ocean represents our busy, active mind. If we duck below the rough seas it gets calmer. The deeper we go the calmer it becomes. We simply sit under the surface with no angry thoughts, devoid of any pleasure or pain, loss or gain and passively observe. Wonderful place to be...

The mind cannot produce silence by thinking noisily. When the mind slows down, we are suddenly aware of our true self. In this consciousness mode, a trained mathematician's mind will suddenly see the answer to an algorithm, which hitherto had gone unnoticed. As will a chef discover parsley is tastier in a dish, if one takes into account the temperature of the food when it's added. A mechanic discovers what that mystery small knocking sound is in an engine. As will an artist discover, using burnt umber instead of cadmium yellow with cobalt blue works better for what a painting's sunset emotionally needs. These nuances are drowned in a mind existing only in a cacophony of noise and mind clutter. Stilling the mind has so many advantages, which only meditation can offer.

Meditation also teaches us to relive the simple things in life. Your basic senses like: tasting fresh food; smelling the damp sea air or rain; feeling the wind on your face; witnessing cloud formations above you and so on are all examples encompassing a form of mindfulness.

Meditation teaches us tolerance. We learn to overcome frustrations, which could be work related or personal problems. The pain will still be there but via meditation we no longer have the desire to aggravate the situation, we simply let go. These new sensations indicate a rebalancing of your psyche. You've finally moved on, thrown away the shackles and climbed the ladder. It's a wonderful feeling of being light and that's where you want to be – light, very light.

Our bodies are surrounded by *'light'* (Aura), we mentally generate *'light'* brainwaves, our psyche gives off sensitive *'light'* frequency waves that resonate in the form of vibrations and we are constantly drawn to the *'light'*, like the breaking of a new day.

You can also use meditation for healing. Group meditation sessions obviously work better as the focused energy vibrations are far more powerful. When doing healing, you need to be able to feel the suffering of the patient whilst still being able to observe the problem from a distance. As you breathe in, focus on absorbing the suffering and as you exhale, release the suffering. Absorb and release, absorb and release. Healing takes a lot of patience and intensity. It is usually best suited to those who are more advanced and comfortable with their meditation.

Mantras...

A personal mantra is usually a positive phrase, expression or affirmative statement, you repeat to yourself, either out loud or within, for the purpose of motivation or encouragement. It is typically your favourite quote, proverb, spiritual truth or religious maxim that motivates and inspires you. Mantras in meditation, are used as a simple focusing tool to block the busy Conscious thought process and help restore the mind into the present. By repeating a word or a string of words, in sync with your breathing, helps you to stay focused and prevents external thoughts from entering your mind.

A mantra originates from the combination of two syllables: *'man'*, meaning *'to reflect'* or *'be aware'*, and *'tra'*, meaning *'tool for'* or *'agent of'*. So, a mantra is a tool for reflection and the development of awareness, used for both concentration and contemplation on the source.

When you chant a mantra during meditation, you need to try and resonate with the vibration of the sound you are chanting and become one with the energy. If you use a well-known mantra like *'Om'* then the possibility of millions of other people using the same mantra simultaneously always exists, resulting in you resonating with everyone throughout the world who is chanting the same mantra, connecting you with them on a spiritual level.

Whether you chant aloud or silently, a simple chant like *'Om'* is energising, healing, cleansing and calming, because when you put it out to the Universe with love and intent you will likewise receive the same in return. Mantras invoke colours and even visualisations. They are often musically based and have rhythm, which helps carry the mantra. They are meaningless sounds used solely for assisting concentration and focus. They are definitely not a form of prayer to heathen Gods, which is a popular belief in the Western world. Two popular meditation mantras are:

- Om – (pronounced - A U Mmmmm)
- Om Mani Padme Hum – (Om Ma-Ni Pin-Me Hum)

These are very easy, almost addictive mantras used world-wide, repeated either out loud, softly to oneself, or internally within the mind. The faith, devotion and pure spiritual empathy with which these mantra's have been chanted, by so many devotees, for so many years, is sufficient cause for the mantras to be charged with positive spiritual energy, always referring back to the Oneness.

Using a Mantra...

To begin - learn the meaning of your mantra because you need to resonate with the meaning. You need to feel and experience the meaning deep within. Grasp its objective, its intensity, its rhythm, its message and then imagine it pictorially and keep it there, alive within you.

When you are ready, repeat your mantra slowly and

steadily, concentrating on its sound as fully as you can. Repeat it in unison with the natural rhythm of your breath. Either split it so you repeat half the mantra when you inhale and the other half when you exhale, or repeat it on both the inhalation and the exhalation. After several recitations, repeat the mantra silently by moving only your lips (this helps maintain a steady rhythm). After several more repetitions, recite it internally without moving your lips. As thoughts arise, simply return to the mantra, knowing this is a natural part of the process. Gently bring your attention back and be mindful of the internal sound as deep as possible. Continue for the period of time you set aside for meditation. Return by taking a few deep slow breaths and sit quietly to mindfully experience your session. You may feel calm and centred or you may be flooded with thoughts and sensations. Take comfort in knowing, this meditative passive action can enable you to experience the present moment in absolute stillness.

You can also download any of the familiar mantras off 'You Tube' and listen to them while you are working, chilling or while in a meditative session. They will bring calm and serenity to whatever it is you're doing.

Music...

The mystics of the east have used music for centuries to induce a specific state of mind, even using music to control pain amongst other things. Throughout the world, music has often been used as a calming method to encourage sleep and relax the active mind.

For meditation, the use of calming, melodic music can produce responsive results fairly quickly. A piece of specific music created for meditation needs to perfectly resonate with the Subconscious mind, producing an almost immediate effect of calm and relaxed alertness, which is the ideal meditative state. The perfect rhythm for achieving this type of music is 60 beats per minute. A range of instruments is preferred as opposed to a single instrument. Instruments can vary from strings to keyboard and soft, melodic wind instruments, not necessarily classically composed, unless in a mellow format but usually with an eastern twist, which includes the subtle sounds of the sitar, flute/recorder and even soft falsetto human voices in split octave harmony.

Music moves in waves like all energy. Our entire Universe consists of waves of energy in so many formats but music is probably one of the more accessible formats, which is why it has such a profound effect on us. Include soft background meditation music when next you meditate and you'll subtly slide into the realms of your Subconscious mind.

If anyone asks you for money to teach you religion, meditation or any other holistic practice, walk away. Meditation is not a 'quick-fix' to enlightenment. You don't have to change your lifestyle or the way you dress. With regular meditation your lifestyle and the way you think and see the world will adjust accordingly as you progress. It's more like a gentle unfolding of the psyche. Your desire to see and learn, to live more in the present, become aware of your spiritual direction, sharpen your senses and understanding of people and the way life works, nursing your tolerance and patience levels, growing your awareness of the environment and God's perfect world around you, embracing that warm fuzzy feeling of genuine love and joy, plus so much more, will happen in a perfectly natural process, if you can calm your mind, relax and simply let go...

The Fox & the Turtle...

This is an old Buddhist story - One day a fox came upon a turtle and decided he would make a tasty meal. The turtle watched the fox approach with teeth bared so he withdrew into his shell, denying the fox his meal. The fox eventually lost interest and moved on. By withdrawing into his shell, the turtle had time to consider his next move and realised, simply by waiting, the fox would move on, then he could continue with his journey.

The morale of the story is not about withdrawing every time a situation or challenge arises, it's about giving yourself some space, some time for reflection before instantly jumping into a situation. By merely observing the problem you're able to remove the fear. Often in life, we are faced with challenges. We need to think through issues, check out all the angles, pros and cons, before making a decision. This is what the turtle did and it saved his life, thanks to a little mindful observing…!

'The more you meditate, the sooner you'll find your centre of peace.'

Setting the Scene…

Now that we've covered an overview of what meditation is all about, we can get practical.

To set the scene, you need a quiet room or space where you're not going to be disturbed. If you have your own meditation room you regularly use then you can decorate the room accordingly with pleasant, soothing emerald green or sky-blue walls. If you're comfortable with a symbolic deity, erect a cross if you're Christian, a Buddha if you're a Buddhist and so on for whatever your religion may be. Adorn the walls with pictures or paintings or photos of serene settings. Install a television and play scenic videos or play soft melodic meditation music.

Have cushions to sit on and be comfortable. Light a candle or several candles. This space must feel special to you. Don't wear shoes of any kind in this room. Instil a level of respect. You can burn incense or use soothing camphor oils or essences to invoke a beautiful aroma, which your senses will come to accept and associate with meditation every time you smell the wonderful scents. You can even dress the room every day with fresh flowers.

Clear the lungs by exhaling completely. Release all that

old stale air in your lungs. To help get the lungs clear and the body completely relaxed you can do a few *'compressions.'* These exercises are designed to build up muscle tension, which you then release and relax. It's a *'contract and release'* exercise. This is accompanied by a wonderful sensation when you liberate the tension and let go.

Stand with your legs shoulder width apart, your arms loosely at your side but slightly raised. As you breathe in, raise your arms above you and reach for the ceiling, stretch for the ceiling and slowly exhale. Now slowly and evenly breathe in deeply, as deep as you can, while you bring your arms down in front of you with your hands facing together in the typical standing prayer position. The exercise now is to hold your breath for as long as possible while you use all your strength to push one hand against the other. The veins around your shoulders should become visible. If they don't, you're not pushing hard enough. Your hands should be shaking from the pressure as tension builds up in and around your shoulders and arms. When you can no longer hold the pose, release the tension and slowly exhale. You'll experience a wonderful feeling of relief as you exhale. All the tension subsides as your muscles now completely unwind. Do this a few times and your body will feel incredibly relaxed.

You can now take up your meditation position. Normally a comfortable sitting position is good. If you can sit in the Lotus position great, if you can't, sit as straight up as you can but sit comfortably. You can sit on a chair or on cushions on the ground. Try and sit upright. Maybe sit against a wall or the back of a chair or couch to begin. This will help give your spine some support. Be careful not to sit so comfortably you'll easily fall asleep. The reason for sitting upright is so your base (coccyx) can make contact with the floor. It's all about being grounded.

Just an informal note on the Lotus position: There are many advanced meditators who advocate, sitting in a comfortable position is far better than trying to force yourself into an uncomfortable Lotus position as the Lotus position can initially create tension in the lower back, hips and knees, thereby restricting the flow of energy throughout the body, which will also deviate you from trying to sit still and relax.

Cup your hands in front of you on your lap or rest your hands on your knees with your hands open, palms upwards (receiving) with the bottom three fingers extended, the forefinger curled to touch the thumb or you can sit in the prayer position with your hands clasped together in front of you in the shape of a pyramid or triangle. Whatever works for you.

When meditating you should be relaxed and comfortable, with your mind alert and focused. Smile. Not a big goofy smile, just a little smile that turns the edges of your lips up. This simple facial move changes everything. It releases tension and boosts positive energy throughout the body because smiling releases endorphins and *'feel good'* serotonin in the brain.

Suzuki Roshi once said, a frog represents the perfect act of meditation because a frog can sit very still for long periods of time and yet still stay so alert, its eyes miss nothing, not even the stealthiest insect can venture past without being noticed. This simple analogy captures the dynamics of meditation so profoundly but then what else would one expect from the Zen Master himself. In our youth we are taught to make things happen, whereas, in meditation we learn to let things happen.

Meditation is also about balance. This is two-fold because we not only look for a mental balance between our brainwave patterns; we also want a physical balance. When you sit down for your meditation session, you need to feel balanced. Both the left and right sides of the body need to feel united. It's that complete feeling of being *'one'*, one with yourself and one with your higher spiritual self. As you begin meditating and focusing within, you soon forget you even have a left and right side to your body. This is when you start feeling balanced. You stop thinking about the material and focus only within.

If you run a hypothetical perfect spiritual line vertically and horizontally on a person, the vertical line runs from the centre of the coccyx, up the spine and out through the centre of the crown on top of the head. The horizontal line runs across the breastbone. In Christendom, the sign of the cross represents these vertical and horizontal lines.

For Roman Catholics, the sign of the cross is made

using the right hand to touch the forehead at the mention of the *Father*; the lower middle of the chest at the mention of the *Son*; the left shoulder on the word *Holy* and the right shoulder on the word *Spirit*, forming a perfect Trinity Triangle. When meditating, a well-known technique is to focus on these vertical and horizontal lines of the body, whilst chanting simple mantras. These lines represent a perfect *'balance'* of the body's energy.

Once you're sitting with your back straight, roll your head forward. Not your shoulders, just your head, almost as if you're tucking your chin into your chest. Don't exaggerate the move. Be comfortable. Now extend the chin back out. This move will help to straighten your back a little. We want to activate the energy Chakras and a bent or rounded spine won't do it. Close your eyes and imagine the world and all its complexities are moving away from you. You are now safe within your inner world, a place of infinite space and infinite peace. Let all your stress thoughts go as we move onto controlled breathing exercises.

Breathing...

As previously mentioned, when we are born, God blesses us with the breath of life and every second thereafter we strive to continue breathing. Our entire human life is meant for purification but we cannot achieve this without breathing. Fact is, we cannot achieve anything without breathing. If your breathing is chaotic, your mind and emotions will be chaotic. If your breathing is steady, your mind and emotions will be steady. By mentally stopping during a chaotic moment and connecting with your breath you can slow your breathing down and refocus. It works every time. By having control of your breathing, you can then control your mind and your emotions.

Important to note here – breathing through your nose is always better than breathing in through your mouth because the nose has filters which filter the air. The mouth has no filters, so always opt for nasal breathing, no matter where you are or what you are doing, keep your mouth shut and breathe via your nose. If you snore at night when sleeping, shut your mouth and you won't snore…!

The seven most important steps for breathing in everyday life are as follows:

1.) Always breathe in via your nose
2.) Breathe slowly. You can control your body tempo via breathing slowly and it helps you get a full breath
3.) Try to breathe less, which is why you need fuller breaths on the inhale
4.) Avoid short breaths as it raises your adrenalin
5.) Exhale via your mouth fully, slowly
6.) Control your breathing with an even tempo
7.) Be consciously aware of your breathing

Take time out to mindfully explore your breathing in

everyday life. It affects your moods, emotions and overall body health. Get used to breathing in slowly via your nose and exhaling even slower out your mouth. Make it a continual habit. It doesn't matter if you're in the gym or walking in the street or even at work. Once you get your breathing into a routine, you will appreciate not only the health benefits but also the control you will have over your entire body as well as your psyche by reducing your emotions down to a calm and serene state and you can do all this just by controlling your breathing...!

In meditation, focusing on your breath gives you a natural feeling of emptiness, an open mind, serene and at peace. We can do this because as explained, our breath is the conduit to life. Whenever the mind gets too active and we start losing our connection, all we do is re-focus on our breathing. This simple action brings us back to our observer position. This is why we call our breath, an 'anchor' in meditation.

Now that you're comfortable, begin breathing by blocking one nostril by pressing against the side of your nose with your forefinger. Breathe for a count of three, hold it in for a count of three and exhale for a count of three. Slowly count to yourself and focus on your breathing technique as you breathe. Keep it as even as you can. Now block the other nostril and breathe through the exposed nostril. Alternate breathing through each nostril at least ten times. By now you'll start to feel a little light-headed.

This is quite normal. Return to breathing normally and completely relax. Breathe evenly through your nose and out through your mouth. Feel all the tension subside out of your upper body with every exhale as you continue focusing on your breathing. Allow your breathing to slow down naturally. You can also breathe by relaxing your stomach and letting it extend outwards on the inhale.

A popular breathing method is to focus only on the tip of the nose. Sit and breathe normally and calmly focus on the tip of your nostrils while breathing in and out, just where the inner and outer skin meets. Try breathing in and out through your nostrils as you read this, but focus on the breath as you inhale and exhale, your breath passing gently through the tip of your nose. You can clearly feel it, making it easy to sense. Focus on this as you sit in meditation and just breathe evenly. Now observe. As thoughts rise and your mind saunters into the future (planning) or gets dragged back to the past (memory) simply acknowledge each thought and return to your focused breath through the tip of the nose, which has now become your anchor. Never force your breaths, let them flow freely, easily. You can also focus on the space between the breaths, which is a deeper, more meaningful meditation technique, very popular in Buddhism.

To help you focus, block your ears with ear plugs. Try blocking your ears with the tip of your little fingers right now as you read this and you'll immediately hear how your voice echoes when you speak. Plus, you'll be able to hear how loud your breathing actually is.

The tip of your tongue should just touch the roof of your mouth. Start breathing slow and shallow via your nose and gradually increase the depth. Imagine you are breathing through your belly button and exhaling through the trapdoor in the crown of your head. Feel each breath, inhale, exhale, inhale, exhale...experience each sensation. You'll notice and hear the exhale more than the inhale. This is normal. Be patient. It all depends on what kind of active day you've had, which is why meditating in the early morning is recommended. However, any level of restfulness is okay to begin.

It can take several minutes before you settle your mind down. With practice, your level of calmness increases. Every day, you'll go a little deeper. On any given day, one may have encountered a lot of activity, so the nervous system may not settle as well as the previous day when you were less challenged. Don't give up just because you feel you are not in the zone today. Consistency pays off.

Feel the calm and joy spreading through you as you become more aware of yourself. You may experience body sensations like minor aches and pains, itches, tingling nerves or twitches that come and go. It's normal. As you relax deeper, you mentally push all thoughts aside. Alpha brainwaves replace Beta brainwaves. Passive observing is in this realm. It's like being in your '*happy place*'. This is all good, the body is winding down as you gently let go. Slowly become aware of each of your senses. Explore each sense, your body gently expanding and contracting as you evenly inhale and exhale. Now conduct a simple body scan. Start by focusing on your toes. Gently contract and release your toes. Slowly work your way up your legs, knees and thighs, contracting and releasing every muscle. Move into your pelvic area and then up into the abdominal area. Contract and release, contract and release. Continue up through the chest into the neck and down each arm to your hands and fingers, slowly contracting and releasing. Experience each sensation. Move back up the arms, feel the shoulders relax completely as you continue up the neck. From here, move up into the head and stop at the 'third eye' position and focus outward. This is not a race. Go with the flow. Slowly and evenly, count each breath from one to seven and back to one again repeatedly whilst still focusing on your 'third eye' position. Don't rush. From focusing on your 'third eye', slowly work all the way down until you arrive at your base (coccyx). Once you feel yourself starting to drift off, take control, do not fall asleep even though your mind feels sleepy. It's at this point of almost dropping off to sleep that you need to be aware. Focus. Be alert. Theta brainwaves have now replaced Alpha brainwaves. Observe. Your body is relaxed and asleep but your mind is vigilant and by now, completely in the present. You remain ever mindful as your ego slowly subsides. You feel incredibly peaceful and relaxed in this wonderland. You are aware of all the energy around you.

There is no threat once you're in this zone. All external noises are now shut off. You are mindfully aware of your breath and body sensations. When you feel ready, shift your focus to your heart and feel warm, heartfelt love flowing through you. Mentally express your love for God and the Universe. Focus only on love. You can also do this by visualising a 'cross' to represent God if you're Christian (choose whatever symbol represents your particular religion). Visualise each member of your family and friends, the same with your enemies, your household pets, include whoever you want. Love with all your heart. If it brings tears to your eyes, it's okay. Let the tears flow. This is a wonderful cleansing process.

Do not fall asleep, as you need to experience and remember what transpires. Whatever happens from here on, don't fight it. Merely observe your thoughts as they develop. Don't get involved. Afterwards, you'll feel calmer and be acutely more aware of your senses. Always return to your breath.

I Choose to Let Go...

This is a favourite meditation practice with a lot of meditation teachers. Once you're sitting comfortably and you've done your breathing exercises, picture your favourite beach. You are sitting on the beach watching the waves out in front of you, gently unfolding onto the shoreline. It is a beautiful sunny day with a slight offshore breeze blowing from behind you. As each wave builds, breathe in slowly and evenly, hold it for a bit as you watch the wave peak. Breathe out slowly and evenly as the wave unfolds onto the sand and races up the beach towards you before receding back into the ocean. You can hear the sound of the waves breaking, the water bristling with energy as it discharges over the sand and shells and races towards you, stopping a few metres in front of your feet. It's music to your ears. As each wave breaks, chant this mantra, *"I choose to let go."* You can break the chant up into two parts, i.e. chant, *"I choose..."* as the wave builds and then *"To let go...!"* as the wave breaks.

Repeat this mantra constantly until you feel completely relaxed. Your busy Beta brainwaves will slowly disperse, replaced with calm Alpha brainwaves as you become more and more focused on the wave building and breaking out in front of you. This vision becomes your anchor. Every time you feel yourself drifting, gently return to the waves until they eventually dissolve and you are left with just the sound of your breath as you gradually slip into the zone, in autopilot mode, in the intangible but incredibly creative Subconscious world of wonder. Afterwards, you'll feel completely relaxed, calm, serene and at peace. Enjoy...!

' The quieter you become, the more you are able to hear'
Rumi

Healing Light...

Once you're sitting comfortably and you've done your

breathing exercises, focus on your sensory feelings. Experience the sensations. If you feel the need, focus on your breath. Don't force trying to feel anything because sensations will naturally come to you. Be aware and receptive in a relaxed manner. Be mindful of space, silence, stillness, your presence, your breath. As you release, you feel happy, anchored in the present moment. Thoughts come and go. Pay them no attention. They are not part of your present moment in time. They are about issues, sometimes the past, other times the future, mostly idle imaginative chatter. Enjoy the peace. Let it flow through you. You feel so light, you are floating. Go with the flow.

Now, imagine a beautiful healing crystal white beam of light entering your third eye position, illuminating throughout your entire inner body, section by detailed section. Observe, as the white light gently reflexes and heals your entire structure, focusing on every bone, every muscle, every organ, every cell, every atom, every molecule. Relax and enjoy the moment, follow the healing light as it moves through you until you feel completely tranquil and healed, left only with an extraordinary sense of overwhelming love.

To come back to reality, begin by flexing your fingers and toes. Work your way through all your muscle groups while breathing evenly. Open your eyes when you feel ready. Come back slowly. There's no rush. As you sit there with your eyes open, try and recall what happened during your meditation session. Write it down. It's good to record it.

Namaste...

'Namaste' is generally used as a greeting or salutation by Hindus, Jains, Buddhists and Yogis. 'Namaste', signifies respect and love for another person. It means: *'The divine in me greets the divine in you'.*

The divinity of 'Namaste' is that it joins two people when they greet with the Oneness that resides within all of us. In essence there is no separation. As one looks at the other, he or she is only a reflection. We are merely looking back at ourselves and realising we are *'One'* and therefore inseparable from God.

Overview...

In meditation, by stilling the busy mind and focusing within or on the breath, you get to strip away all mind clutter, thoughts, concerns, emotions, etc. The ego has left the room, leaving the *'Real You'* naked, alone, completely exposed. Initially, it's a little overwhelming but once you become mindful of what's happening, it's an astounding revolutionary feeling.

The ego will constantly strive to return and dominate, pulsing you with random thoughts but with time you learn to ignore them and focus only on the moment. It's illuminating and enchanting at the same time because every meditation session is different. What you witness, learn and comprehend is infinite. It never stops.

Sometimes its spiritual, other times personal and then there are situations where random images of people you've never seen before, pop in and out of your zone, sometimes ignoring you, busy with things, other times, persistently trying to tell you something or other. You don't get involved; you merely observe. It's like dreaming or watching live theatre. You are fully awake and aware of what is happening. Very trippy...!

The following is a brief list of tips, to guide you on those off-weather days when your inspiration is weak...

- Don't meditate if you are in a hurry, with a need to rush off to do something else. Always make time to be in the present
- There will be good and not so good meditations. However, even those meditations when thoughts don't settle, are still a resemblance of peace of mind and therefore beneficial
- When you finish meditating don't think it's over. Maintain a positive thought that your meditative state will remain with you for the remainder of the day
- There's no use worrying about how much time you need to allocate to meditate because there is no set time. Even a few minutes, to draw your awareness to your inner centre, is time well spent
- Always bear in mind, when you're meditating, there are probably millions of people throughout

the world in meditation with you at the same time...!

Why do a lot of people fail at meditation...? It's because not everyone understands the real intention of meditation, which isn't only to calm or silence the mind. It's more about gradually becoming more familiar and comfortable with the mind. This is why it takes time and perseverance.

Once you're familiar with the mind it becomes your purpose, you discover there is no such thing as a bad meditation. The experience then becomes softer and frictionless. If you have any big expectations from your meditations, you could become disappointed when they are not achieved. Have faith, it all comes together eventually.

You need to put in the hard yards with everything in life if you want to really achieve anything. It's no different with meditation, the more time and dedication you apply to meditating, the more you'll understand the process and enjoy the benefits.

This chapter is an elementary meditation introduction. There are many influences and styles of meditation you can add. With time and patience, you will eventually find your comfort zone.

Most of all – enjoy it...!

Namaste...!

Life Is...

I love to live simply, to live in the now
Enjoying every precious moment
For life is short on this earth plane
And quality is better than quantity

I like to socialise with like-minded souls
Liberated spirits filled with positive and vibrant energy
Givers not takers, no judges or wannabees
Those who are free and caring, do it for me

I like sitting sedentary at a window to idly witness
The incredible energy of a summer storm
The pouring rain drumming a mesmerising staccato
Against the transparent window pane
Watching raindrops splashing effortlessly, endlessly
Each drop singular and yet together
Joining seamlessly, powerfully, silently, in Oneness

I love to read books
Books I'll never be tested on
Books I can openly enjoy
And share with those who care

Breathing deeply, filling my lungs with untainted air
Or languishing in a hot, steamy tub
Seasoned with scented oils
Bathing in the warm, soaking fragrances, is my pleasure

I like to write songs, create music
And write stories because I want to
Not because I have something to prove
I enjoy playing guitar and the piano
Releasing the creative influence from deep within
Caressing those timeless ancient woods and dulcet curves
Experiencing each subtle note with sonic resonance

My morning practice is yoga
This teaches me to surrender and receive
Enhancing stillness, balance and alignment
All part of the eternal balance of opposites
The energy force that controls our Universe

I enjoy watching a beautiful sunrise
Across a glassy ocean in the early dawn
Witnessing a fiery sunset ablaze in the late afternoon
Enjoying a full moon and the entrancing mood
Laying back on a dark night to peacefully behold
The celestial landscape of stars above
Pondering on the infinity of space
These are my peaceful times

I like to wake up effortlessly with the morning glow
Drinking in the light while I decide where to go
I prefer casual, loose fitting clothes
Cannot dress to impress
And I choose to eat less

I'm uncomfortable with control
Being governed by time, money and those who know
I get high drinking pure, clean rain water
Consuming organic natural green food from Mother Earth
And seasonal fresh fruit in abundance
For this is my essence in Life

I give daily thanks to our Creator
The divine spirit within and without
Walking a path of light and love
In the presence of the Great Spirit, I have no doubt

Love to be in the presence of animals
For they never judge you
Only love you, unconditionally love you
True harmony and depth with these sentient, loyal beings

There are times when I like to be alone
Wrapped in complete silence
Lost in the presence of my idle thoughts
Having time to explore my individual senses

Walking on an undulating shore line
Feeling the soft crush of beach sand underfoot
The warm sun on my exposed back
The gentle, fresh windswept sting of saltwater on my face
The sight of dolphins frolicking across the mid reef
The timeless sound of waves discharging on naked sand
The world around me is 'right' in this moment

I like to travel
And explore this incredible planet
Observe other cultures and make new friends
I enjoy good movies, especially comedies
And laugh unashamedly until it hurts

I love the scent of a wind-swept ocean
A gentle offshore breeze
Paddling out at first light
Catching a surreal wave
The glassy perfection
The flowing energy, timeless, infinite
Pulling into a liquid barrel
Emerging exhilarated
Overcome with pure joy

This is Life...this is me
This is where I want to be

Namaste...!

Robin Morris

Acknowledgments

It's always difficult to express oneself personally, in bare-bones reality, exposed for all to witness my wholesome take on spirituality and how I perceive this wonderful world. One's spiritual perspective is very individual and private for most, not something readily aired overtly, so thank you to all and one for allowing me to have my say and thank you to the following for your assistance and many wise words…

Craig Mackay - For the beautiful cover design

Professor Tim Mtshali - For his valuable input and dedication in proof reading the manuscript

Professor Ian Schulz - Foreword

Kiko Michel - For sagely direction and all the wise words

Derek Sivers - For so many wise words

Paul M. Sutter - Magnetic energy in space

Bob Newhart - For his tobacco story

Dr Winfried Otto Schumann – The Schumann Resonance

Claude Bernard – Biofeedback

Paul MacLean - Triune brain theory

Roger W. Sperry – Right brain, left brain theory

Carl Zimmer - Right brain, left brain theory

Sigmund Freud – Mind states

Dr Masaru Emoto – The Hidden Messages in Water

Paul Hawken - Findhorn

Pascal Fries - Neuronal Synchronisation

Billy Connolly – Funnies

Patrice Bouchardon – Trees

Kübler-Ross – Grief

Carlos Santana – Musical chills

John Peters - Sharing

Pamela Stephenson – Billy Connolly

Darwin – The Descent of Man

Temple Grandin – Animal Behaviour

Ben Thouard – Water Photographer

Jim B. Tucker – Reincarnation

COSI Science Centre – Magnetic Fields

Science & Sound – Water absorption and the resonance theory of consciousness

Rene Descartes - *'I think, therefore I am'*

'Let there always be Spiritual Light in your Life'

About the Author – Tim Mtshali

Robin Morris lives in Jeffreys Bay, South Africa. His passion in life is surfing, having travelled the world in search of the perfect wave. He has written and published several books to-date, ranging from fiction to holistic, including marketing, humour and surfing. Robin is also an accomplished musician, guitarist, pianist and songwriter with over twenty-five albums available online. His genre is primarily Rock & Blues but he also enjoys acoustic.

Robin's spiritual interest began many years ago when he became part of a research group, tasked by a local University to gather information on ESP and meditation skills in African culture. This eventually led to a lasting relationship with the east and a voyage of self-discovery that convinced him of the need to introduce meditation at local school level.

During his twenty something years heading up an Advertising Agency, Robin studied Psychology, specialising in Consumer Behaviour Patterns, which provided him with an insight into People Dynamics and hence, a lot of material for this book.

It is the essence of the written word that captures his passion for writing.

www.robinmorris.co.za

Made in the USA
Columbia, SC
12 October 2022

69328773R00241